Visit us at

www.syngress.com

Syngress is committed to publishing high-quality books for IT Professionals and delivering those books in media and formats that fit the demands of our customers. We are also committed to extending the utility of the book you purchase via additional materials available from our Web site.

SOLUTIONS WEB SITE

To register your book, visit www.syngress.com/solutions. Once registered, you can access our solutions@syngress.com Web pages. There you may find an assortment of valueadded features such as free e-books related to the topic of this book, URLs of related Web sites, FAQs from the book, corrections, and any updates from the author(s).

ULTIMATE CDs

Our Ultimate CD product line offers our readers budget-conscious compilations of some of our best-selling backlist titles in Adobe PDF form. These CDs are the perfect way to extend your reference library on key topics pertaining to your area of expertise, including Cisco Engineering, Microsoft Windows System Administration, CyberCrime Investigation, Open Source Security, and Firewall Configuration, to name a few.

DOWNLOADABLE E-BOOKS

For readers who can't wait for hard copy, we offer most of our titles in downloadable Adobe PDF form. These e-books are often available weeks before hard copies, and are priced affordably.

SYNGRESS OUTLET

Our outlet store at syngress.com features overstocked, out-of-print, or slightly hurt books at significant savings.

SITE LICENSING

Syngress has a well-established program for site licensing our e-books onto servers in corporations, educational institutions, and large organizations. Contact us at sales@syngress.com for more information.

CUSTOM PUBLISHING

Many organizations welcome the ability to combine par[illegible] as well as their own content, into a single volume for th[illegible] us at sales@syngress.com for more information.

SYNGRESS®

Nmap
In the Enterprise Your Guide to Network Scanning

Angela Orebaugh
Becky Pinkard

KEY	SERIAL NUMBER
001	HJIRTCV764
002	PO9873D5FG
003	829KM8NJH2
004	BAL923457U
005	CVPLQ6WQ23
006	VBP965T5T5
007	HJJJ863WD3E
008	2987GVTWMK
009	629MP5SDJT
010	IMWQ295T6T

PUBLISHED BY
Syngress Publishing, Inc.
Elsevier, Inc.
30 Corporate Drive
Burlington, MA 01803

Nmap in the Enterprise: Your Guide to Network Scanning

Printed in the United States of America
1 2 3 4 5 6 7 8 9 0

ISBN 13: 978-1-59749-241-6

Publisher: Andrew Williams
Technical Editor: Aaron Bayles
Page Layout and Art: SPi

For information on rights, translations, and bulk sales, contact Matt Pedersen, Commercial Sales Director and Rights, at Syngress Publishing; email m.pedersen@elsevier.com.

Authors

Angela Orebaugh is an information security technologist, scientist, and author with a broad spectrum of expertise in information assurance. She synergizes her 15 years of hands-on experiences within industry, academia, and government to advise clients on information assurance strategy, management, and technologies. Ms. Orebaugh is involved in several security initiatives with the National Institute of Standards and Technology (NIST) including technical Special Publications (800 series), the National Vulnerability Database (NVD), Security Content Automation Protocol (SCAP), and secure eVoting.

Ms. Orebaugh is an adjunct professor at George Mason University where she performs research and teaching in intrusion detection and forensics. Her research includes peer-reviewed publications in the areas of intrusion detection and prevention, data mining, attacker profiling, user behavior analysis, and network forensics.

Ms. Orebaugh is the author of the Syngress best seller's *Wireshark and Ethereal Network Protocol Analyzer Toolkit* and *Ethereal Packet Sniffing*. She has also co-authored the *Snort Cookbook* and *Intrusion Prevention and Active Response*. She is a frequent speaker at a variety of security conferences and technology events, including the SANS Institute and the Institute for Applied Network Security.

Ms. Orebaugh holds a Masters degree in Computer Science and a Bachelors degree in Computer Information Systems from James Madison University. She is currently completing her dissertation for her Ph.D. at George Mason University, with a concentration in Information Security.

Angela would like to thank Andrew Williams and Syngress/Elsevier for providing the opportunity to write this book. It would not have been possible without my security guru co-author, Becky Pinkard. Thank you for your amazing technical expertise, constant dedication, and much needed comic relief. I would also like to thank Tim Boyles for his helpful insights and assistance. I would like to thank Fyodor and the Nmap developers for creating such a full-featured, versatile tool.

I am fortunate to have such loving and supportive family and friends, who bring joy and balance to my life. Thank you for always being there. Most of all, I would like to thank Tammy Wilt. Your love and encouragement gives me strength to follow my dreams and your patience and support allows me to make them a reality. I am eternally grateful.

Becky Pinkard got her start in the information technology industry in 1996, answering phones and configuring dial-up networking for GTE Internetworking. She is currently a senior security manager with a Fortune 20 company where she is lucky enough to work with security technology on a daily basis.

Becky is a SANS Certified Instructor and has taught with the SANS Institute since 2001. She has participated as a GIAC GCIA advisory board member and on the Strategic Advisory Council for the Center for Internet Security. She is a co-author of the Syngress book, *Intrusion Prevention and Active Response, Deploying Network and Host IPS.* Becky also enjoys speaking at technical conferences, conventions and meetings. Basically anywhere security geeks can get together and have a few laughs while learning something cool! Additionally, Becky has setup enterprise intrusion detection systems, designed patch, vulnerability and firewall strategies, performed network and web security audits, led forensics cases, and developed security awareness training in small and large environments.

***Becky** would like to thank the following folks for their support, kindness and general, all-around, nice-to-work-withedness in making this book possible.*

Syngress Publishing, Elsevier and especially Andrew Williams for his enthusiasm with this project, sense of humor and much-tested patience.

A huge thank you to Eric Ortego for his assistance with Chapter 6 – may our fingerprints never show up on your assets! ☺

Thanks to Dan Cutrer for being, without a doubt, the funniest and nicest lawyer I know. Your insights and assistance were greatly appreciated.

Acknowledgements would not be complete without mentioning Fyodor and all the incredibly talented people who have made Nmap what it is today. Many, many thanks to you all.

A special thank you goes out to Angela Orebaugh - I will always be indebted to you for asking me to share this wild book ride with you. Here's to the only person I now consider one of my best friends to have never met face-to-face!

Here's a huge shout out to my Mom, just because I know she will get a kick out of it. I love you so much – thank you for all your help over the past few months.

Last, but without whom nothing else matters – Kim, Ben, Jake, and our beautiful, happy baby, Luke. Some day when you get big enough, I will teach you how to scan stuff.

Technical Editor

Aaron W. Bayles is an INFOSEC Principal in Houston, Texas. He has provided services to clients with penetration testing, vulnerability assessment, risk assessments, and security design/architecture for enterprise networks. He has over 12 years experience with INFOSEC, with specific experience with wireless security, penetration testing, and incident response. Aaron's background includes work as a senior security engineer with SAIC in Virginia and Texas. He is also the lead author of the Syngress book, *InfoSec Career Hacking, Sell your Skillz, Not Your Soul*, as well as a contributing author of the First Edition of *Penetration Tester's Open Source Toolkit*.

Aaron has provided INFOSEC support and penetration testing for multiple agencies in the U.S. Department of the Treasury, such as the Financial Management Service and Securities and Exchange Commission, and the Department of Homeland Security, such as U. S. Customs and Border Protection. He holds a Bachelor's of Science degree in Computer Science with post-graduate work in Embedded Linux Programming from Sam Houston State University and is also a CISSP.

Contents

Chapter 1

Introducing Network Scanning

Solutions in this chapter:

- What is Network Scanning?
- Networking and Protocol Fundamentals
- Network Scanning Techniques
- Common Network Scanning Tools
- Who Uses Network Scanning?
- Detecting and Protecting
- Network Scanning and Policy

☑ Summary

☑ Solutions Fast Track

☑ Frequently Asked Questions

Introduction

About ten years ago I was working as a Network Administrator managing a medium size network. One of my first tasks in this position was to create a network asset database for all network devices. We already had a high-priced, although functionally deficient, network management tool that just wasn't making the cut. Using the output from the management tool as a starting point I began painstakingly connecting to each network device, and documenting them to inventory the network. This also involved a lot of hours physically traversing buildings, basements, and wiring closets. Finally, it seemed that I had visited every nook and cranny and identified every router, bridge, switch, hub, and archaic telecommunications device retrofitted to the network. For security, I wrote a UNIX script to connect to the known devices and disable physical ports that weren't being used and enable security features on the devices. This is when things started to get complicated. Suddenly the help desk phones started ringing and people were complaining of lost network connectivity. Alas, there were even more devices out there that we didn't know about! Luckily the UNIX script was easily reversible. After hearing my woes that evening a "hacker" friend of mine pointed out a new tool for scanning networks that he read about in Phrack magazine. It was a bit controversial, but it was free and it looked like it could do the job. The next day became my first experience with Nmap, a network scanner, and since that day it has been making my life a whole lot easier.

What is Network Scanning?

Network scanning is the process of discovering active hosts on the network and information about the hosts, such as operating system, active ports, services, and applications. Network scanning is comprised of the following four basic techniques:

- **Network Mapping** Sending messages to a host that will generate a response if the host is active
- **Port Scanning** Sending messages to a specified port to determine if it is active
- **Service and Version Detection** Sending specially crafted messages to active ports to generate responses that will indicate the type and version of service running

- **OS Detection** Sending specially crafted messages to an active host to generate certain responses that will indicate the type of operating system running on the host

In addition to these basic techniques, advanced network scanners can perform other techniques such as masking the origin of the scanning, enabling timing features for stealthy scans, evading perimeter defenses such as firewalls, and providing reporting options.

The following is an example of the type of output you would expect from a network scan:

- Host 192.168.100.1 is responding
- Open ports include:
  - 135/tcp open msrpc
  - 139/tcp open netbios-ssn
  - 445/tcp open microsoft-ds
  - 3389/tcp open ms-term-serv
  - 8081/tcp open blackice-icecap
- The operating system is Windows XP SP2

NOTE

Throughout this book the terms device, host, and system may be used interchangeably.

Networking and Protocol Fundamentals

This section provides background information on how networks and protocols work. However, there are many other excellent resources available, including the most popular and undoubtedly one of the best written, Richard Stevens' "TCP/IP Illustrated, Vol. 1–3."

Explaining Ethernet

Ethernet is the most popular protocol standard used to enable computers to communicate. A protocol is like speaking a particular language. Ethernet was built around the principle of a shared medium where all computers on the local network segment share the same cable. It is known as a *broadcast* protocol because it sends that data to all other computers on the same network segment. This information is divided up into manageable chunks called *packets*, and each packet has a header containing the addresses of both the destination and source computers. Even though this information is sent out to all computers on a segment, only the computer with the matching destination address responds. All of the other computers on the network still see the packet, but if they are not the intended receiver they disregard it.

Ethernet addresses are also known as Media Access Control (MAC) addresses and hardware addresses. Because many computers may share a single Ethernet segment, each one must have an individual identifier hard-coded onto the network interface card (NIC). A MAC address is a 48-bit number, which is also stated as a 12-digit hexadecimal number. This number is broken down into two halves; the first 24 bits identify the vendor of the Ethernet card, and the second 24 bits comprise a serial number assigned by the vendor.

The following steps allow you to view your NIC's MAC address:

- **Windows 9x/ME** Access **Start | Run** and type **winipcfg.exe**. The MAC address will be listed as the "Adapter Address."
- **Windows NT, 2000, XP, and 2003** Access the command line and type **ipconfig /all**. The MAC address will be listed as the "Physical Address."
- **Linux and Solaris** Type **ifconfig –a** at the command line. The MAC address will be listed as the "HWaddr" on Linux and as "ether" on Solaris.
- **Macintosh OS X** Type **ifconfig –a** at the Terminal application. The MAC address will be listed as the "Ether" label.

You can also view the MAC addresses of other computers that you have recently communicated with, by typing the command **arp –a**. The Address Resolution Protocol (ARP) is responsible for mapping IP addresses to MAC addresses.

MAC addresses are unique, and no two computers should have the same one. However, occasionally a manufacturing error may occur that causes more than one NIC to have the same MAC address. Thus, people may choose to change their MAC addresses intentionally, which can be done with a program (e.g., *ifconfig*) that allows you to fake your MAC address. Faking your MAC address (and other types of addresses) is also known as *spoofing*. Also, some adapters allow you to use a program to reconfigure the runtime MAC address. And lastly, with the right tools and skill you can physically re-burn the address into the NIC.

NOTE

Spoofing is the process of altering network packet information (e.g., the IP source address, the MAC address, or the e-mail address). This is often done to masquerade as another device in order to exploit a trust relationship or to make tracing the source of attacks difficult. Address spoofing is also used in DoS attacks (e.g., Smurf), where the return addresses of network requests are spoofed to be the IP address of the victim.

Understanding the Open Systems Interconnection Model

The International Standards Organization (ISO) developed the Open Systems Interconnection (OSI) model in the early 1980s to describe how network protocols and components work together. It divides network functions into seven layers, each layer representing a group of related specifications, functions, and activities (see Figure 1.1). Although complicated at first, the terminology is used extensively in networking, systems, and development communities. Understanding what these layers represent and how they work together will facilitate your comprehension of network scanning.

Figure 1.1 Seven Boxes Corresponding to the OSI Model

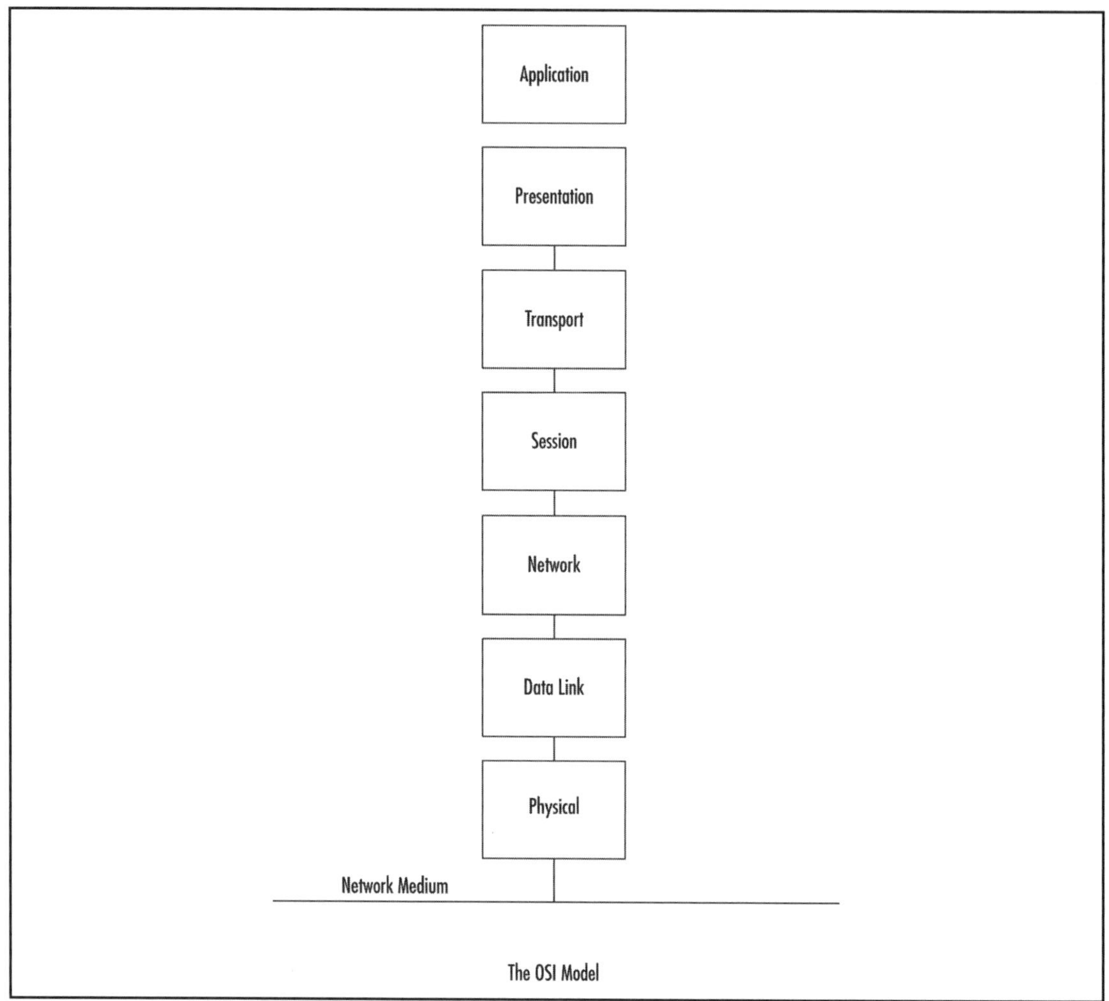

NOTE

The OSI model is not necessarily reflective of the way that applications and OSes are actually written. In fact, some security tools use the differences in protocol implementations to extract information from computers (including their OSes) and specific patches and services packs that may have been installed.

"We still talk about the seven layers model, because it's a convenient model for discussion, but that has absolutely zero to do with any real-life software engineering. In other words, it's a way to talk about things, not to implement

them. And that's important. Specs are a basis for talking about things. But they are not a basis for implementing software."

– Linus Torvalds, project coordinator for the Linux kernel, in an e-mail dated September 29, 2005 (http://lkml.org/lkml/2005/9/29/233).

The following sections define the seven layers of the OSI model.

Layer 1: Physical

The first layer of the OSI model is the *Physical* layer, which specifies the electrical and mechanical requirements for transmitting data bits across the transmission medium (cable or airwaves). It involves sending and receiving the data stream on the carrier, whether that carrier uses electrical (cable), light (fiber optic), radio, infrared, or laser (wireless) signals. The Physical layer specifications include:

- Voltage changes
- The timing of voltage changes
- Data rates
- Maximum transmission distances
- The physical connectors to the transmission medium (plug)
- The topology or physical layout of the network

Many complex issues are addressed at the Physical layer, including digital vs. analog signaling, baseband vs. broadband signaling, whether data is transmitted synchronously or asynchronously, and how signals are divided into channels (multiplexing).

Devices that operate at the Physical layer deal with signaling (e.g., transceivers on the NIC), repeaters, basic hubs, and simple connectors that join segments of cable). The data handled by the Physical layer is in bits of 1s (ones) and 0s (zeros), which are represented by pulses of light or voltage changes of electricity, and by the state of those pulses (*on* generally representing 1 and *off* generally representing *0*).

How these bits are arranged and managed is a function of the Data Link layer (layer 2) of the OSI model.

Layer 2: Data Link

Layer 2 is the *Data Link* layer, which is responsible for maintaining the data link between two computers, typically called *hosts* or *nodes*. It also defines and manages the ordering of bits to and from packets. *Frames* contain data arranged in an organized manner, which provides an orderly and consistent method of sending data bits across the medium. Without such control, the data would be sent in random sizes or configurations and the data on one end could not be decoded at the other end. The Data Link layer manages the physical addressing and synchronization of the data packets. It is also responsible for flow control and error notification on the Physical layer. Flow control is the process of managing the timing of sending and receiving data so that it doesn't exceed the capacity of the physical connection or host. Since the Physical layer is only responsible for physically moving the data onto and off of the network medium, the Data Link layer also receives and manages error messaging related to the physical delivery of packets.

Network devices that operate at this layer include layer 2 switches (switching hubs) and bridges. A layer 2 switch decreases network congestion by sending data out only on the port that the destination computer is attached to, instead of sending it out on all ports (hubs). Bridges provide a way to segment a network into two parts and filter traffic, by building tables that define which computers are located on each side of the bridge, based on their MAC addresses. Conversely, bridges also can be used to join separate networks and allow traffic to pass between them.

The Data Link layer is divided into two sublayers: the Logical Link Control (LLC) sublayer and the MAC sublayer.

NOTE

On Ethernet NICs, the physical or MAC address (also called the *hardware* address) is expressed as 12 hexadecimal digits arranged in pairs with colons between each pair (e.g., 12:3A:4D:66:3A:1C). The initial three sets of numbers represent the manufacturer, and the last three bits represent a unique NIC made by that manufacturer.

Layer 3: Network

Moving up the stack, the next layer is the *Network* layer (layer 3), which is where packets are sequenced and logical addressing is assigned. Logical addresses are nonpermanent, software-assigned addresses that can only be changed by administrators. The IP addresses used by the TCP/IP protocols on the Internet, and the Internet Package Exchange (IPX) addresses used by the IPX/Sequenced Packet Exchange

(SPX) protocols on NetWare networks are examples of logical addresses. These protocol stacks are referred to as *routable* because they include addressing schemes that identify the network or subnet and the particular client on that network or subnet. Other network/transport protocols (e.g., NETBIOS Extended User Interface [NetBEUI]) do not have a sophisticated addressing scheme and thus cannot be routed between different types of networks.

NOTE

To understand the difference between physical and logical addresses, consider this analogy: A house has a physical GPS address that identifies exactly where it is located. This is similar to the MAC address on a NIC. A house also has a logical address assigned to it by the post office that consists of a street name and number. The post office occasionally changes the names of streets or renumbers the houses located on them. This is similar to the IP address assigned to a network interface.

The Network layer is also responsible for creating a virtual circuit (i.e., a logical connection, not a physical connection) between points or nodes. A node is any device that has a MAC address, which typically includes computers, printers, and routers. This layer is also responsible for routing, layer 3 switching, and forwarding packets. *Routing* refers to forwarding packets from one network or subnet to another. Without routing, computers can only communicate with computers on the same network. Routing is the key to the global Internet, and is one of the most important duties of the Network layer.

Finally, the Network layer provides additional levels of flow control and error control. From this point on, the primary methods of implementing the OSI model architecture involve software rather than hardware.

Devices that operate at the network layer include routers and layer 3 switches.

Layer 4: Transport

Layer 4 is the *Transport* layer, and is responsible for transporting the data from one node to another. It provides transparent data transfer between nodes, and manages the end-to-end flow control, error detection, and error recovery.

The Transport layer protocols initiate contact between specific ports on different host computers, and set up a virtual circuit. Transmission Control Protocol (TCP) is one such layer 4 protocol. As an example, TCP verifies that the application sending the data is authorized to access the network and that both ends are ready to initiate the data transfer. When this synchronization is complete, the data is sent. As the data is being transmitted, the TCP protocol on each host monitors the data flow and watches for transport errors. If transport errors are detected, TCP provides error recovery.

The functions performed by the Transport layer are very important to network communication. Just as the Data Link layer provides lower-level reliability and connection-oriented or connectionless communications, the Transport layer does the same thing but at a higher level. The two protocols most commonly associated with the Transport layer are TCP, which is connection-oriented, and User Datagram Protocol (UDP), which is connectionless.

NOTE

What's the difference between a connection-oriented protocol and a connectionless protocol? A connection-oriented protocol (e.g., TCP) creates a connection between two computers before sending the data, and then verifies that the data has reached its destination by using acknowledgements (ACKs) (i.e., messages sent back to the sending computer from the receiving computer that acknowledge receipt). Connectionless protocols send the data and trust that it will reach the proper destination or that the application will handle retransmission and data verification.

Consider this analogy: You need to send an important letter to a business associate that contains valuable papers. You call him before e-mailing the letter, to let him know that he or she should expect it (establishing the connection). A few days later your friend calls to let you know that he received the letter, or you receive the return receipt (ACK). This is how connection-oriented communication works. When mailing a postcard to a friend, you drop it in the mailbox and hope it gets to the addressee. You don't expect or require any acknowledgement. This is how connectionless communication works.

The Transport layer also manages the logical addressing of ports. Think of a port as a suite or apartment number within a building that defines exactly where the data should go. Table 1.1 shows the most commonly used Internet ports.

Table 1.1 Commonly Used Internet Ports

Internet Protocol (IP) Port(s)	Protocol(s)	Description
80	TCP	Hypertext Transfer Protocol (HTTP), commonly used for Web servers
443	TCP	HTTP Secure sockets (HTTPS) for secure Web communications.
53	UDP and TCP	Domain Name Service (DNS) for resolving names to IP addresses
25	TCP	Simple Mail Transport Protocol (SMTP) for sending e-mail
22	TCP	Secure Shell (SSH) protocol for encrypting communications
23	TCP	Telnet, a plaintext administration protocol
20 and 21	TCP	File Transfer Protocol (FTP) for transferring data between systems
135–139 and 445	TCP and UDP	Windows file sharing, login, and Remote Procedure Call (RPC)
500	UDP	Internet Security Association and Key Management Protocol (ISAKMP) key negotiation for Secure Internet Protocol (IPSec) virtual private networks (VPNs)
5060	UDP	Session Initiation Protocol (SIP) for some Voice over IP (VoIP) uses
123	UDP	Network Time Protocol (NTP) for network time synchronization

A computer may have several network applications running at the same time (e.g., a Web browser sending a request to a Web server for a Web page, an e-mail client sending and receiving e-mail, and a file transfer program uploading or downloading information to and from an FTP server). The mechanism for determining which incoming data packets belong to which application is the function of port numbers. The FTP protocol is assigned a particular port, whereas the Web browser and e-mail clients use different protocols (e.g., HTTP and Post Office Protocol (POP3) or Internet Message Access Protocol [IMAP]) that have their own assigned ports; thus the information intended for the Web browser doesn't go to the e-mail program by mistake. Port numbers are used by TCP and UDP and consist of ports found within a range of 0–65535. Ports 0–1023 are assigned by the Internet Assigned Numbers Authority (IANA) and are considered static. Ports >=1024 are ephemeral ports, although many are commonly used for specific applications.

NOTE

The Internet Assigned Numbers Agency (IANA) has a website of port assignments that cross-references registered services to ports. It is located at www.iana.org/assignments/port-numbers.

Layer 5: Session

After the Transport layer establishes a virtual connection, a communication session is made between two processes on two different computers. The *Session* layer (layer 5) is responsible for establishing, monitoring, and terminating sessions, using the virtual circuits established by the Transport layer.

The Session layer is also responsible for putting header information into data packets that indicates where a message begins and ends. Once header information is attached to the data packets, the Session layer performs synchronization between the sender's Session layer and the receiver's Session layer. The use of ACKs helps coordinate the transfer of data at the Session-layer level.

Another important function of the Session layer is controlling whether the communications within a session are sent as full-duplex or half-duplex messages. Half-duplex communication goes in both directions between the communicating computers, but information can only travel in one direction at a time (e.g., radio communications where you hold down the microphone button to transmit, but cannot hear the person on the other end). With full-duplex communication, information can be sent in both directions at the same time (e.g., a telephone conversation, where both parties can talk and hear one another at the same time).

Whereas the Transport layer establishes a connection between two machines, the Session layer establishes a connection between two processes. An application can run many processes simultaneously to accomplish the work of the application.

After the Transport layer establishes the connection between the two machines, the Session layer sets up the connection between the application process on one computer and the application process on another computer.

Layer 6: Presentation

Data translation is the primary activity of the *Presentation* layer (layer 6). When data is sent from a sender to a receiver, it is translated at the Presentation layer (i.e., the sender's application passes data down to the Presentation layer, where it is changed into a common format). When the data is received on the other end, the Presentation layer changes it from the common format back into a format that is useable by the application. Protocol translation (i.e., the conversion of data from one protocol to another so that it can be exchanged between computers using different platforms or OSes) takes place here.

The Presentation layer is also where *gateway* services operate. Gateways are connection points between networks that use different platforms or applications (e.g., e-mail gateways, Systems Network Architecture (SNA) gateways, and gateways that cross platforms or file systems). Gateways are usually implemented via software such as the Gateway Services for NetWare (GSNW). Software redirectors also operate at this layer.

Data compression takes place in layer 6, which minimizes the number of bits that must be transmitted on the network media to the receiver. Data encryption and decryption take place in the Presentation layer as well.

Layer 7: Application

The *Application* layer is the point at which the user application program interacts with the network. Don't confuse the networking model with the application itself. Application processes (e.g., file transfers or e-mail) are initiated within a user application (e.g., an e-mail program). Then the data created by that process is handed to the Application layer of the networking software. Everything that occurs at this level is application-specific (e.g., file sharing, remote printer access, network monitoring and management, remote procedure calls, and all forms of electronic messaging).

Both FTP and Telnet function within the Application layer, as do SMTP, POP, and IMAP, all of which are used for sending or receiving e-mail. Other Application-layer protocols include HTTP, Network News Transfer Protocol (NNTP), and Simple Network Management Protocol (SNMP).

You have to distinguish between the protocols mentioned and the applications that might bear the same names, because there are many different FTP programs made by different software vendors that use FTP to transfer files.

The OSI model is generic, yet provides the appropriate guidelines to be used to explain the majority of network protocols. Various protocol suites are often mapped against the OSI model for this purpose. A solid understanding of the OSI model aids in network analysis, comparison, and troubleshooting. However, it is important to remember that not all protocols map well to the OSI model (e.g., TCP/IP was designed to map to the U.S. Department of Defense (DoD) model). In the 1970s, the DoD developed its four-layer model. The core Internet protocols adhere to this model.

The DoD model is a condensed version of the OSI model. Its four layers are:

- **Application/Process Layer** This layer defines protocols that implement user-level applications (e.g., e-mail delivery, remote login, and file transfer.
- **Host-to-host Layer** This layer manages the connection, data flow management, and retransmission of lost data.
- **Internet Layer** This layer delivers data from the source host to the destination host across a set of physical networks that connect the two machines.
- **Network Access Layer** This layer manages the delivery of data over a particular hardware media.

NOTE

The five layer TCP/IP model is a popular model; however it is not recognized as a standard. The five layers include: Application, Transport, Network/Internet, Data link, and Physical.

Carrier Sense Multiple Access/Collision Detection (CSMA/CD)

Ethernet uses the CSMA/CD protocol in order for devices to exchange data on the network. The term *multiple access* refers to the fact that many network devices attached to the same segment have the opportunity to transmit. Each device is given an equal opportunity; no device has priority over another. *Carrier sense* describes how an Ethernet interface on a network device listens to the cable before transmitting. The network interface ensures that there are no other signals on the cable before it transmits, and listens while transmitting to ensure that no other network device transmits data at the same time. When two network devices transmit at the same time, a *collision* occurs. Because Ethernet interfaces listen to the media while they are transmitting, they can identify the presence of others through *collision detection*. If a collision occurs, the transmitting device waits for a small, random amount of time before retransmitting. This function is known as the *back off delay*. It has also been referred to as a back off timer or exponential back off.

Traditionally, Ethernet operation has been half-duplex, which means that an interface can either transmit or receive data, but not at the same time. If more than one network interface on a segment tries to transmit at the same time, a collision occurs. When a crossover cable is used to connect two devices, or a single device is attached to a switch port, only two interfaces on the segment need to transmit or receive; no collisions occur. This is because the transmit (TX) of device A is connected to the receive (RX) of device B, and the TX of B is connected to the RX of device A. The collision detection method is no longer necessary, therefore, interfaces can be placed in full-duplex mode, which allows network devices to transmit and receive at the same time, thereby increasing performance.

The Major Protocols: IP, TCP, UDP, and ICMP

The next four protocols are at the heart of how the Internet works today.

NOTE

Other, different protocols are used across the Internet, and new protocols are constantly created to fulfill specific needs. One of these is Internet Protocol version 6 (IPv6), which seeks to improve the existing Internet protocol suite by providing more IP addresses, and by improving the security of network connections across the Internet using encryption. For more information on IPv6, see www.ipv6.org/ or http://en.wikipedia.org/wiki/IPv6.

IP

Internet Protocol (IP) is a connectionless protocol that manages addressing data from one point to another, and fragments large amounts of data into smaller, transmittable packets. The major components of Internet Protocol datagrams are:

- **IP Identification (IPID)** Used to uniquely identify IP datagrams and for reassembly of fragmented packets.
- **Protocol** Describes the higher-level protocol embedded within the datagram.
- **Time-to-live (TTL)** Attempts to keep datagrams and packets from routing in circles. When TTL reaches 0, the datagram is dropped. The TTL allows traceroute to function, identifying each router in a network by sending out datagrams with successively increasing TTLs, and tracking when those TTLs are exceeded.
- **Source IP Address** The IP address of the host where the datagram was created.
- **Destination IP Address** The destination where the datagram should be sent.

Notes from the Underground…

IP Address Source Spoofing

It is possible to spoof any part of an IP datagram; however, the most commonly spoofed IP component is the source IP address. Also, not all protocols function completely with a spoofed source IP address (e.g., connection-oriented protocols such as TCP require handshaking before data can be transmitted, thereby reducing the ease and effectiveness of spoofing-based attacks).

Spoofing can also be used as part of a DoS attack. If Network A sends a datagram to Network B, with a spoofed source IP host address on Network C, Network C will see traffic going to it that originates from Network B, perhaps without any indication that Network A is involved at all. This type of spoofing is common in Smurf and Fraggle attacks.

The best practice for network administrators is to ensure that the network can only originate packets with a proper Source IP address (i.e., an IP address in the network itself). It is also common practice for network administrators to deny inbound packets with source IP addresses matching those of their internal networks.

Internet Control Message Protocol

The Internet Control Message Protocol (ICMP) manages errors and provides informational reporting for IP networks. ICMP messages are defined by RFC 792-defined *types* and *codes*. The following are common types of ICMP messages:

- **Echo Request (Type 8)/Reply (Type 0)** Used by programs such as *ping* to calculate the delay in reaching another IP address.
- **Destination Unreachable (Type 3):** An unreachable message is sent to the source IP address of a packet when a network, host, protocol or port cannot be reached. This can happen when a host or network is down or if there is a network problem. There are a number of subtypes of Destination Unreachable messages that are helpful at diagnosing communication issues.
- **Time Exceeded (Type 11)** Occurs when a packet's TTL reaches 0.

TCP

TCP packets are connection-oriented, and are used most often to transmit data. The connection-oriented nature of TCP packets makes it a poor choice for source IP address spoofing. Several applications use TCP, including the Web (HTTP), e-mail (SMTP), FTP, SSH, Telnet, POP and many others.

The TCP Handshake

An important concept of TCP is *handshaking,* as depicted in Figure 1.2. Before any data can be exchanged between two hosts, they must agree to communicate. Host A sends a packet to Host B with the synchronize (SYN) flag set. If Host B is willing and able to communicate, it returns the SYN packet and adds an acknowledgement (ACK) flag. Host A indicates to Host B that it received the ACK from B. This is called a TCP 3-way handshake. At this point, data transmission can begin. When the communication between the hosts ends, a packet with the finish (FIN) flag is sent, and a similar acknowledgement process is followed. This process makes up graceful 4-way close as each side of the communication must send a FIN and ACK. If one side of the communication sends a reset (RST) packet during the sequence, the transmission is quickly aborted.

Figure 1.2 TCP 3-Way Handshake

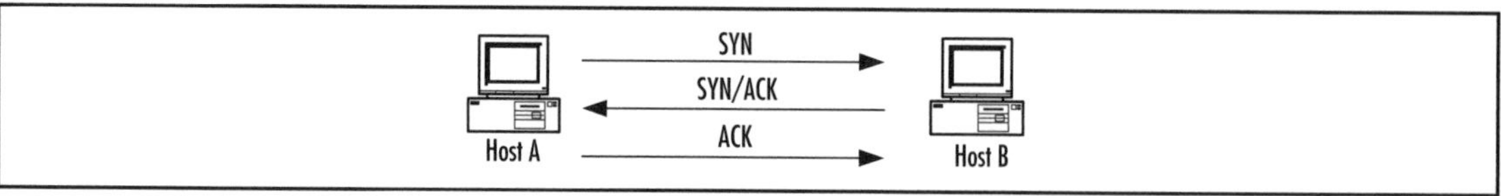

TCP Sequence

Another important component of TCP is *sequence identification*, where each packet sent is part of a sequence. Through these sequence numbers, TCP handles complex tasks such as retransmission, acknowledgement, and packet ordering.

UDP

UDP packets are the connectionless equivalent to TCP, and are used for many purposes, the most important being that DNS uses UDP for a majority of its name resolution work. DNS has the ability to perform reverse and forward lookups, necessary to determine which IP address corresponds to which hostname and vice versa (e.g., *www.example.com* is not routable if utilized inside an IP datagram; however, through a DNS system it can find the IP address and include that in the IP datagram to route traffic to). Due to the connectionless nature of UDP, it is considered a speedy protocol and has a wide range of uses, especially for applications that must transmit data very quickly like VoIP, instant messaging, online games, Peer-to-peer (P2P applications, online radio, broadcasts and other streaming media types.

Network Scanning Techniques

Host Discovery

The first part of network scanning is identifying active hosts, known as host discovery. Network scanners perform host discovery by attempting to solicit a response from a host. You can perform host discovery on a single IP address, a range of IP addresses, or a comma-separated list of IP addresses. Some network scanners also allow you to provide an input file that contains a list of IP addresses to scan or an exclude list of IP address not to scan.

Network scanners use a variety of techniques to solicit responses from a target. Host discovery is often performed by the following basic techniques:

- **ICMP ECHO Request** An ICMP ECHO request is an ICMP type 8 packet, commonly referred to as a *ping*. If the target IP address is active, an ICMP ECHO reply (ICMP type 0) is received. Sending ICMP ECHO requests to multiple hosts is known as a *ping sweep*.
- **ICMP Timestamp** An ICMP Type 13 message is a timestamp query. If the target IP address is active it will respond with the current time (ICMP type 14).
- **ICMP Address Mask Request** An ICMP Type 17 message is an address mask request. If the target IP address is active it will respond with its netmask (ICMP type 18).
- **TCP Ping** A TCP ping sends a TCP SYN or TCP ACK packet to a target IP address. You will need to provide a target port number to send the packet to, such as 21, 25, or 80. If the target IP address is active it will respond, however the type of response depends on the type of packet sent, the target's operating system, and the presence of firewalls or router access lists.
- **UDP Ping** A UDP Ping sends a UDP packet to a specific UDP port at the target IP address. If the target IP address is active, but the UDP port is closed, the system will send an ICMP Port Unreachable. However, due to the connectionless nature of UDP, this type of UDP ping is unique in that no response from the target also indicates the possibility that the port (and therefore, the host) is active.

These host discovery methods are not fool proof. While no response could give an indication of the target's active status, it could also mean that a router or firewall is dropping the packets. Also, some operating systems may not comply with the requests and drop the packet.

NOTE

Although network scanning identifies active hosts, ports, services, and applications, vulnerability scanning goes one step further to identify weaknesses and vulnerabilities on a system that may be exploited by an attacker.

NOTE

Inverse mapping is the ability to determine potential active hosts by gathering information about inactive IP addresses. A firewall or router that is blocking pings will not respond to an ICMP ECHO request packet if the target IP address is active on the network. However, they often respond with an ICMP host unreachable packet if the target is not active.

Port and Service Scanning

Once you have identified an active host you can attempt to identify the ports and services running on that host by performing port scanning. When an attacker performs port scanning, it is often compared to a burglar checking for unlocked doors and windows on a house. Knowing the open ports and services helps attackers further investigate vulnerabilities that can be possible entry points into the system. Port scanning sends a request to solicit a reply from ports on a target computer. There are many different types of port scanning techniques. Most of them can be loosely categorized as the following:

- **Connect scan.** Connect scans perform a full TCP three way handshake and open a connection to the target. These scans are easily detected and often logged by the host. If a TCP port is listening and not firewalled it will respond with a SYN/ACK packet, otherwise the host responds with a RST/ACK packet.
- **Half-open scan.** A half open scan does not complete the full TCP three way handshake. It is also referred to as a SYN scan. With a half open scan, when the scanner receives a SYN/ACK from the target host, implying an open port on the target, the scanner immediately tears down the connection with a RST. This type of scan used to be considered a stealth scan because the connection was not completed and therefore not logged by the host; however it is easily detected by intrusion detection systems.
- **Stealth scan.** Stealth scans use various flag settings, fragmentation, and other types of evasion techniques to go undetected. Some examples are a SYN/ACK scan, a FIN scan, an ACK scan, a NULL scan, and a XMAS (Christmas Tree) scan. Each of these scan types are covered in detail later in the book.

Port scanning solicits a variety of responses by setting different TCP flags or sending UDP packets with various parameters. Both TCP and UDP each have 65,536 possible ports (0 through 65,535). You may scan all of them or a subset, such as the most commonly used ports. For example, it is routine to scan the well-known ports below 1024 that are associated with common services such as FTP, SSH, Telnet, SMTP, DNS, and HTTP. Once a port is discovered, a network scanner may perform additional examination to determine the actual version of the service running on the open port. As with host discovery, port scanning is also subject to intervention by routers and firewalls, thus port responses may be dropped. Also, some operating systems may not comply with the requests and drop the packet.

NOTE

Because UDP is a connectionless protocol, it does not send replies like TCP. UDP uses ICMP to respond to requests involving closed UDP ports. Active UDP ports will not provide any response to UDP pings. They must be further probed by actual application-level queries.

OS Detection

Operating system detection, also called fingerprinting, is used to determine the type of operating system that is running on the target. Fingerprinting can be performed both actively and passively. With active fingerprinting the network scanner sends several packets to the target with various settings. The responses to the settings are analyzed and compared to a list of known request/response values to find a match. Operating systems are all built with identifying characteristics within their TCP/IP stacks and configurations. This includes settings such as the TCP window size and TCP initial sequence numbers. Passive fingerprinting also looks at deviations in TCP/IP stack implementations; however it looks for these deviations by analyzing the traffic on the network. Passive fingerprinting does not send any packets to the target; it passively monitors the target's communications.

Optimization

There are several performance optimization techniques for network scanning; however they are dependant on the features of the scanner. High performance network scanners will perform many functions in parallel and utilize efficiency algorithms. For example, a common technique is the ability to scan many targets in parallel. Some scanners allow you to modify timing parameters such as timeouts. Decreasing the time that the scanner waits for a response or the time between retries may increase performance. Another optimization technique is to narrow the number of targets and number of ports to scan. For example, instead of scanning the entire network at once, scan each network segment separately or scan for a particular port or service type.

Evasion and Spoofing

A secure network blocks scanning techniques and alerts when a scan is detected. Firewalls block scanning attempts or drop responses to request packets. Intrusion detection systems (IDS) monitor network and host activity and create alerts when traffic matches predefined signatures. Most scanning techniques are easy to detect and will easily trigger IDS alarms. Attackers therefore use a variety of techniques to scan in stealth mode to evade firewalls and IDSs, including the following:

- **Low and slow scanning** Security applications and IDSs watch for a large number of connections during a short period of time to hosts and ports. *Low and slow* scanning is a painfully slow technique that limits the number of hosts and ports that are scanned in a specified time period. Scanning over a long period of time reduces the chance of triggering an alert. If the attacker is patient, this type of scan can be very successful simply because it has a higher chance of not being detected.
- **Fragmentation** Fragmentation splits up TCP-based scan requests over several packets in an attempt to evade detection.
- **Spoofing and decoys** Attackers often spoof their IP addresses and use decoys to evade detection. Spoofing changes the source IP address of the scanner. This technique isn't effective for obtaining scan results since the scanner won't receive replies; it won't be able to obtain any information about the targets. Decoys are fake hosts that appear to be scanning your network at the same time the real attacker is also scanning. This makes it difficult to determine which IP address is the valid scanner.
- **Source ports** Another firewall evasion technique is to specify a source port that is allowed through a firewall such as port 53 (DNS).

- **IP options** Some scanners also allow you to modify IP protocol options to evade firewalls and specify a route to the target.
- **Advanced techniques** Other advanced evasion techniques include FTP bounce scans, idle scans, or proxy tunneling. These will be covered in more detail later in this book.

Common Network Scanning Tools

There are numerous network scanners available including free, open source and commercial products. The following list contains a few of the more popular scanners:

- **Nmap** Nmap is a free open source network scanning utility. It runs on most operating systems including Linux, Windows, and MacOSX. Nmap is the most widely used network scanner and there are many third party tools that integrate with Nmap. It can be downloaded from http://insecure.org.
- **Superscan** Superscan is a free Windows-based network scanner developed by Foundstone. It can be downloaded from www.foundstone.com/us/resources-free-tools.asp.
- **YAPS** Yet Another Port Scanner (YAPS) is a free Windows-based port scanner. It has a simple graphical interface and can scan many targets simultaneously. It can be downloaded from www.steelbytes.com.
- **Angry IP Scanner** Angry IP Scanner is a small, fast IP and port scanner. It runs on Windows, Linux, and Mac OSX. It can be downloaded for free from www.angryziber.com/ipscan/.
- **NEWT** NEWT is both a freeware and commercial Windows-based network scanner. The freeware version has not been updated since 2003, but the commercial version is updated frequently. It is available at www.komodolabs.com.

Who Uses Network Scanning?

System administrators, network engineers, auditors, and security engineers all use network scanners for various reasons including the following:

- Security auditing
- Compliance testing

- Asset management
- Network and system inventory

For example, OS and version scanning is used to manage patches, upgrades and to monitor device and service uptime. Port scanning is used to identify services on a host for policy compliance. Network scanning is also used to verify the firewall filter operation.

Network scanning is a double-edged sword. While network, system, and security professionals use it for assessing and managing systems and networks, intruders use network scanning for harmful purposes. A network scanner is a tool, and like all tools, it can be used for both good and bad purposes. Once an intruder has a profile of the organization from performing reconnaissance or *footprinting*, he or she uses network scanning to gather specific information about the target systems. The intruder scans the target network and systems to identify active hosts, operating systems, and available services and applications. The attacker then uses this information to exploit potential vulnerabilities.

TIP

Host discovery is a great way to audit your network for unauthorized devices.

Notes from the Underground…

Footprinting

Footprinting is a reconnaissance technique that an attacker uses to gather information about the target organization or network. Attackers perform footprinting prior to scanning. The type of information gathered may include:

- Contact information such as employee names, email addresses, phone and fax numbers
- IP addresses
- Identified servers such as DNS and mail

Often an organization's own web page provides this type of information! One point to remember is that footprinting is non-intrusive. No target systems are accessed (with the exception of public websites) at this point. Footprinting relies solely on public information and information collected from the organization.

There are several methods used for footprinting including the following:

- Domain Name Lookups (ARIN, INTERNIC, Samspade, nslookup, dig)
- Newsgroups
- Web searches
- Organization or departmental websites
- Traceroute
- Dumpster Diving
- Physical access
- Social engineering

DNS lookups often reveal IP address, ISP, contact, and DNS server information. Forum or *newsgroup* postings include email addresses, IP addresses, devices used, applications used, and more. Company techies often give away a lot of information when looking for an answer to a problem. *Web searches* may reveal vendor articles and other news articles may reveal the specific types of devices (such as Cisco routers or Check Point firewalls) and applications (such as Peoplesoft) an organization uses. The *organization website* often includes anything from phone numbers, email addresses, and contact information, to partners, mergers, and acquisitions. *Traceroute* is a tool that is used to map the path a packet takes from the source to the destination. It comes installed by default on Windows and UNIX operating systems. For each hop the packet makes, traceroute shows the IP address and DNS name of that hop. If the packet makes it all the way to the destination without being blocked it is a good chance that the hop before the final destination is the border gateway or firewall for the network. Sometimes the names will even reveal what the devices are, such as router.company.org or firewall.company.org. *Dumpster diving* is a valuable way to find printouts, manuals, diagrams and all kinds of other important information that is thrown away. It's not a very fun or pleasant job but it can have great rewards. Having *physical access* to the target site is also helpful, even if is means sitting in the public lobby or better yet, sitting in the cafeteria and listening in on lunch meetings. Last, but certainly not least, *social engineering* is a great source of information. If you smooth talk someone well enough, or impersonate someone well enough you can get anything from IP addresses to passwords.

Detecting and Protecting

Because attackers also use network scanning, you must detect when your organization is a target and protect against network scanning activity. Monitoring for port scans can be a tricky task. You must find the right balance between performance and security. For example, it would not be effective to monitor for SYN scanning by alerting on every SYN packet. Most products perform scan detection by monitoring connection attempts to a large number of hosts or ports from a single source IP over a period of time. To keep false alarms at a minimum it is recommended to set realistic thresholds for alerting. For example, you could set a threshold for 25 SYN packets sent to closed ports within a 5 second interval. Keep in mind this is an example figure, the acceptable number of packets received in a given time period will depend on your own specific environment. You could implement filters to detect a variety of scan attempts such as monitoring for a large number of ACK or FIN packets, or packets with strange combinations of TCP flags. These types of rules should also be tested in your infrastructure for efficiency and to minimize pesky false positives or negatives.

One of the easiest methods of protecting against network scanning is to block ping sweeps by not allowing ICMP ECHO requests to enter your network. This can be performed with a router access control list or with a firewall rule. However, remember there are many non-ICMP ECHO techniques used to scan a network. You can also implement a firewall or inline intrusion prevention system (IPS) that monitors connection state. It will block or alert on connection attempts to enter a network with flags such as ACK or FIN, that are not part of a pre-existing connection. Performing your own network scans from outside the network is a great way to protect your network and systems by determining what the attackers can see. Then you can close ports and implement firewall rules as necessary.

There are also open source port scan detection tools available. One such tool is the Linux-based Port Scan Attack Detector (PSAD), nicely maintained by Cipherdyne and available here: www.cipherdyne.org/psad/.

Network Scanning and Policy

There is one very important topic that we would like to take time to address. Before running your newly installed network scanner at work, please read your company policy! A properly written and comprehensive "Appropriate Use" network policy will more than likely prohibit you from running network scanners. Usually the only exception to this is if network scanning is in your job description. Also, just because you may provide security consulting services for company clients, this does not mean that you can use your scanner on the company network. However, if you are an administrator and are allowed to legitimately run a network scanner, you can use it to manage your network, perform security audits, enforce the company's security policy, and much more. If the policy on the use of network scanners is not clear in your organization, take the time to get permission in writing from the appropriate departments before using a network scanner or any other security-related tools.

Also, if you provide security services for clients, such as an ethical hacker who performs penetration testing, be sure that the use of network scanning is included in your Rules of Engagement. Be very specific about how, where, and when it will be used.

Another word of caution: many ISPs prohibit the use of network scanning in their "Appropriate Use" policy. If they discover that you are scanning devices attached to their network, they may disconnect your service. The best place to experiment with network scanning is on your own home network that is not connected to the Internet. Most network scanners will let you scan your local system. If you get bored with local scanning you can use two computers with a crossover cable between them, or a virtual machine application. You can configure one as a client, and install server services on the other, such as Telnet, FTP, Web, and mail. Install the network scanner on one or both computers and have fun!

Summary

Network scanning is a key component to maintaining secure networks and systems. Proactive management can help find issues before they turn into serious problems and cause network downtime or compromise of confidential data. In addition to managing network and system security, your network scanner may be used for a number of network and system administration tasks.

This chapter provided an overview of network scanning and the specific techniques used to scan networks and systems. To do this adequately it was also necessary to provide some background information on how TCP/IP works. A good networking and protocol reference should be on every administrator's bookshelf. We provided a list of network scanning tools and some potential uses of network scanning by both the good guys and bad guys. While network scanning is a beneficial tool for a system, network, or security administrator, attackers may also use it against us. Thus, we provided an overview of ways to detect and protect against network scanners.

Now that you have been introduced to network scanning and the techniques used to discover active hosts, ports, services, and operating systems you are armed with the knowledge to start exploring a network scanning product. This book covers the Nmap network scanner and its plethora of uses and add-ons. It was touched on in this chapter, but as you read through this book you will continue to discover the variety of ways to use Nmap in the enterprise environment.

Finally, remember to only use network scanning if you have permission and the law is on your side. A curious, up-and-coming administrator could easily be mistaken for an intruder. Make sure you have permission, or use your own private network to experiment.

Solutions Fast Track

What is Network Scanning?

- ☑ Network scanning discovers active hosts on the network and information about the hosts, such as type of operating system, active ports, services, and applications.
- ☑ Network scanning often uses network mapping, port scanning, service and version detection, and operating system detection.
- ☑ Advanced network scanners include scanning optimization and stealthy scanning techniques.

Networking and Protocol Fundamentals

- ☑ Ethernet is a shared medium that uses MAC or hardware addresses.
- ☑ The OSI model has seven layers and represents a standard for network communication.
- ☑ The IP protocol contains the source and destination IP addresses used for network scanning.
- ☑ TCP performs a three way handshake to make a connection between two devices.
- ☑ Both TCP and UDP use ports to communicate.

Network Scanning Techniques

- ☑ Host discovery identifies active hosts on the network.
- ☑ Host discovery often uses ICMP ECHO requests to solicit a reply from a host, but non-ICMP methods may also be used.
- ☑ Firewalls and border routers may block host discovery attempts.
- ☑ Port scanning identifies open ports and services by attempting to solicit a reply from a specific port on a device.
- ☑ Port scanning uses a variety of TCP flags or UDP parameters to solicit replies from hosts and to attempt to evade firewalls and border routers.
- ☑ Active fingerprinting sends several packets to a device with a variety of parameters in order to evaluate the replies and determine the operating system against a known list of requests and replies by OS.
- ☑ Parallelism and timing parameters provide performance optimization for network scanners.
- ☑ Low and slow scanning, fragmentation, and spoofing are methods used by advanced network scanners to evade detection by firewalls and intrusion detection systems.

Common Network Scanning Tools

- ☑ Nmap is the most popular and widely used free network scanner.
- ☑ Superscan is a popular free Windows-based network scanner.
- ☑ NEWT is a popular network scanner available for free or as a commercial product.

Who Uses Network Scanning?

☑ Network, system, and security professionals use network scanning for a variety of administrative functions such as security auditing, compliance testing, asset management, and network and system inventory.

☑ Network scanning may be used to manage patching and upgrades, monitor system uptime, assess policy compliance, verify firewall filter operation, and discover unauthorized devices and applications.

☑ Attackers use network scanning to identify active hosts, open ports and services on a target device. The attacker may then exploit discovered vulnerabilities.

Detecting and Protecting

☑ Most products perform scan detection by monitoring connection attempts to a large number of hosts or ports from a single source IP over a specific period of time.

☑ Refining thresholds for your specific infrastructure reduces false positives.

☑ Protect your network from ping sweeps by not allowing ICMP ECHO requests to enter your network.

☑ Products that monitor connection state will detect packets that are not part of an existing connection.

☑ Regularly perform your own network scan attempts from outside of the network, (if you have permission) to see what attackers can see.

Network Scanning and Policy

☑ A good Appropriate Use policy will prohibit the use of network scanners by anyone not specifically designated to perform this function.

☑ Make sure you have permission to use a network scanner on a network that is not your own.

☑ Read the appropriate use policies of your ISP before using a network scanner.

Frequently Asked Questions

Q: Our security administrator uses a network scanner all the time to look for open ports and potential security issues, but as a network and system administrator I never thought about using it. How do I make sure that I am allowed to use a network scanner as part of my job?

A: First, locate the individual that is responsible for the overall security of the organization. This may be the Chief Security Officer (CSO) or Director of IT, or someone else. This is likely the same person that is responsible for the Appropriate Use policies. Next, meet with this person and explain how and why you intend to use a network scanner. Make sure you get signed permission in writing so that you can proceed with these activities.

Q: I keep seeing messages in my logs about port scanning activity, how do I know if this is something legitimate or an attacker?

A: First, report the activity to the security department or team. If they are unaware of this activity they will most likely use a network sniffer, such as Wireshark or tcpdump, to start tracing the source of the scanning.

Q: I see scanning attempts daily on the outside of my border router, should I be concerned?

A: Unfortunately scanning is a typical activity on the Internet. It may be script kiddies, worm traffic, spammers, or other intruders. If you run an IDS outside of your network at the border router you will see a lot of this activity. Make sure your border router and firewall are blocking the scans from reaching inside the network. Also make sure you are using an IDS on the internal network to identify attacks that may result from an attacker or worm successfully scanning, identifying, and exploiting a vulnerability on your network or systems.

Q: Can I trust the results of my network scanner 100%?

A: No. The biggest problem is that routers and firewalls may block responses to a scanner. Thus, the scanner may report that certain systems are inactive, when they are actually active, or that certain ports are closed when they are actually open.

Another reason not to fully trust a network scanner is the availability of tools to trick the scanner. For example, there are tools, discussed later in this book that can send fake responses to OS detection. So a system may be a Linux system that is reporting as a Windows system. This doesn't mean that you shouldn't run a network scanner, or trust it at all. It just means that you keep this in mind as you perform scanning and analyze the results.

Chapter 2

Introducing Nmap

Solutions in this chapter:

- What is Nmap?
- Using Nmap in the Enterprise
- Securing Nmap
- Optimizing Nmap
- Advanced Nmap Scanning Techniques

☑ Summary

☑ Solutions Fast Track

☑ Frequently Asked Questions

Introduction

In the first chapter, we learned about network scanning at a high level and discussed some of the different technologies and methodologies available to perform scans. Now we're going to start our deep dive into one of the most popular network scanning tools of all time, Nmap, which can be found at http://insecure.org/nmap/index.html. Having a background in IT audit, information security or even system administration will definitely help as you start to learn about this tool. However, the neat thing about Nmap is both the ease with which it can be installed and utilized, as well as how advanced you can get with the tool as you become more familiar with it and learn more about how it can meet your own scanning needs.

We'll properly introduce Nmap in this chapter, talking a bit about its history and some of the scanning ideas that the author, Fyodor, integrated into that first release. Ten short Internet-years have passed since the release of Nmap and we'll discuss how Nmap has evolved and where it continues to help us with current enterprise scanning needs. We'll dig into a section devoted to securing and optimizing. Finally, the chapter will close with information related to advanced Nmap scanning techniques. These are ways of not only setting up and running the scans in your environment but also for interpreting the feedback.

What is Nmap?

Nmap, or Network Mapper, is a free, open source tool that is available under the GNU General Public License as published by the Free Software Foundation. It is most often used by network administrators and IT security professionals to scan enterprise networks, looking for live hosts, specific services, or specific operating systems. Part of the beauty of Nmap is its ability to create IP packets from scratch and send them out utilizing unique methodologies to perform the above-mentioned types of scans and more. In addition, Nmap comes with command-line or GUI functionality and is easily installed on everything from Unix and Windows to Mac OS X. Installation requirements are dependent on the Nmap version you are installing and consist mainly of network library dependencies specific to that version.

History of Nmap

In the grand scheme of things, Nmap is a relative newcomer to the world at the tender young age of 10 years old. However, in Internet-parlance, Nmap is practically a great-grandfather. The application was originally released to the world in September of 1997 via an article Fyodor posted in Phrack, www.phrack.org/issues.html?issue=51&id=11#article. His article included the entire source code for the application, including all his code comments, interesting variables, and error messages:

```
/* gawd, my next project will be in c++ so I don't have to deal with this crap…
simple linked list implementation */
```

to:

```
struct in_addr bullshit, bullshit2;
```

and:

```
if (gethostname(myname, MAXHOSTNAMELEN) ||
!(myhostent = gethostbyname(myname)))
fatal("Your system is fucked up.\n");
```

and:

```
if (portarray[i] > 1023) {
      fprintf(stderr, "Your ftp bounce server sucks, it won't let us feed bogus
ports!\n");
      exit(1);
```

As Nmap gained followers and began drawing more and more interest, Fyodor was launched into geek fame, developer-style. The proof of Nmap's fame was enforced by the use of Fyodor's application in one of the most innovative movies of all times: *The Matrix*. In the sequel, *The Matrix Reloaded*, one of the main characters whips out a laptop, executes a perfect example of an Nmap port scan, and then proceeds to follow it up with an SSH-based exploit.

Figure 2.1 Matrix Reloaded Nmap Scan Screenshot

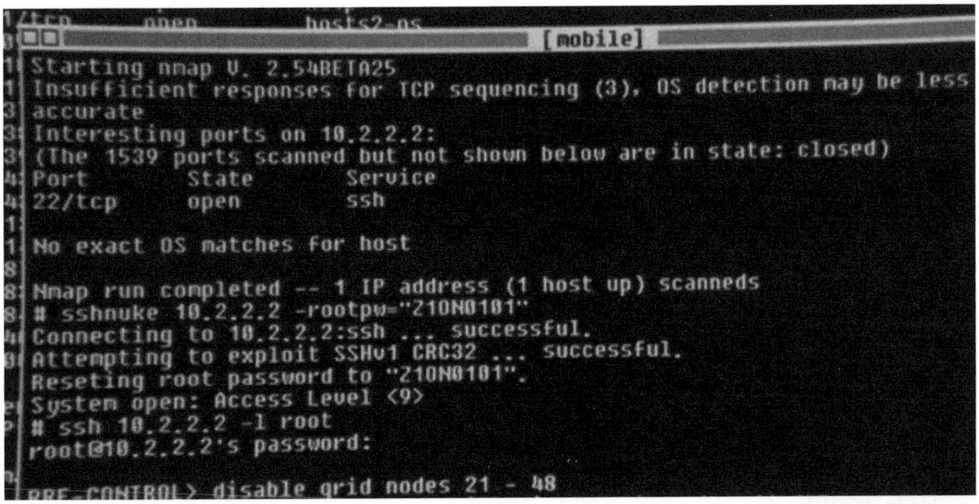

TIP

In enterprise architecture, it is considered best practice to allow server administration via secure shell (SSH). Having an accessible SSH port was not actually the issue with the CityPower Grid server, in *The Matrix Reloaded*. Their big problem was having an outdated, vulnerable instance of SSH running on the server! Once Trinity (the main character who runs the attack) was inside the protected environment of the heavily-guarded datacenter, she was able to succeed in her attack due to a vulnerable version of SSH. If you look closely at Figure 2.1, you will see that first she runs Nmap to identify open ports on the server and the operating system type. The OS type is not discernible; however she finds one port open (SSH). Normally an attacker might attempt to utilize the Nmap service version scan, which was not present in the version 2.54 used above, against this open port to determine first-hand if the open service is running a vulnerable version or not. In Trinity's case, she goes straight to the sshnuke exploit and finds success. See, even in the movies, they know you should always stay on top of the latest security patches and application updates.

Nmap was created with thoughts of firewall subversion and has always been very good at staying abreast of network and operating systems updates that impact the scanning capabilities of the tool. Fyodor has actually come under verbal attack from many administrators for continuing to refine and include evasive measures in the application. In Nmap's defense, Fyodor's stance has always been in support of the administrator. In documentation and forum postings submitted by Fyodor, he describes the necessity for administrators to stay one step ahead of attackers. His opinion is that an attacker will find a way to scan your network, so why shouldn't you? As an example of trying to stay ahead of the challenges, halfway through 2004 Microsoft introduced certain changes to their XP operating system with Service Pack (SP) 2 that impacted the way raw sockets could be constructed. Since Nmap requires the ability to create and manipulate raw sockets to produce and send packets, this created a huge impact for the Windows XP version of the tool. Fyodor and developers working with him on Nmap reported on all the changes and then promptly began coding an XP SP2-specific release of Nmap in order to work around the constraints imposed by Microsoft. This type of response had been previously duplicated when Fyodor discovered that many IDS tools started creating signatures to detect Nmap scans based on timing and patterns utilized by the various scan types. In order to defeat this, he introduced new timing capabilities and types of scans, including the capability to fragment packets, spoof source addresses, and craft packet options.

Nmap Features

Nmap is packed with features. It has the capacity to perform basic, bare-bones scans, such a simple ICMP pings to determine if hosts are up or down. It also has the means to command advanced scans containing a multitude of options and scanning across a huge spectrum of IP address space while logging to specific file types or systems. The reporting functionality also contains a myriad of options with available types from stdout (displayed to the screen), normal (which contains fewer runtime messages and warnings) to XML, s|<rIpt kIddi3, and a grepable format. We will cover many of these features and scan types throughout the book as we continue to discuss the application itself and various enterprise situations showcasing it.

Notes from the Underground...

Script Kiddie Format

At first glance, the script kiddie output format seems like a silly diversion for such a hard-working tool; however the developer responsible for integrating this output format, Peter Kosinar, did so with grander intentions of showcasing Nmap's output capabilities. As infrastructures' reliance on XML grew, output flexibility became a spotlight issue for many tools. Peter's "sl<rIpt kIddi3" output format was a showcase for demonstrating the new output power and potential of Nmap.

Here's a sample scan run with the script kiddie output option. This was posted to the forum by Fyodor when the output type was first introduced in January 2000:

```
amy# nmap -sS -oS - -O -v vectra
$TartInG nmap V. 2.3B3tA14 bY fy0D0r@!n$ecure.org (www.ins3cuR3.0Rg/nmap/)
    !nt3r3$t|nG pOrtz On v3cTrA.yuma.nEt (192.168.0.5):
    P0rt $tate PrOtOcOL $3rv!c3
    13 Op3n tCp Dayt|m3
    21 Open tcp ftp
    22 OpEn Tcp $SH
    23 open tcp tEln3t
    37 OpEn Tcp tim3
```

Continued

```
    79 op3N tcp f!ng3r
    111 0p3n TcP sunrpC
    113 Open tcp auTh
    513 0peN Tcp lOgIn
    514 OpEn tcp $h3ll
TcP S3QuEncE PReDiCtion: ClA$s=random p0$|TivE incr3m3nts
                         DIffIculty=24696 (WorthY Challeng3)
s3quEnce numb3rz: 61B825b7 61b83793 61B88114 61b8B073 61B90DB2 61BA306B
    R3m0t3 operAtInG sy$t3m gue$z: OpeNBSD 2.2 - 2.3
NMAP run c0mpleteD -- 1 IP adDR3ss (1 h0sT up) $CAnNed in 1 SEC0nd
```

As you can see, you must be very "L33t" indeed to interpret this output.

Nmap's User Interface

Traditionally, Nmap is utilized as a command-line driven, UNIX-based tool. This is the way it was originally written and since command-line based applications have an advantage when it comes to creating batch scripts, geeks have flocked to this version for years. The GUI versions of Nmap have seen a rise in popularity in recent years as federal regulations, international, state and local laws have created an urgency surrounding data security and more organizations have been forced to find a way to locate and track things like open ports and service types in their infrastructures. For folks newer to these security roles, using a GUI in front of the application is a comfortable way to gain understanding of how Nmap works and learn more advanced usage techniques. Another factor in pushing more techies to Nmap and GUI-based versions of Nmap was the rise in worm-based vulnerabilities, starting around 1999-2000. Finding infected machines on a network became a challenge. Nmap came to the rescue in the form of a solid tool, with a great reputation and the price of 'free'.

From the command-line, Nmap is executed by simply calling the name of the application (nmap or nmap.exe) and applying the appropriate parameters or switches. It is very helpful, especially for the new user or for advanced configuration, to have a copy of the help instructions close-by. These can be easily accessed from the command-line by typing `nmap -h`.

Once you start investigating GUI renditions of the tool, you will find that historically there were a couple of different options depending on your platform type and which version of the tool you downloaded. There were versions maintained at the Insecure.org website (Nmapwin, NmapFE) and separate versions maintained by developers at other sites (like NmapNT). It was confusing at times to determine which version was the latest and greatest. Fortunately for us now, this has all been replaced with Zenmap. In November 2007, Insecure.org posted a Windows installer that includes a checkbox for installing the Zenmap front-end (see Figure 2.2).

Figure 2.2 Nmap Windows installer, Zenmap option screenshot

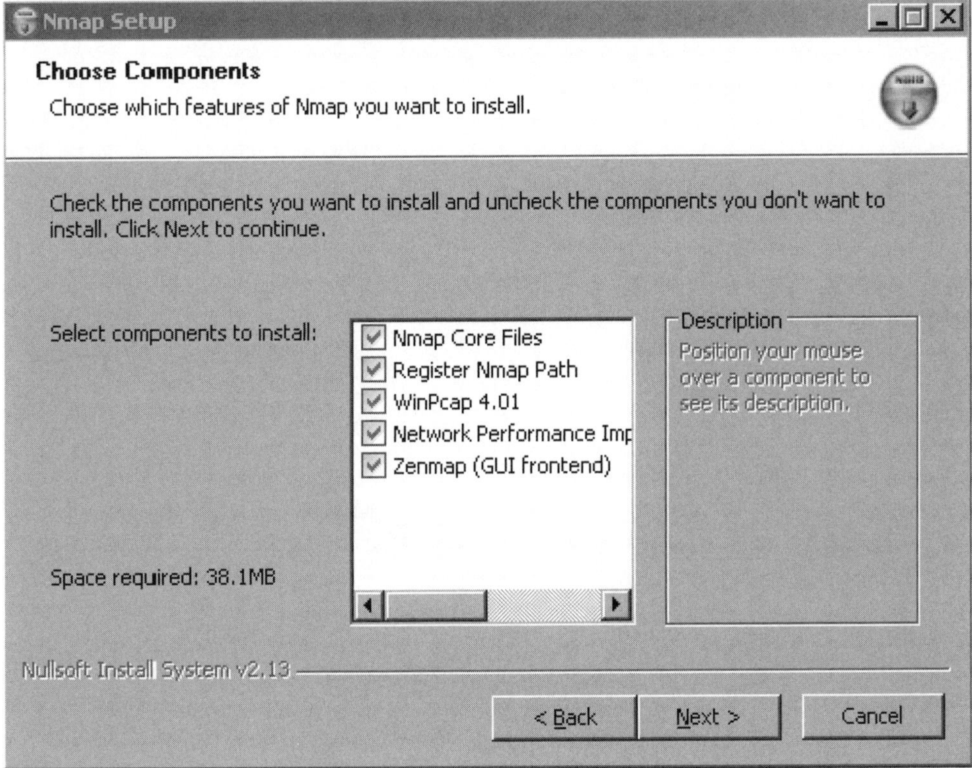

Once installed, a Zenmap icon appears on the desktop and when double-clicked, the user is presented with the ability to work with all Nmap configuration options and parameters (see Figure 2.3).

Figure 2.3 Nmap GUI–Zenmap screenshot

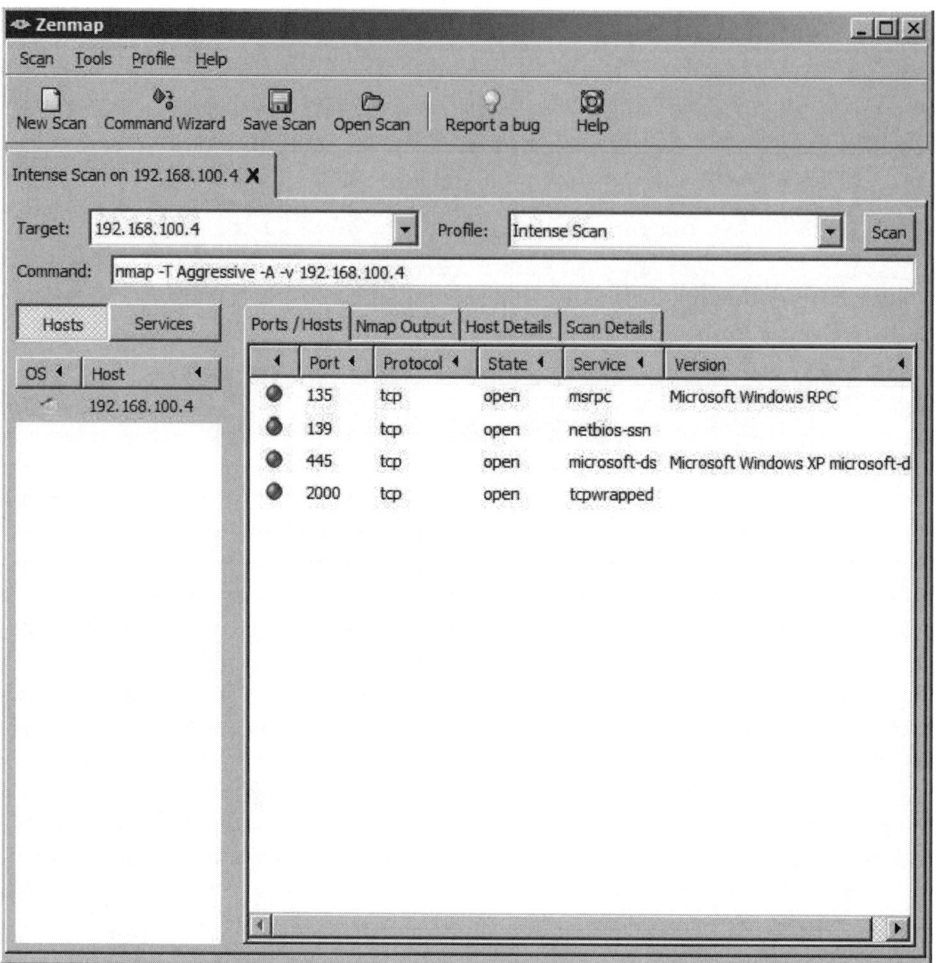

NOTE

The Zenmap GUI was first included as part of the Windows Nmap development package 4.23RC2.

Additional Nmap Resources

Like many of the popular open source applications that exist today, Nmap has a huge following from the developer community. Many developers have spent considerable time and effort to port Nmap to different platforms, integrate it into other pieces of software, and create new ways of working with it or create output from it. You can find an extensive list of these related projects on the insecure.org website at http://insecure.org/nmap/projects.html. Here is a sampling of some of the additional tools and capabilities that have been designed:

- *Nmap Online* http://nmap-online.com/, is a web-based interface to Nmap, written and hosted by Matousec Security. This is a handy way to scan yourself and see what your computer looks like from the Internet side.
- *Nmap-CGI* is a web-based application for scanning your network with Nmap. It offers user management and privilege levels to control who can scan what.
- *Nmap::Scanner* performs Nmap scans programmatically using perl. It was written by Max Schubert <nmap@webwizarddesign.com>.
- *Nmap-Parser* is a perl module for parsing Nmap's XML output. It was created by Anthony Persaud <apersaud@gmail.com>.
- *Cancerbero* is an Nmap-based port scan engine which automates regular scans, storing results in MySQL and generating alerts, change reports, etc. A web interface is provided for configuration and data mining.
- Jens Vogt has created a useful Windows frontend for Nmap called *NMapWin*. It offers many cool features, such as automatic service scheduling.
- *Nmap-Audit* is a perl script which automates port scans, running them in parallel and producing a report of differences between successive scans. It was written by Keith Resar <nmap-audit@heavyk.org>.
- *Inprotect* offers free (GPL) web front-end software for Nmap and Nessus, as well as certain services.
- Julio David Quintana has created a Web PHP front-end for Nmap called *nmapWebFE*.
- Alexandre Sagala has created a Qt/KDE front-end called *KNmap*.
- Ian Zepp <icszepp&at&islc.net> has created another excellent Nmap front end, this time with Qt along with KDE integration. It is called *kmap*.
- Joshua Grubman <jg@false.net> has created this extremely cool *Network Tool* which is a CGI form allowing you to conduct OS scans, traceroutes, and other tests on arbitrary machines. This is a great anti-spam resource!

- The *Zaurus Developer Community* has created an Nmap package for the Sharp Zaurus handheld!
- Dennis Webb has created *Qpenmapfe* – A graphical (QTopia) frontend for Nmap on handhelds like the Sharp Zaurus or specially configured IPAQ.
- Chris Martin has created another ARM Nmap package for the Zaurus or Linux-equipped IPAQ. It is available at www.killefiz.de/zaurus/showdetail.php?app=340 and works with the front-end above.
- Joshua D. Abraham <jabra@ccs.neu.edu> has created *Pbnj*, a tool for running Nmap scans and diff'ing the results.
- Jay Freeman (saurik) (saurik@saurik.com) has created *Nmap+V* – a patch that allows Nmap to capture version numbers for numerous services.
- *Remote nmap* (Rnmap) is a pair of client and server programs which allow for various authorized clients to run their port scans from a centralized server. It was written by Tuomo Makinen <tmakinen@pp.htv.fi>.
- The *Alldas defacement mirror* uses Nmap for port scanning and OS detection of compromised hosts. Their defacement/announce lists are mirrored at seclists.org.
- Nat <natritmeyer@mac.com> has created a Mac OS X frontend for Nmap known as *XNmap*.

Keep in mind that these projects are owned and maintained separately from the tools you will find on the insecure.org website, so your mileage may vary (YMMV) as you start to explore some of them. It is common to find open source offshoots that are no longer maintained or not maintained to the same high standards as the original piece of software. However, you will still often come across that rare gem that does exactly what you need.

Using Nmap in the Enterprise

Nmap has achieved mass following from system administrators, security and network engineers, incident response teams, firewall administrators, penetration testers, desktop administrators, and domain administrators – the list goes on. Anyone who has ever had a job function that required locating a system, testing for an open port, determining what service might be running on a given port, or identifying a target's operating system has looked to Nmap to help fulfill these service needs. As any IT professional can attest, the biggest hurdle to fixing a problem is how much money a particular fix might cost. Being able to utilize well-known, well-maintained, open source tools is a huge bonus for administrators and engineers. Some locations will have difficulties getting approval to use open source technology. Usually these organizations are interested in vendor support, maintenance agreements, and a sense of assurance about the security built into the software. The opposing side to these requirements is that well-supported open source software generally has very extensive testing and excellent ongoing maintenance. Additionally, it is easy to find large, very involved and very vocal user communities associated with these types of open source software. Wireshark, Snort, and Nessus are some other examples that spring to mind.

TIP

Nmap has a great forum for development information, bug reporting, and latest release info. You can find out more about it here: http://cgi.insecure.org/mailman/listinfo/nmap-dev.

We'll be discussing different scenarios you might find in any given enterprise infrastructure, regardless of size, where Nmap capabilities might fit the bill. We'll talk about using Nmap when testing for policy compliance, for desktop and server inventory assistance, for security auditing purposes and finally for general system administration needs.

Using Nmap for Compliance Testing

Testing for compliance can be one of the most important detective security controls you perform in a enterprise infrastructure. The purpose of compliance testing is to measure the critical components of the organization to the policies and controls that govern them. Normally this function falls to either an internal or external audit team. An internal team is generally comprised of employees of the organization and perhaps some long-term contractors, while an external team is often part of a managed services or consulting package. The audit team is responsible for conducting compliance testing against controls they have developed that are specific to meeting regulatory and legal requirements. These requirements vary based on the *type* of business your organization is in (the vertical market), in addition to *where* your organization is located or does business. International, state and local laws all come into play. It is the audit team's responsibility to stay on top of the latest requirements and also to ensure that compliance testing is done in both an orderly and timely fashion. Much like designing and maintaining the policies themselves, compliance testing requires persistent and ongoing attention.

There are many different types of compliance testing where Nmap could be utilized as part of the solution. Some examples:

- Testing for open ports on the interfaces of a firewall.
- Performing scans across workstation IP address ranges to determine if any unauthorized networking applications are installed.
- Determining if the correct version of web service is installed in your De-Militarized Zone (DMZ).
- Locating systems with open file sharing ports.
- Locating unauthorized File Transfer Protocol (FTP) servers, printers or operating systems.
- Any number of needs specific to the controls written around your organization's policies.

Let's take the example of determining what version of web service is running on the server located in your DMZ. We'll pull out our trusty Nmap application and use the Version Scan, `-sV`, setting:

```
nmap -sV host.example.com
Starting Nmap 4.50 (http://insecure.org) at 2007-12-13 19:41 Central
Standard Time
Interesting ports on host.example.com (192.168.10.10):
Not shown: 1686 closed ports
PORT STATE SERVICE VERSION
21/tcp open tcpwrapped
80/tcp open http Microsoft IIS webserver 5.0
135/tcp open msrpc Microsoft Windows RPC
443/tcp open https?
445/tcp open microsoft-ds Microsoft Windows 2000 microsoft-ds
1025/tcp open msrpc Microsoft Windows RPC
1027/tcp open msrpc Microsoft Windows RPC
1433/tcp open ms-sql-s?
2301/tcp open http Compaq Diagnostis httpd (CompaqHTTPServer 4.2)
3389/tcp open ms-term-serv?
49400/tcp open http Compaq Diagnostis httpd (CompaqHTTPServer 4.2)
Service Info: OS: Windows
```

In this example, we see that Nmap believes the server to be running Microsoft IIS 5.0.You can also see a lot of other port information that isn't really specific to our current question.We'll discuss how to narrow down our Nmap query in order to facilitate the scan. First though let's telnet to port 80 on the server and see if Nmap has given us the correct information.

```
telnet host.example.com 80
GET/HTTP/1.0
HTTP/1.1 200 OK
Server: Microsoft-IIS/5.0
Date: Wed, 13 Dec 2007 21:24:22 GMT
X-Powered-By: ASP.NET
X-AspNet-Version: 2.0.50727
Cache-Control: private
Content-Type: text/html; charset=utf-8
Content-Length: 9578
```

Keep in mind that it is very easy to mask this information at the server, but if you are checking organization owned assets for version compliance, most likely you have found an outdated system. Now, if you wanted to narrow down your Nmap scan to only check ports 80 and 443 (or any other ports you know your organization might be using for web-based applications), it is fairly easy to scan specific ports with the –p command.

WARNING

This is common sense for most IT people, but as a word of caution: Always make sure you have appropriate *documented* permission from the organization to scan and that you have the appropriate network access. Jobs have been lost because organization have been caught unaware and labeled scanning as "rogue" when appropriate permissions were not in place.

The most important point to keep in mind when scanning for policy compliance is that you should have an established set of controls that map back to and describe the particular piece of policy you are checking.As an example, let's say your organization has a policy mandating the usage of AV (anti-virus) software on all desktops. Depending on the type of anti-virus application that is deployed, you might find that you have an open port on each system running the AV client. By creating a control that describes this port and the fact that it should be present on systems in your Desktop VLANs, you can then utilize Nmap to locate active systems and subsequently query for this specific port. The beauty of Nmap and its various output capabilities is that you can script this entire process and end up with a small report of online systems having this AV port. One thing to keep in mind (and this goes for any discovery process) is that an end-user's workstation could make it onto the "has AV installed" list and *not* be running the AV client. This happens when users inadvertently or purposely reassign ports to other networked applications. This author once came across the elite port of 31337 (default port for the Back Orifice Trojan) during a scheduled port scan of a small intranet and then discovered that a programmer was beta-testing a new application and had chosen this port because it was "fun to use infamous ports"! Needless to say, the programmer was asked to change the default port setting of the application.

Using Nmap for Inventory and Asset Management

There are many commercial applications designed to track assets, manage inventory counts, relay information about installed services, and monitor system uptime. Luckily for non-commercial application owners, this is another area where Nmap's ease of use pays off with succinct results. In a matter of minutes, an administrator can generate a scan request for a range of IP addresses, an entire subnet, or even re-scan pre-identified systems. The options for identifying services and Operating System (OS) type come in handy when you are trying to identify existing desktops or servers in the infrastructure.

Let's assume you have been tasked with identifying any outdated OS in your network. Step one is to use Nmap to identify *up* systems. This will help us narrow down the number of IP addresses that we have to scan more in-depth. Step two is to use Nmap to query those systems to determine what OS is installed. We'll do this in an Nmap 2-step process first to get used to the idea:

```
nmap -n -sP 10.0.0.1-10 (ok, it's a small network)
Starting Nmap 4.50 (http://insecure.org) at 2007-12-13 19:52 Central Standard Time
Host 10.0.0.1 appears to be up.
MAC Address: 00:0F:B5:6C:DE:E0 (Netgear)
Host 10.0.0.2 appears to be up.
MAC Address: 00:02:E3:13:36:4B (Lite-on Communications)
Host 10.0.0.3 appears to be up.
MAC Address: 00:19:C5:D5:70:EA (Unknown)
Host 10.0.0.4 appears to be up.
Host 10.0.0.5 appears to be up.
MAC Address: 00:14:A5:13:17:75 (Gemtek Technology Co.)
```

```
Host 10.0.0.6 appears to be up.
MAC Address: 00:10:A4:7C:22:AF (Xircom)
Host 10.0.0.7 appears to be up.
MAC Address: 00:0C:29:E9:43:0A (VMware)
Nmap finished: 10 IP addresses (7 hosts up) scanned in 1.000 seconds
```

Here we utilized the `-sP` parameter to perform a ping scan and determine which hosts are up on this small ten host network. We also used the `-n` option to disable DNS lookups of the IP addresses. This is a common practice to help speed up the performance of the network mapping scan (although Nmap is extremely efficient, even when performing DNS lookups). Notice that the 10.0.0.4 host did not report a MAC address. This is because the scan was performed from this system.

Now let's use the `-oN` parameter to write our results to a *normal* output file, to try and make it easier to perform step two:

```
nmap -n -oN up-systems -sP 10.0.0.1-10
```

If we open the *up-systems* file in Wordpad (or whatever your text viewer of choice might be), we find the following (see Figure 2.4):

Figure 2.4 –oN Results of Nmap –sP Scan

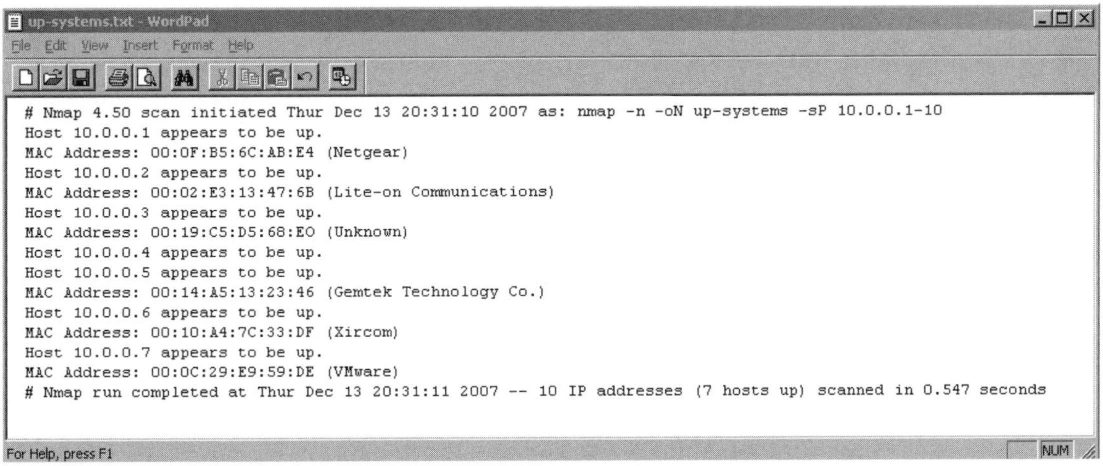

```
up-systems.txt - WordPad
File Edit View Insert Format Help

# Nmap 4.50 scan initiated Thur Dec 13 20:31:10 2007 as: nmap -n -oN up-systems -sP 10.0.0.1-10
Host 10.0.0.1 appears to be up.
MAC Address: 00:0F:B5:6C:AB:E4 (Netgear)
Host 10.0.0.2 appears to be up.
MAC Address: 00:02:E3:13:47:6B (Lite-on Communications)
Host 10.0.0.3 appears to be up.
MAC Address: 00:19:C5:D5:68:E0 (Unknown)
Host 10.0.0.4 appears to be up.
Host 10.0.0.5 appears to be up.
MAC Address: 00:14:A5:13:23:46 (Gemtek Technology Co.)
Host 10.0.0.6 appears to be up.
MAC Address: 00:10:A4:7C:33:DF (Xircom)
Host 10.0.0.7 appears to be up.
MAC Address: 00:0C:29:E9:59:DE (VMware)
# Nmap run completed at Thur Dec 13 20:31:11 2007 -- 10 IP addresses (7 hosts up) scanned in 0.547 seconds

For Help, press F1                                                    NUM
```

While this is a great format for viewing the results off-line or at a later point in time, this does not easily lend itself to our step two. In order to submit a list of online hosts to Nmap, we need to have just a listing of hosts without any extraneous information. If you try to submit this list, Nmap will complain that it is unable to determine what the hosts are:

```
nmap -sV -iL up-systems
```

```
Starting Nmap 4.50 (http://insecure.org) at 2007-12-13 20:47 Central Standard Time
Invalid target host specification: #
QUITTING!
```

What we need is a nice, well-ordered list that we can work with for our step two submission to Nmap. Let's try a different output option to see what impact it has. In this example, we'll use the `-oG` or 'grepable' format. This format has been deprecated but is still very popular for this very reason: It is simple to create a file that can later be searched and manipulated.

```
nmap -sP -oG up-systems2 10.0.0.1-10
```

This produces a report with output that is very easy to read:

```
# Nmap 4.50 scan initiated Thur Dec 13 22:03:28 2007 as: nmap -sP -oG
up-systems2 10.0.0.1-10
Host: 10.0.0.1 ()     Status: Up
Host: 10.0.0.2 ()     Status: Up
Host: 10.0.0.3 ()     Status: Up
Host: 10.0.0.4 ()     Status: Up
Host: 10.0.0.5 ()     Status: Up
Host: 10.0.0.6 ()     Status: Up
Host: 10.0.0.7 ()     Status: Up
# Nmap run completed at Thur Dec 13 22:03:29 2007 -- 10 IP addresses
(7 hosts up) scanned in 0.922 seconds
```

At this point, we can simply delete the top and bottom status lines and then use a combination of *cut* and *tr* to cull the IP addresses from our resulting file and create a new file of only active IP addresses that can be fed into Nmap for our OS scan. As an example for this file, we can use *cut* to create a list with only our active IP addresses in it (see Figure 2.5).

```
cut -b7-15 up-systems2 > IPs-only
```

Figure 2.5 Resulting List of Active IP addresses only

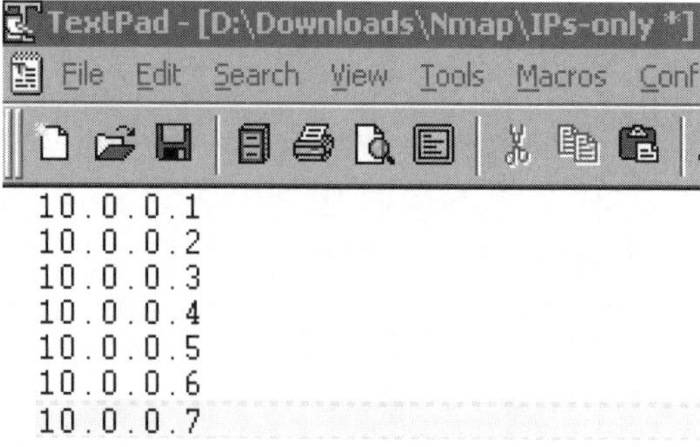

As our final prep step, we'll use the *tr* command to delete the carriage returns and prep our IP address list so that it is ready to be fed into our Nmap OS scan:

```
tr -d '\r' < IPs-only > Nmap-ready_IPs
```

If you take a peek into the *Nmap-ready_IPs* file, you will see the IP addresses are all on one line, each separated by a space. It's not very easy to manually read, but this is the perfect format for Nmap:

```
10.0.0.1 10.0.0.2 10.0.0.3 10.0.0.4 10.0.0.5 10.0.0.6 10.0.0.7
```

As another alternative, this single command line will create a CR delimited list of IP addresses that Nmap can use as an input file:

```
cat up-systems2 | grep Host | awk '{print $2}' > Nmap-ready_IPs
```

Now we are ready for our second Nmap step: Let's run this *Nmap-ready_IPs* file as an input file to an Nmap `-A` scan to detect service and OS versions of these live hosts. We'll output the data to a file named *OS-Svc-info* and then peek into the contents of the resulting file (edited for length) to get our OS info:

```
Nmap -A -iL Nmap-ready_IPs > OS-Svc-info
Starting Nmap 4.50 (http://insecure.org) at 2007-12-13 23:48 Central
Standard Time
Insufficient responses for TCP sequencing (1), OS detection may be less accurate
Interesting ports on 10.0.0.1:
Not shown: 1694 filtered ports
PORT STATE SERVICE VERSION
23/tcp open telnet?
80/tcp open tcpwrapped
1723/tcp closed pptp
MAC Address: 00:0F:B5:6C:AB:E4 (Netgear)
Device type: remote management|firewall|media device
Running: Compaq embedded, Enterasys embedded, Phillips embedded
OS details: Compaq Inside Management Board, Enterasys XSR-1805 Security Route,
Phillips ReplayTV 5000 DVR
Network Distance: 1 hop
<Author's Note: This host is a Netgear 54Mps Wireless Router WGR614 v5>
Interesting ports on 10.0.0.2:
Not shown: 1694 closed ports
PORT STATE SERVICE VERSION
135/tcp open msrpc Microsoft Windows RPC
139/tcp open netbios-ssn
1026/tcp open mstask Microsoft mstask (task server - c:\winnt\system32\Mstask.exe)
MAC Address: 00:02:E3:13:47:6B (Lite-on Communications)
```

Device type: general purpose|firewall|VoIP adapter|specialized

Running (JUST GUESSING) : Microsoft Windows NT/2K/XP|95/98/ME|2003/.NET|PocketPC/CE (97%), NetBSD (92%), IBM OS/400 V5 (92%), Secure Computing embedded (92%), Cisco embedded (91%), Ixia embedded (90%), Apple Mac OS X 10.2.X (90%)

Aggressive OS guesses: Microsoft Windows 2000 Professional SP2 (97%), Microsoft Windows XP Pro SP1/SP2 or 2000 SP4 (95%), Microsoft Windows Millennium Edition (Me), Windows 2000 Professional or Advanced Server, or Windows XP (94%), Microsoft Windows 2003 Server or XP SP2 (93%), Microsoft Windows 2000 Professional RC1 or Windows 2000 Advanced Server Beta3 (93%), Microsoft Windows 2003 Server Enterprise Edition (93%), NetBSD 1.6.2 (alpha) (92%), IBM AS/400 running OS/400 5.1 (92%), Microsoft Windows NT 3.51 SP5, NT 4.0 or 95/98/98SE (92%), Secure Computing Sidewinder firewall 5.2.1.06 (92%)

No exact OS matches for host (test conditions non-ideal).

Network Distance: 1 hop

Service Info: OS: Windows

<Author's Note: This host is running Windows 2000, SP4>

Warning: OS detection for 10.0.0.3 will be MUCH less reliable because we did not find at least 1 open and 1 closed TCP port

All 1697 scanned ports on 10.0.0.3 are closed

MAC Address: 00:19:C5:D5:68:EO (Unknown)

Device type: general purpose

Running: NetBSD

OS details: NetBSD 4.99.4 (x86)

Network Distance: 1 hop

<Author's Note: This is actually a Playstation 3, v. 2.01 on a wireless connection>

Skipping SYN Stealth Scan against 10.0.0.4 because Windows does not support scanning your own machine (localhost) this way.

Skipping OS Scan against 10.0.0.4 because it doesn't work against your own machine (localhost)

All 0 scanned ports on 10.0.0.4 are

Insufficient responses for TCP sequencing (0), OS detection may be less accurate

<Author's Note: This is my scanning system and it is a Windows XP SP2 box>

Interesting ports on 10.0.0.5:

Not shown: 1695 closed ports

PORT STATE SERVICE VERSION

135/tcp open msrpc?

912/tcp open ftp vsftpd or WU-FTPD

MAC Address: 00:14:A5:13:23:46 (Gemtek Technology Co.)

Too many fingerprints match this host to give specific OS details

Network Distance: 1 hop

<Author's Note: This host is running XP SP2 and connecting wirelessly using an internal Broadcom 802.11b/g WLAN adapter>

```
Interesting ports on 10.0.0.6:
Not shown: 1693 closed ports
PORT STATE SERVICE VERSION
135/tcp open msrpc?
139/tcp open netbios-ssn
445/tcp open microsoft-ds Microsoft Windows XP microsoft-ds
1025/tcp open NFS-or-IIS?
MAC Address: 00:10:A4:7C:33:DF (Xircom)
Device type: general purpose|firewall|VoIP adapter|specialized
Running (JUST GUESSING) : Microsoft Windows NT/2K/XP|95/98/ME|2003/.NET|PocketPC/
CE (97%), NetBSD (92%), IBM OS/400 V5 (92%), Secure Computing embedded (92%),
Cisco embedded (91%), Ixia embedded (90%), Apple Mac OS X 10.2.X (90%)
Aggressive OS guesses: Microsoft Windows 2000 Professional SP2 (97%), Microsoft
Windows XP Pro SP1/SP2 or 2000 SP4 (95%), Microsoft Windows Millennium Edition
(Me), Windows 2000 Professional or Advanced Server, or Windows XP (94%), Microsoft
Windows 2003 Server or XP SP2 (93%), Microsoft Windows 2000 Professional RC1 or
Windows 2000 Advanced Server Beta3 (93%), Microsoft Windows 2003 Server Enterprise
Edition (93%), NetBSD 1.6.2 (alpha) (92%), IBM AS/400 running OS/400 5.1 (92%),
Microsoft Windows NT 3.51 SP5, NT 4.0 or 95/98/98SE (92%), Secure Computing
Sidewinder firewall 5.2.1.06 (92%)
No exact OS matches for host (test conditions non-ideal).
Network Distance: 1 hop
Service Info: OS: Windows
<Author's Note: This is another Windows 2000 SP4 system>
Interesting ports on 10.0.0.7:
Not shown: 1694 closed ports
PORT STATE SERVICE VERSION
22/tcp open tcpwrapped
111/tcp open rpcbind?
631/tcp open ipp?
MAC Address: 00:0C:29:E9:59:DE (VMware)
Device type: general purpose
Running: Linux 2.4.X
OS details: Linux 2.4.22-ck2 (x86) w/grsecurity.org and HZ=1000 patches
Network Distance: 1 hop
<Author's Note: This is a Vmware box running SuSe Linux 10.0 with a 2.6.13-15kernel>
OS and Service detection performed. Please report any incorrect results at http://
insecure.org/nmap/submit/.
Nmap finished: 6 IP addresses (6 hosts up) scanned in 223.859 seconds
```

Now you are probably saying "That definitely was not a quick, easy method" and since our test environment is really just a small, home network, this really is overkill. However, once you start scanning class C and larger networks, it is often very handy to have a separate file that contains just live host information. This is true both from an ongoing *live hosts* comparison perspective and also from the proficiency angle when you start firing up service and OS scans.

TIP

If you are more comfortable using Nmap from a Windows system, yet you appreciate UNIX file and text tools, then you will probably be interested in obtaining the GNU core utilities from http://gnuwin32.sourceforge.net/. As of this writing, this will install 84 different unix-based file, text and shell utilities on your Windows platform.

Using Nmap for Security Auditing

Security auditing can be defined as creating a set of controls specific to the technology or infrastructure being reviewed and then applying those controls, like a filter, to your environment. Any gaps in or outside that filter become audit points and could negatively impact the audit's overall assessment of your security framework.

Nmap can assist with such audit needs as:

- Auditing firewalls by verifying the firewall filters are operating properly.
- Searching for open ports on perimeter devices (perimeter being anything from Internet-edge, to extranet or intranet boundary lines).
- Performing reconnaissance for certain versions of services.
- Utilizing the OS detection feature to pin-point outdated or unauthorized systems on your networks.
- Discovering unauthorized applications and services.

Tools & Traps...

Knoppix-based ISOs

Thanks to Knoppix-based bootable live CDs, it has become quite easy to get up and running with a well-rounded arsenal of security tools at your fingertips.

With the power of Knoppix, you can put a CD or DVD into your workstation and boot up into a full-blown Linux operating system. Going a step further, many sites have sprung up over the past few years that have taken Knoppix and tweaked the available tools to create bootable distributions (distros) with specific security toolsets. For example, let's imagine you are new to Linux and would like to test out Nmap on the Linux platform, but don't have the time to install the Linux operating system and then figure out how to get Nmap compiled and running. Instead you can grab a copy of BackTrack, a very popular security Knoppix-based distro available from www.remote-exploit.org/backtrack.html. BackTrack contains approximately 255 different security and hacking tools, including some of the more well-known ones like Nmap.

Using Nmap for System Administration

Although it is normally seen as a go-to application for security professionals, its wide-range of port scanning, service and OS identification capabilities make it perfect for the system administrator. If you decide to make Nmap available to administrators outside IT Security, keep in mind that this could increase unwanted scanning activity in your network. This is a perfect lead-in to our next subject–important security facets of employing Nmap.

Securing Nmap

Nmap is a security tool, but it must also be utilized in your infrastructure with security in mind. Any administrative tool running in your environment, security-related or otherwise, will require certain policies and procedures to ensure a successful deployment and operation. When you start specifically addressing security-related tools, you have to be sure to incorporate everything from separation of duties to principle of least privilege, as well as access tracking and usage reporting.

Executable and End-User Requirements

As with almost any security-related application, the first things to think about when starting the installation process includes security of the user context for the application and what permissions are required to manipulate the executable. Commonly you will find that the user must have root permissions on a UNIX system and administrator rights on a Windows box for both application installation and execution. Security best practices for accountability dictate that in order for administrative access to be properly tracked, Nmap users must have credentials that are individually identifiable. For example,

John must have a personal use account *and* an administrative use account, both of which personally identify John as the account holder. If a common administrative username is utilized across the team, you have lost all tracking and auditing abilities. Shared "administrator" or "root" usage can be a hard habit to break; however it only takes getting caught by one auditing requirement to justify making the break.

This is connected to another important security best practice, the principle of least privilege. If John's day-to-day work does not require administrative access, he should be logged in with his personal use account the majority of time. He must only switch to the administrative account when and if the details of his work require those extra access privileges. The theory behind this practice is that by limiting his access to the administrative account, he is helping to limit exposure to any vulnerability that might be associated with the use of that account. For example, many worms have achieved superior results for the simple reason that users were logged on at the time of infection with higher-than-necessary privilege. There are also ways of limiting users' access by properly setting up and utilizing user groups or granting temporary access via commands like *run as* in the Windows Active Directory environment. Access control can also be implemented in the UNIX world via the use of group permissions and commands like *sudo*.

NOTE

Sudo is a command that gives system administrators the ability to grant individual users or groups of users special access to run commands with root access or as another user. Sudo also tracks the user's input during their sudo session. A *sudoers* file must be configured on the system where the user requires access. You can learn more about this command by reading the UNIX man page associated with it.

System Environment

What is the organization's policy for acceptable use of security tools? When you get ready to incorporate Nmap into your enterprise infrastructure, there are a few things to think about in terms of the infrastructure and Nmap environment:

- Should Nmap be installed on a workstation contained in a separate domain?
- Is Nmap part of your open source software repository?

- Is Nmap maintained by your package installation team or maintained separately by IT Security?
- Do you have hash definitions of acceptable versions of Nmap?
- Have you updated your IDS/IPS teams so that they can recognize the Nmap scanning footprint?
- Do Nmap users scan from a segregated, remote system or do they scan from their own workstation?

The answers to these questions will help determine the organization's overall posture towards scanning and Nmap's place in the infrastructure.

Security of scan results

Once you have started to obtain results with Nmap, you have to decide if you are going to store them on a short- or long-term basis. Either decision will require careful consideration of what data classification is assigned to the results information, as well as what your organization's policy for data retention and storage dictates. This is a direct proportion formula. These classification decisions will become more critical as the sensitivity of your scanned assets increases. Here are some additional questions to address:

- Does this information require encryption at rest (in storage)?
- Will we need to back up the scanning reports?
- What is our ongoing retention schedule?
- What permissions will we establish for report accessibility?

Addressing all of these questions will help meet what security personnel like to call the *non-functional requirement of auditability*. Properly securing your Nmap scanning workstation, user permissions, and output creates an auditor's paradise of controls. Separation of duties is employed, principle of least privilege applied, authorized access is required and monitored, and report output and storage are carefully controlled.

TIP

The SANS Institute maintains a great site on security policies if you are still in the process of establishing policies for your organization or have been tasked with updating existing policies. You can find templates, policy examples, definitions and more information at www.sans.org/resources/policies/.

Optimizing Nmap

Nmap has integrated functionality for helping the efficiency of your scans. You can make the scan run faster or slower depending on the timing option you choose. You can also manipulate the number of probe retransmits and other facets of the scan operation. This type of functionality has a dual purpose: It helps create more efficiently-run scans, and it can also be used to make scans stealthier. Attackers love this functionality of course, but we can also use it to our advantage when scanning in the enterprise. For example, if you are concerned about impacting servers during a scan of new IP address space, you can set the timing option (`-T`) so that the probes are sent very far apart. As a matter of fact, by using the `-T0` option, Nmap will only send probes every 5 minutes! On the opposite end of the spectrum, using the `-T5` option will cause Nmap to send probes approximately every 5 milliseconds. The concern with sending probes at such an insane rate is that you create a greater potential for upsetting the server you are trying to scan. The `T5` option is also called the *insane* timing parameter for this very reason.

Here is the tcpdump output from a Windows host that has been hit with a `-T5` timed scan (shortened and trimmed for clarity). In the output below, 10.129.0.196 is the host conducting the Nmap scan. Notice the *SYN (S)* probes are sent within 80-100 thousandths of a second of each other:

```
11:22:51.181872 IP 10.129.0.196.50900 > 10.129.0.193.321: S
11:22:51.181956 IP 10.129.0.196.50900 > 10.129.0.193.2766: S
11:22:51.182044 IP 10.129.0.196.50900 > 10.129.0.193.1495: S
11:22:51.182146 IP 10.129.0.196.50900 > 10.129.0.193.887: S
11:22:51.182329 IP 10.129.0.196.50900 > 10.129.0.193.1467: S
11:22:51.182456 IP 10.129.0.196.50900 > 10.129.0.193.6347: S
11:22:51.182541 IP 10.129.0.196.50900 > 10.129.0.193.2046: S
11:22:51.182630 IP 10.129.0.196.50900 > 10.129.0.193.975: S
11:22:51.182717 IP 10.129.0.196.50900 > 10.129.0.193.1373: S
11:22:51.182843 IP 10.129.0.196.50900 > 10.129.0.193.351: S
```

The Nmap help documentation includes a section specific to timing and performance. For reference, here are some of the options and information available from that documentation:

- Options which take <time> are in milliseconds, unless you append 's' (seconds), 'm' (minutes), or 'h' (hours) to the value (e.g. 30m).
- –T[0-5]: Set timing template (higher is faster); timing options from 0 (paranoid) to 5 (insane).

- –min-hostgroup/max-hostgroup <size>: Parallel host scan group sizes.
- –min-parallelism/max-parallelism <time>: Probe parallelization.
- –min-rtt-timeout/max-rtt-timeout/initial-rtt-timeout <time>: Specifies probe round trip time.
- –max-retries <tries>: Caps number of port scan probe retransmissions.
- –host-timeout <time>: Give up on target after this long.
- –scan-delay/–max-scan-delay <time>: Adjust delay between probes.

By default Nmap will *sometimes* perform DNS resolution of hosts it is scanning. You can avoid any potential performance hit by using the –n switch. Many UNIX-based networking and security tools use the –n switch to mean "Do not DNS resolve hosts".

Advanced Nmap Scanning Techniques

In this section, we'll be covering some Nmap advanced scanning techniques as applicable to an enterprise. There are many advanced options and combinations available; we'll cover some of the more useful ones for assisting with the types of scans you might find yourself needing to run in an enterprise infrastructure. Advanced scanning options cover a wide range of possibilities:

- TCP scan flags customization
- Packet fragmentation
- IP and MAC address spoofing
- Adding decoy scan source IP addresses
- Source port specification
- Ability to add random data to sent packets
- Manipulatable time-to-live field
- Ability to send packets with bogus TCP or UDP checksums

One thing to be careful of when working with advanced scanning options is that your results will vary based on the type of scan you create. It sounds easy, but depending on what is going on behind the scenes, you might end up with a port being reported closed that is really open. It's critical to have an understanding of TCP flags, for example, if you start customizing your scans with this option. Here's a great example of the difference in results if we select a *synchronize* (SYN) flag as our customization versus selected the *push* (PSH) flag. Notice in the first scan, we are looking to determine if port 135 is open by sending a packet with the PSH flag enabled. The results come back and let us know that port 135 appears closed ... why? In this example, 10.129.0.197 is the host running Nmap and 10.129.0.196 is the server being scanned. We are using Windump to capture the packets being sent. (Trimmed for clarity)

```
vm1:~ # nmap --scanflags PSH -p135 10.129.0.196
10.129.0.197.49671 > 10.129.0.196.135: P win 1024
10.129.0.196.135 > 10.129.0.197.49671: R 0:0(0) ack 4148940485 win 0

Interesting ports on 10.129.0.196:
PORT      STATE    SERVICE
135/tcp   closed   msrpc
```

Let's contrast this scan with one that uses the SYN flag. What is the difference? Why does the port now appear open?

```
vm1:~ # nmap --scanflags SYN -p135 10.129.0.196
10.129.0.197.50224 > 10.129.0.196.135: S 2609233962:2609233962(0) win 2048
<mss 1460>

10.129.0.196.135 > 10.129.0.197.50224: S 3256184574:3256184574(0) ack 2609233963
win 65535 <mss 1260>

10.129.0.197.50224 > 10.129.0.196.135: R 2609233963:2609233963(0) win 0

Interesting ports on 10.129.0.196:
PORT      STATE    SERVICE
135/tcp   open     msrpc
```

Now we can tell that with the first scan attempt, the box being scanned replied to our *push* packet with a *reset* (R) packet. At this point, to our scanner, it appears that the port is not open and it reports that finding. However, when we contrast that with our second attempt and the *synchronize* packet, we see the server respond first with a *synchronize/acknowledge* or SA packet. This tells our scanner that the port is open and ready to complete the 3-way handshake. Since this scan customization conforms to TCP standards for setting up a socket, we see the server respond accordingly, and now Nmap is able to tell that the port is actually open. If you want to conduct different types of scans against your external firewall interface utilizing the scanflags option to see what responses an attacker might see, remember to complete your test with a valid connection scan and look for responsive ports.

Another advanced scanning technique that Nmap performs is the ability to pad out a packet's length with random data to make it equal a set length. This is useful for testing intranet or extranet connections where you might have concerns about the allowable maximum segment size. It's also useful for testing a link's capacity for handling potential packet fragmentation. This can also be accomplished with the `-f` option to fragment Nmap packets. From the security perspective, these advanced features can give the penetration test team a real advantage when it comes to testing the IDS logging capability or IPS response.

Summary

We've seen Nmap's ability to provide assistance across the enterprise: everything from maintaining lists of available systems, mapping open ports to running services, and identifying operating systems.

This chapter provided an overview of Nmap and high-level techniques used to scan networks and systems. To do this adequately it was also necessary to provide background information on securely implementing Nmap in your enterprise framework. We provided various scanning scenarios and potential uses of network scanning by security professionals, auditors, and system administrators. Lastly, we discussed different ways of optimizing your Nmap scans and a few advanced scanning techniques.

Now that you have been introduced to network scanning and the techniques used to discover active hosts, ports, services, and operating systems you are armed with the knowledge to start exploring your organization's infrastructure. This chapter introduces the Nmap network scanner and its many uses across the enterprise. As you continue reading through this book, you will discover even more ways to use advanced Nmap features in the enterprise environment.

Finally, it's worth reiterating that you must remember to only use network scanning if you have permission and the law is on your side. A security administrator could be mistaken for an attacker from the IDS or IPS point of view. If non-security IT professionals, like auditors, are given permission to use the tool make sure it is documented that they are allowed to do so. Always make certain you have permission, or use your own private network to experiment with Nmap or any other security tools.

Solutions Fast Track

What is Nmap?

- ☑ Nmap, or Network Mapper, is a free, open source tool that is available under the GNU General Public License as published by the Free Software Foundation.
- ☑ Nmap has capabilities for network mapping, port scanning, service and version detection, and operating system detection.
- ☑ Nmap can be installed on Windows, Linux, or Mac OS X.

Using Nmap in the Enterprise

- ☑ Make sure you have well-documented permission from the appropriate upper-management to conduct Nmap scans.

- ☑ Identify change control windows for scanning of critical assets.
- ☑ Post an email address or phone number to reach the Nmap team in case of scanning-caused outage.
- ☑ Approach reconnaissance of your networks as an attacker would. Start with a wide-reaching scan to determine available systems, and then gradually narrow down your scans to identify specific operating systems, ports or services.

Securing Nmap

- ☑ Nmap requires administrative privilege in order to successfully install and run.
- ☑ Employees conducting Nmap scans should be utilizing special access accounts in order to maintain accountability and the principle of least privilege.
- ☑ According to your data classification policies, it may be necessary to securely store Nmap results of critical assets.
- ☑ Create a solid working relationship with your internal IT audit team to help facilitate your understanding of their audit controls.

Optimizing Nmap

- ☑ Nmap has integrated timing policies that vary from T0 (very, very slow) to T5 (extremely fast).
- ☑ You can tell Nmap to never perform DNS resolution of the IP addresses it is scanning by using the -n option.
- ☑ Additional parameters give Nmap the power to control parallel scanning of a certain number of IP addresses.

Advanced Nmap Scanning Techniques

- ☑ Nmap comes with additional parameters that can provide scanning capabilities beyond the basic syn – syn/ack – ack connect scan.
- ☑ Manipulating options like the time-to-live, packet size or fragmentation can be used to test your organization's intrusion detection or prevention teams.
- ☑ Understanding how TCP and UDP respond to certain stimuli is critical to working with advanced Nmap scanning features.

Frequently Asked Questions

Q: Which OS should I install Nmap on? Is one better than the other?

A: It used to be that Nmap was much better on Linux, simply because that was the original platform for the tool. However, over the past few years, Nmap's popularity has led to more developments in the application for other operating systems. These days, you should download and start working with Nmap on whichever supported platform you are most comfortable with.

Q: Can I scan systems that are not on the same local network as my scanning system?

A: You bet! There are a couple of things to keep in mind when scanning through a router or firewall. For example, access controls on the firewall may impact whether or not your scan-generated packets will be able to pass through or if certain types of responses will be able to get back to the scanner. Oftentimes, firewall and network administrators will block protocols that Nmap relies on for certain scan types, such as ICMP or UDP. Your best chance for running successful scans across networks is to become good friends with your network and firewall teams. You will need upper management support and their assistance to setup the appropriate access control rules for your scanners.

Q: Can Nmap scans for service and OS version cause a system to crash?

A: It is not common for an Nmap scan to cause a system to crash, however this does not detract from the fact that you should have established scanning permission in your environment and also be certain to perform the scans during a change control window or a pre-established scanning window.

Q: Nmap's OS scanning option doesn't seem very exact, how is it going to benefit me when I need to identify systems in my enterprise infrastructure?

A: As you begin working with this –O Nmap option in your environment, you will get a feel for how it responds to different system builds. At that point, anomalies will pop out and you can zero in on those hosts to perform further testing on or attempt to track down.

Chapter 3

Getting and Installing Nmap

Solutions in this chapter:

- Getting Nmap
- Installing Nmap on Windows
- Installing Nmap on Linux
- Installing Nmap on Mac OS X
- Installing Nmap from Source

☑ Summary

☑ Solutions Fast Track

☑ Frequently Asked Questions

Introduction

In this chapter, we will cover all of the steps necessary to complete a functioning installation of. Due to the overwhelming amount of Linux/UNIX-based distributions available today, installation instructions can vary from distribution to distribution, and are beyond the scope of this chapter. For this reason, we will be focusing on information specific to installation on the Linux Fedora platform. We have chosen Fedora because it is the most commonly used Linux distribution in the world, and serves as a good starting point upon which to base further installations. Most of what we cover here should apply to most other popular distributions without significant modification. If the instructions do vary, however, the difference should be minimal. For the Windows side, we will be focusing on Windows XP, due to its common use. Lastly, we have included several installation options for Mac OS X.

For this chapter, we started with fresh installations of Fedora, Windows XP, and Mac OS X. We accepted the default installation parameters for each of the operating systems (OSes). These types of installations often install needless software, and leave many security vulnerabilities wide open. You should follow security best practices when installing new systems and also when subsequently applying operating system security procedures. These methods are beyond the scope of this book, but you should pick up a good reference for securing your particular operating system. Please make sure your operating system is current, patched, and secured. You will also need to verify that your network is set up and functioning properly, or you might not be able to send and receive packets!

Let's take a moment to introduce you to the way we approached this chapter. When it comes to computers, networking, and security, some of you are beginners and some are pros. Based on the varying technical abilities of the target audience of this book, we tried to approach almost every subject as if we were learning it for the first time. Our only assumption was that you do have a basic understanding of the operating system and how to use it. For the beginners, we made the step-by-step instructions for each installation easy to find and read. This chapter will serve as an excellent reference for the more experienced reader. The only time we will have a lengthier explanation with the procedures is when there is possibly some pitfall to watch for, or during description of certain side notes that might be helpful. You will find our longer descriptions and discussions *outside* of the chapter installation instructions. So, let's start installing Nmap!

NOTE

Fyodor has a detailed Nmap installation guide located at *http://insecure.org/nmap/install/*. It includes information on installing Nmap on other operating systems.

Getting Nmap

Fyodor maintains the official website for Nmap at http://insecure.org. You can download Nmap from http://insecure.org/nmap/download.html. Nmap is available for many operating systems, including Linux, Windows, and Mac OS X. Both binaries and source code are available, depending on your preference. The source code is available in zipped archive (tar.gz or bz2) format. Another source for obtaining Nmap may be your OS itself, or related repositories. Nmap is typically included in most Linux variants. However, some of these may not be the most recent release and it is worth the time to download the latest version.

NOTE

You can check to see if Nmap is already installed by typing **nmap** and pressing Enter. If it is installed you see will Nmap usage output.

Nmap has no dependencies. It requires libpcap, libpcre, and libdnet to operate, so it comes with these packages included as part of the installation. Nmap uses the optional OpenSSL cryptography libraries to probe SSL-encrypted services if the packages are already installed on the system.

NOTE

Libpcap is used as the basis for many security tools, mostly sniffer-related. Besides Nmap, tools such as Wireshark, Nessus, Kismet, dsniff, and ettercap use libpcap. Some tools are ported to Windows and take advantage of WinPcap.

Now is a good time to talk about the basic requirements needed to run Nmap. In general, Nmap will run on any platform for which there is source code or binaries available. There are no published hardware/software specifications that are required to run Nmap. However, as one might expect, newer, faster hardware usually yields some measure of better performance. Conversely, remember that most of what's happening when you run Nmap is on the network.

You may want to download the latest version of the software before beginning. Feel free to do so; just make sure to substitute package names when necessary. For example, the current, stable version of Nmap at this writing is 4.50. So if we reference the file nmap-4.50.tar.gz and you have nmap-4.80.tar.gz, use *your* filename because it's newer.

NOTE

You can get the latest Nmap source code release from the Subversion (SVN) repository. This version has the newest fixes and features, but they are not considered stable releases. SVN is mostly used by developers and advanced users. You can download the latest code using the following command **svn co –username guest –password "" svn://svn.insecure.org/nmap/**.

NOTE

You can verify the integrity of your Nmap download by using PGP and the Nmap Project Signing Key. You will need to import the key and then use it to verify downloaded file signatures. For more information please refer to http://insecure.org/nmap/nstall/index.html#inst-integrity.

Notes from the Underground…

Verifying Binary Integrity

A good habit to have is to perform some level of integrity verification of your download. Typically that involves checking a file *hash* for verification. There are many hashing algorithms available, but a couple of the more commonly-used ones are MD5 and SHA1. MD5 and SHA1 checksum tools exist for both Linux and Windows. Be sure to download these from a reputable source! Another means of integrity checking is by verifying against a trusted source's PGP (Pretty Good Privacy) signature. The program owner signs their executable (or any file) by applying their private key to create a *signed hash* or *signature*. When you download that signed file, you must have and trust the public key of the program owner in order to verify their signature. This type of signature is considered the best and most secure method for verification. If you don't own PGP, an open source alternative is Gnu Privacy Guard (GnuPG). It is supported on Linux, Windows, and Mac OS X. If a PGP signature is not available, most vendors provide MD5 or SHA1 checksums to verify the integrity of the file. While this is not necessarily the most secure, in the absence of any other method, it affords the minimum check for some level of sanity.

Platforms and System Requirements

So, what operating system platforms support the installation of Nmap? The following list shows a number of platforms that have readily available Nmap binaries or come pre-loaded with Nmap:

- Mac OS X
- Debian GNU/Linux
- FreeBSD
- Gentoo Linux
- HP-UX
- Suse Linux
- Mandriva Linux
- Windows
- NetBSD
- OpenPKG
- Red Hat/Fedora/Enterprise Linux
- Ubuntu Linux
- Sun Solaris/i386
- Sun Solaris/Sparc

This list is constantly expanding as developers *port* the Nmap source to new platforms. If your operating system is not listed, and you are feeling brave, go ahead and download the source code and begin building it for your system! Check out the "Installing Nmap from Source" section in this chapter for tips.

NOTE

Sun Solaris users will be happy to know that there is an excellent repository for Solaris x86 and Solaris Sparc packages at www.sunfreeware.com. There are Nmap packages there for every release of Solaris dating back to version 2.5, not to mention many other fine packages. Thanks to Steven Christensen for maintaining the site!

Installing Nmap on Windows

In the early years of Nmap, Windows support was almost non-existent. Today a large portion of users run Nmap on Windows. The Windows install can be performed in the follow three ways:

- **Windows self-installer package.** This is the easiest and most common method of installing Nmap for Windows. This method includes the command line version of Nmap and the Zenmap GUI frontend.
- **Command-line Zip files.** This method is also easy to install, but you must also install WinPcap. This method installs the command line version of Nmap and does not install a GUI.
- **Source code compile.** Typically, you would perform Windows source code installation if you are interested in assisting with Nmap development. It requires Microsoft Visual C++ 2005 to compile.

In this chapter we provide examples of installing Nmap for Windows using the self-installer package and the command-line zip files. The source code compilation is beyond the scope of this book and we suggest you refer to the Nmap website or the Nmap development (nmap-dev) list.

NOTE

The Windows version of Nmap does have some differences from the UNIX version. The Nmap Windows version, does not allow you to scan yourself by using the 127.0.0.1 loopback address (or any other IP address the interface might have.) You can work around this issue by using a TCP connect scan without pinging (-sT -PN). Also the Windows port will only support Ethernet interfaces (and most 802.11 wireless cards as well.) It does not support RAS connections such as PPP dialup. You can work around this for some interfaces by using a TCP connect scan without pinging (-sT -PN). Both of the above issues are largely due to Microsoft dropping support for raw TCP/IP socket support. The other limitation is that version detection does not support SSL scan-through.

Installing Nmap from Windows Self-Installer

A Windows self-installer is created for each stable Nmap release. The self-installer executable is named **nmap-*version*-setup.exe**.

1. Download the Nmap executable from http://insecure.org/nmap/download.html.
2. Begin the installation process by double-clicking the installer: **nmap-*version*-setup.exe**. The first screen is the Nmap GNU General Public License Agreement. After reading the terms of the license, click **I Agree** to accept the license and continue.
3. The next screen allows you to choose the following Nmap components to install:
   - **Nmap Core Files** Installs Nmap executables and script files.
   - **Register Nmap Path** Registers Nmap path to system path so you can execute it from any directory.
   - **WinPcap** Installs WinPcap (required for most Nmap scans unless it is already installed).
   - **Network Performance Improvements (Registry Changes)** Installs recommended modifications to the Windows registry values to improve TCP connect scan performance.

- **Zenmap GUI frontend** Installs the multi- platform graphical Nmap front end and results viewer.

Accept the default settings and click **Next** to continue.

4. The next screen allows you to choose the folder where you would like to install Nmap. Accept the default of C:\Program Files\Nmap and click **Install**.
5. The Nmap installation screen shows the status of the installation process, giving line-by-line details of what is happening behind the scenes, as well as an overall progress bar. If WinPcap is already installed you will see a Window stating that the installer is skipping the WinPcap installation. Click **OK** to continue, and proceed to step 7. If you don't have WinPcap already installed, the Nmap installer will now install it for you.
6. A new window appears to allow you to install WinPcap. Click **I Agree** to accept the license agreement. The next screen allows you to choose the folder where you would like to install WinPcap. Accept the default of C:\Program Files\WinPcap and click **Install**. A screen shows the status of the WinPcap installation process will appear. It gives line-by-line details of what is happening behind the scenes, as well as an overall progress bar. Once the WinPcap installation is completed click **Close** to close this window.
7. Once the Nmap installation is complete click **Next** to continue.
8. The next screen allows you to create an Nmap start menu folder and add an Nmap GUI desktop icon. Accept the defaults or uncheck the boxes if you don't want a start menu folder or desktop icon. Click **Close** to complete the installation.

All done! Nmap is now installed and ready to go. You can double-click the Nmap – Zenmap GUI desktop icon to open the Nmap GUI, or you can run the command line version of Nmap from C:\Program Files\Nmap. The C:\Program Files\Nmap directory also includes the Nmap uninstall.exe file.

NOTE

A nice feature of the completed installation box is the ability to save the installation log to a file. Simply right-click one of the lines in the box and a small window pops up that says "Copy Details To Clipboard." Select this option and paste the results into Notepad or your favorite text editor.

Installing Nmap from the Command-line Zip files

A Windows zip file is created for each stable Nmap release. The zip file is named **nmap-*version*-win32.zip** and includes the command-line binaries and other Nmap files. This release does not include a GUI. You will need to install WinPcap, version 4 or later, if you haven't already. To install WinPcap, you need to have the right to install new drivers to your system, and you will need to be logged in as Administrator or have Administrator rights. Perform the following steps to install WinPcap:

1. Download the WinPcap executable from www.winpcap.org.
2. Begin the installation process by double-clicking the installer, **WinPcap_*version*.exe**. The first screen is a general welcome screen for the installation wizard. Click **Next** to continue.
3. The next screen displays information on the WinPcap license. Once you have read the terms of the agreement, click **I Agree** to accept the license and continue.
4. The Setup Status window appears, showing the files being copied and displaying a progress bar. Once the installation is complete, click **Finish** to exit the setup.

Perform the following to install Nmap:

1. Download the Nmap executable from http://insecure.org/nmap/download.html.
2. Begin the installation process by double-clicking the installer: **nmap-*version*-win32.zip**. Uncompress the zip file into C:\Program Files, or another directory of your choice. The zip file will create a folder named nmap-*version* when it extracts. This folder includes the Nmap executable and other Nmap files.

All done! Nmap is now installed and ready to go. You can run Nmap by opening the command prompt, changing to the directory where Nmap is installed and typing **nmap** and pressing **Enter**.

NOTE

You will need a zip compression utility to unzip the Nmap zip file. Windows XP and Vista have a zip utility included with the operating system. There are several open source zip utilities available, such as 7-zip (www.7-zip.org). Winzip may also be used, but it is now commercial software.

Installing Nmap on Linux

There are a variety of ways to install Nmap on Linux, including binary packages and source code. Binary packages are typically easier to install than source code, and they offer ease of management for upgrading and removing software. Binary packages are also customized to use the proper settings for your specific operating system. One thing to keep in mind is that binary packages may not include the latest release of Nmap; some distributions stay current, while others may be several versions behind. In this section, we cover installing Nmap using the RPMs and using Yellow Dog Updater, Modified (YUM). Each example performs the process of installing Nmap on Fedora. So let's get started installing Nmap!

Installing Nmap from the RPMs

RPM Package Manager, originally called Red Hat Package Manager, is a Linux package management system. Fyodor creates two RPM packages for each release of Nmap, one for the Nmap command-line version and one for the optional Zenmap GUI front end. These packages work for a variety of Linux distributions including Red Hat, Mandrake, Suse, and Fedora. You must have root privileges to install the Nmap RPM package. Make sure you are logged in as root, or switch to root by typing **su root**, pressing **Enter**, and typing the appropriate root password. Perform the following to install the NMAP RPM:

1. Install the Nmap RPM by typing **rpm -vhU http://download.insecure.org/nmap/dist/nmap-4.50-1.i386.rpm** and pressing **Enter**.
2. Install the optional Zenmap GUI bye typing **rpm -vhU http://download.insecure.org/nmap/dist/zenmap-4.50-1.noarch.rpm** and pressing **Enter**.

All done! Nmap is now installed and ready to go. You can run Nmap by typing **nmap** and pressing **Enter**. You can run the GUI by typing **zenmap** and pressing **Enter**. To remove nmap type **rpm -e nmap** and press **Enter**.

NOTE

Once you have used the switch user command to switch to root (su root) you can exit from root by typing **exit** and pressing **Enter**. This will take you back to your regular user account.

NOTE

You may run into dependencies with RPM packages. If so, you will need to download and install the necessary packages.

Notes from the Underground…

A Word about RPMs

The RPM Package Manager is a powerful package management system capable of installing, uninstalling, verifying, querying, and updating Linux software packages. Finding RPMs is relatively easy, and www.rpmfind.net has a well-designed search and download system. However, since RPMs tend to be contributed by various individuals, they are often times a version or two behind the current source-code release. They are created on systems with varying file structures and environments, which can lead to difficulties if your system does not match those parameters. Installing an RPM can sometimes be easier than compiling from source—provided there are no dependency problems.

The RPM system, while an excellent package management tool, is fraught with problems regarding dependencies. It understands and reports which specific files the package requires that you install, but is not yet capable of acquiring and installing the packages necessary to fulfill its requirements. If you are not familiar with the term, *dependencies* are packages and/or libraries required by other packages. The Red Hat Linux OS is built on dependencies, which you can visualize as an upside-down tree structure. At the top of the tree are your basic user-installed programs, such as Nmap. Nmap depends on libpcap to operate, and libpcap requires other libraries to function. This tree structure is nice, but it adds to the dependency problem. For example, you may want to install a new software package and receive an error stating that another library on the system needs to be updated first. OK, so you download that library and attempt to update it. But, now, that library has dependencies too that need to be updated! This can be a never-ending and stressful adventure.

Continued

You can get information about RPMs in several ways:

- *rpm –q* (query) can be used to find out the version of a package installed—for example, *rpm –q nmap*.
- *rpm –qa* (query all) can be used to show a very long list of all of the packages on the system. To make this list shorter, you can *pipe* the query into a *grep* to find what you are looking for: *rpm –qa | grep nmap*.
- *rpm –ql* (query list) shows all of the files that were installed on the system with a particular package—for example, *rpm –ql nmap*.
- *rpm –qf* (query file) can be used to find out which RPM a particular file belongs to—for example, *rpm –qf/usr/bin/nmap*.

When using the RPM utility, you can install software three ways:

- *rpm –i* (install) installs a new RPM file, and leaves any previously installed versions alone.
- *rpm –u* (update) installs new software and removes any existing older versions.
- *rpm –f* (freshen) installs new software, but only if a previous version already exists. This is typically used for installing patches.

You can uninstall an RPM from your system by using the following:

- *rpm –e* (erase) removes an RPM from the system—for example, *rpm –e nmap*.

Sometimes you can be successful by installing a package with the *--nodeps* option (notice it includes two hyphens). This causes the package to install regardless of the dependencies it calls for. This may, or may not, work, depending on whether the package you are installing really does need all of the dependencies to function.

Installing Nmap RPMs Using YUM

YUM is an open-source, command-line package management utility for RPM-compatible Linux systems. It is an automated method of installing, updating, and removing RPM packages. YUM takes care of dependencies and does a lot of the work for us. It is included in several Linux distributions including Fedora, CentOS-5, Red Hat Enterprise Linux 5 and above, Scientific Linux, Yellow Dog Linux and openSUSE Linux. You must have root privileges to install Nmap using YUM. Make sure you are logged in as root, or switch to root by typing **su root**, pressing **Enter**, and typing the appropriate root password. Let's begin the Nmap installation process:

1. Install the Nmap package by typing **yum install nmap** and pressing **Enter**.
2. Likewise you can also install the optional NmapFE GUI by typing **yum install nmap-frontend** and pressing **Enter**.

That's it! YUM downloads Nmap and install it for you. Verify the installation by typing **nmap** and pressing **Enter**. You can run the GUI by typing **nmapfe** and pressing **Enter**. To update Nmap when new versions are released, you can type **yum update nmap** to install available updates to Nmap and other packages. You can remove the Nmap package by typing **yum remove nmap** and pressing **Enter**.

NOTE

NmapFE was the first generation Nmap GUI that was written in 1999. UMIT was later developed to overcome limitations of NmapFE and to provide a robust second generation GUI, which later became called Zenmap. Zenmap has replaced NmapFE, however some binary packages that are not up to date will not yet have Zenmap.

NOTE

If you have a less-than-current version of your Linux OS, you may not be able to update to the latest Nmap. It's always advisable to stay at the most current, stable versions of your OS and Nmap.

Installing Nmap on Mac OS X

There are a number of ways to install Nmap on Mac OS X, including building from source code or installing preconfigured binaries using MacPorts and Fink.

Installing Nmap on Mac OS X from Source

Many people prefer to build Nmap from source because of the control they have over the installation. We performed the source-code method of installing Nmap on

Mac OS X Tiger. Perform the following to install Nmap from the source code (replace *version* with the most recent Nmap version):

1. Prepare your Mac by installing Xcode Tools, which is located on your Mac OS X CD. This installs the gcc compiler and other development tools needed to compile source code, such as the X11 environment. If you are running Tiger, find the **Xcode Tools** folder on the Mac OS X Install Disc 1. Double-click the **XcodeTools.mpkg** in this folder and follow the onscreen instructions to install **Xcode Tools**.
2. Install the X11 user environment, which is also located on your Mac OS X Install Disc 1. The package is located in **System | Installation | Packages | X11User.pkg**. Double-click the **X11User.pkg** and follow the onscreen instructions. This installs the X11 application in the Utilities folder.
3. Download the latest version of the Nmap tarball in bzip or gzip compressed format and save it to your user folder, typically /Users/*username*.
4. Run the X11 application in the Utilities folder by double-clicking it. This will open an Xterminal window. By default, Xterminal should put you into the /Users/*username* directory and you should be able to see your files by typing **ls** and pressing **Enter**.
5. Ensure that /usr/local/bin is in your $PATH. If not, add it by typing **PATH=$PATH:/usr/local/bin** and pressing **Enter**.
6. Uncompress and extract the Nmap tarball by typing **bzip2 –cd nmap-*version*.tar.bz2 | tar xvf -** and pressing **Enter**. (or **gzip –cd nmap-*version*.tgz | tar xvf -**).
7. Change to the Nmap directory by typing **cd nmap-*version*** and pressing **Enter**.
8. Run the configure script by typing **./configure** and pressing **Enter**.
9. Next, compile the source code by typing **make** and pressing **Enter**.
10. Next, you must become root to install Nmap. Type **su root** and press **Enter**. Enter the password for root and press **Enter**.
11. Next, install the files in their appropriate locations by typing **make install** and pressing **Enter**.
12. Once the install process is completed you will see NMAP SUCCESSFULLY INSTALLED. You may run Nmap by typing **nmap** and pressing **Enter**. You will see the Nmap usage information.

Now you have successfully installed Nmap from the source code. Each time you wish to run Nmap, make sure to run the X11 application and run Nmap from the Xterminal window that opens. The Nmap binary installs in /usr/local/bin, so if you don't have that directory in your permanent $PATH, you will need to add it. Once everything is installed, you may also remove the *.tar.gz files from your /User/*username* folder.

Installing Nmap on Mac OS X Using MacPorts

MacPorts (formerly known as DarwinPorts) contains Linux/Unix-based software that has been modified to run on Mac OS X, known as *porting*. MacPorts automates the process of building third-party software for Mac OS X and other operating systems. It also tracks all dependency information for a given software tool. It knows what to build and install and in what order. After you download and install MacPorts, you can use it to easily install all kinds of other software—in our case, Nmap.

1. Prepare your Mac by installing Xcode Tools, which is located on your Mac OS X CD. This will install the gcc compiler and other development tools needed to compile source code, such as the X11 environment. If you are running Tiger, find the **Xcode Tools** folder on the Mac OS X Install Disc 1. Double-click the **XcodeTools.mpkg** in this folder and follow the onscreen instructions to install **Xcode Tools**.
2. Install the X11 user environment located on your Mac OS X Install Disc 1 as well. The package is located in **System | Installation | Packages | X11User.pkg**. Double-click the **X11User.pkg** and follow the onscreen instructions. This installs the X11 application in the Utilities folder.
3. Download the **MacPorts** "dmg" disk image installer from **macports.com**. Double-click the disk image to uncompress it, then double-click the MacPorts package to launch installer. Follow the onscreen instructions to walk through the MacPorts installer. You will also see usage information and other documentation. MacPorts installs in /opt/local/bin, so you may need to add that to your PATH by typing **PATH=$PATH:/opt/local/bin** and pressing **Enter**.
4. Run the **X11** application in the **Utilities** folder by double-clicking it. This will open an Xterminal window. By default, Xterminal should put you into the **/Users/*username*** directory.

5. Update the ports to make sure they are current by typing **sudo port –d selfupdate** and pressing **Enter**.
6. Install Nmap by typing **sudo port install nmap** and pressing **Enter**. MacPorts will then start fetching and installing the appropriate software dependencies and the Nmap binary.
7. Once the installation is complete, run Nmap by typing **nmap** and pressing **Enter**. You will see the Nmap usage information.

Now you have successfully installed Nmap using MacPorts. Each time you wish to run Nmap, make sure you run the X11 application and run Nmap from the Xterminal window that opens. The Nmap binary installs in /opt/local/bin so if you don't have that directory in your permanent $PATH, you will need to add it.

Installing Nmap on Mac OS X Using Fink

The Fink Project modifies UNIX software so it compiles and runs on Mac OS X. This is known as *porting*. Fink will also download and install all necessary dependencies for a software package.

1. The first thing you need to do is prepare your Mac by installing Xcode Tools, which are located on your Mac OS X CD. This installs the gcc compiler and other development tools needed to compile source code, such as the X11 environment. If you are running Tiger, an **Xcode Tools** folder can be found on the Mac OS X Install Disc 1. Double-click the **XcodeTools.mpkg** in this folder and follow the onscreen instructions to install **Xcode Tools**.
2. Install the X11 user environment, which is located on your Mac OS X Install Disc 1 as well. The package can be found by choosing **System | Installation | Packages | X11User.pkg**. Double-click the **X11User.pkg** and follow the onscreen instructions. This installs the X11 application in the Utilities folder.
3. Download the Fink installer disk image from **fink.sourceforge.net**. Double-click the disk image to uncompress it, and then double-click the **Fink pkg file** to launch the installer. Follow the onscreen instructions to walk through the Fink installer.
4. Open the **FinkCommander** directory on the installer image and drag the **FinkCommander** binary to the **Applications** folder.
5. Double-click the **FinkCommand** application to open the GUI.

6. Perform an update by clicking the **Source** menu and choosing **Selfupdate-rsync**. This will ensure that all of the packages are current.
7. Now you are ready to install Nmap. Scroll down through the list of packages and choose the **nmap** package. Click the icon in the upper-left corner of the window to install the binary package.
8. Once the installation is complete, you must open an Xterminal window to run Nmap. Run Nmap by typing **nmap** and pressing **Enter**. You will see the Nmap usage information.

Now you have successfully installed Nmap using Fink. Each time you wish to run Nmap, make sure you run the X11 application and then run Nmap from the Xterminal window that opens. The Nmap binary installs in /sw/bin, so if you don't have that directory in your permanent $PATH, you should add it.

Installing Nmap from Source

Installing Nmap from source is usually the best way to install the latest and greatest version, as binaries sometimes lag being built after source is released. Installing from the source code also give you more control over the installation. Also, binary packages don't usually include additional software such as OpenSSL, which Nmap uses for version detection. Perform the following to install Nmap from the source code (replace *version* with the most recent Nmap version):

1. Download the Nmap tarball in bzip or gzip compressed format from http://insecure.org/nmap/download.
2. Uncompress and extract the Nmap tarball by typing **bzip2 –cd nmap-*version*.tar.bz2 | tar xvf -** and pressing **Enter**. (or **gzip –cd nmap-*version*.tgz | tar xvf -**).
3. Change to the Nmap directory by typing **cd nmap-*version*** and pressing **Enter**.
4. Run the configure script by typing **./configure** and pressing **Enter**.
5. When the *configure* process is complete and the command prompt is displayed, make sure there are no errors. If everything appears trouble-free, run the make utility simply by typing **make** and pressing **Enter**.
6. If the *make* utility completed without errors, you must become root to install Nmap. Type **su root** and press **Enter**. Enter the password for root and press **Enter**.

Next, install the files in their appropriate locations by typing **make install** and pressing **Enter**.

7. After the *make install* process completes, the command prompt will be displayed once again. To run Nmap, type **nmap** and press **Enter**. You will see the list of usage options.

You have now completed your build of Nmap from source. The Nmap binary installs in /usr/local/bin, so if you don't have that directory in your permanent $PATH, you must add it. Once everything is installed, you may also remove the *.tar.bz2 or *.tgz files.

Note

Most installations follow the **configure | make | make install** format. However, in some instances, there may be other steps. Once the tar file has been extracted, there is usually an INSTALL text file included in the software subdirectory. Take a look at this file by typing **more INSTALL** to verify the installation process.

Notes from the Underground...

Compression Utilities

As you are downloading software packages from the Internet, you will encounter numerous compression utilities. Many people are already familiar with the zip compression format used on both Windows and UNIX systems. In this chapter, we discuss the tar format used for archiving files. The tar format does not provide compression. Instead, it merely packages files together into one single file. This single tar file will still take up the same amount of space, plus a little more, as the sum of all of the individual files. Tar files are typically compressed with other utilities such as gzip or bzip2.

Gzip is used to reduce the size of files, thus making it a great tool for compressing large packet captures. Gzip files are recognized by the .gz extension. Files can be compressed by typing the command **gzip *filename***. Files can be *uncompressed* by using the commands **gzip –d *filename*** or **gunzip *filename***.

Bzip2 is a newer file compression utility and is capable of greater compression ratios than gzip. Bzip2 files are recognized by the .bz2 extension. Files can be compressed by typing the command **bzip2 *filename***. Files can be *uncompressed* by using the commands **bzip2 –d *filename*** or **bunzip2 *filename***.

NOTE

Let's take a moment to define the typical variables used for the tar command: *-z, -x, -v,* and *-f* options.

The *-z* option specifies that the file must be processed through the *gzip* filter. You can tell if an archive was created with gzip by the *.gz* extension. The *-z* option is only available in the GNU version of tar. If you are not using the GNU version, you will have to unzip the tar file with a command such as *gunzip* or *gzip –dc filename.tar.gz | tar xvf -*.

The *-x* option indicates you want the contents of the archive to be extracted. By default, this action will extract the contents into the current working directory unless otherwise specified.

The *-v* option stands for verbose, which means that tar will display all files it processes on the screen. This is a personal preference and is not critical to the extraction operation.

The *-f* option specifies the file that tar will process. For example, this could be nmap-*version*.tar.gz. Sometimes it might be necessary to specify a full path if the file you want to work with is located in another directory.

Using the *configure* Script

During the *configure* script portion of the build process, you can pass options to the installer to customize the application to your specific needs. There are many options available, but here are the ones most important to Nmap.

NOTE

Typing *./configure --help* will give you the complete list of information on the optional parameters.

- **--prefix=directoryname** This option determines where Nmap and its components are installed. By default, everything is installed to /usr/local and Nmap gets installed to /usr/local/bin. The man page and data files (OS fingerprint information, services definitions, etc) are installed in sub-directories under /usr/local/man and /usr/local/share/nmap respectively. You can change the path of the separate elements by using the options --bindir, --datadir, or --mandir.
- **--without-zenmap** This parameter prevents the Zenmap graphical frontend from being created. The Zenmap graphical frontend is discussed later in the book.
- **--with-openssl=directoryname** Nmap uses the openssl libraries to probe SSL encrypted services. Nmap will look for these libraries on your host and include the capability if they are found. If the openssl libraries are in a non-standard location or are not in the search path, then you may want to use this option to specify where the libraries are located.
- **--with-libpcap=directoryname** Nmap uses libpcap for capturing raw IP packets. Nmap will check your system for an existing copy of libpcap that is compatible with the version being installed. Otherwise Nmap will install a copy that is included. If you want to use your own version of libpcap that you have already installed, use this option to tell Nmap where it's installed.
- **--with-libpcre=directoryname** LibPCRE is a Perl-compatible regular expression library that is included with Nmap, but you may want to use your own version of libpcre that you have already installed. If so, use this option to tell Nmap where it's installed.
- **--with-libdnet=directoryname** Libdnet is a library used by Nmap for sending raw ethernet frames. An Nmap-specific version is already included in the Nmap build, but if you want to use your own version installed on your system, you will need to tell Nmap where it is located by using this option. It is recommended to use the version of libdnet that is included with Nmap because it has been customized to work properly with Nmap.
- **--with-localdirs** This parameter forces Nmap to look in /usr/local/lib and /usr/local/include for critical library and header files. This is generally not necessary, unless libraries are stored in a non-standard location.

Summary

In this chapter, we covered the basics of Nmap installation for Windows, Mac OS X, and Linux/Unix-based systems. As you can see there are a variety of ways to install Nmap, with pros and cons to each installation method. Remember, installing preconfigured binaries, such as the executable file for Windows, or using YUM for Linux offers the quickest and easiest installation. However installing from source code gives you more control over the installation and ensures that you are using the most up to date version of Nmap.

As previously stated in this chapter, it is important to keep your Nmap installation up-to-date. This includes the packet capture libraries, and the Nmap software itself. Remember that Linux OS distributions frequently have Nmap as part of their software library, but that it may not always be up to date. Package managers such as RPM and YUM have built in utilities to update packages. You should also visit the Nmap site periodically to keep up on the latest announcements, as well as subscribe to some of the mailing lists. We also strongly recommend you keep your OS up-to-date as well, especially when it comes to security updates and patches. Computer security is an ever-changing technology, and staying current is necessary to avoid system compromises.

Nmap is a key element in your bag of tools and will help you greatly in many security and non-security related tasks. You will find it invaluable in troubleshooting and helping to manage and secure your enterprise.

Solutions Fast Track

Getting Nmap

☑ Nmap can be downloaded as a binary package or as source code.

☑ Nmap binaries are available for a number of platforms.

☑ Binary packages may be a version or more behind the latest version of Nmap.

☑ Nmap already exists in many Linux distributions.

Installing Nmap on Windows

☑ Nmap may be installed in three ways on Windows: a self-installer executable, command-line zip files, and source code compile.

- ☑ The Windows self-installer executable installs WinPcap for you by default during the installer process.
- ☑ Uninstall Nmap by using the uninstall.exe program.

Installing Nmap on Linux

- ☑ RPM Package Manager is used to install, update, and remove binary packages.
- ☑ Yellow dog Updater, Modified (YUM) installs Nmap and any of its dependencies automatically.
- ☑ You may also install the Nmap RPMs individually for your Linux system.

Installing Nmap on Mac OS X

- ☑ You may install Nmap on Mac OS X using MacPorts, Fink, or by compiling from source code.
- ☑ MacPorts and Fink will install Nmap and its dependencies for you automatically.

Installing Nmap from Source

- ☑ Source code installs are accomplished with the **configure | make | make install** process.
- ☑ Installing from source code gives you more control over the installation process.
- ☑ Installing from source gives you access to the source code and additional documentation.
- ☑ Nmap installs by default in the /usr/local/bin directory.
- ☑ Many options to the configure script are available to customize your install.

Frequently Asked Questions

Q: Can I mix methods of installation? For example, can I install libpcap with the RPM and then build Nmap from source, or vice-versa?

A: Yes, you can, as long as your OS supports the methods you are trying to use. Depending on the method, you may have to adjust your $PATH variable for the install to find the necessary dependencies. Also keep in mind that the versions of libpcap and libdnet that are included with Nmap have been modified for performance and functionality.

Q: A new version of Nmap was released and I want to upgrade. How do I do that?

A: For Linux, you would use the *rpm –Uvh* command or *yum update*. For Windows, simply run the new executable and it will upgrade your current version. For Mac OS X using MacPorts, you may use the *port upgrade nmap* command. If you have compiled the code from source, you will need to perform the *configure* | *make* | *make install* process again for the new version.

Q: I installed everything and it looks like it worked okay, but when I try to run Nmap it says it can't find it?

A: Make sure the Nmap directory is included in your $PATH settings.

Q: I've heard that Nmap is used within the Nessus security program. If I have Nessus, do I need to install Nmap separately?

A: While there are ways to use Nmap within Nessus, it's best to have separate installations. It will give you greater granularity.

Chapter 4

Using Nmap

Solutions in this chapter:

- Starting Nmap Scanning
- Discovering Hosts
- Port Scanning
- Detecting Operating Systems
- Detecting Service and Application Versions
- Other Scanning Options

☑ Summary

☑ Solutions Fast Track

☑ Frequently Asked Questions

Introduction

There are several reasons to use Nmap in the enterprise in addition to the fact that it is free and supports a variety of operating systems (OSes). Nmap is full of features and is very user-friendly. Its command-line options are easy to use and script, or you can use the Zenmap graphical user interface (GUI) with a point-and-click interface and command wizard. This chapter covers basic Nmap usage, including command-line options for host discovery, port scanning, OS detection, version detection, logging, and more. You will learn how to discover assets on your network for network inventory, manage assets by detecting OSes and services, and audit your network and systems for compliance and potential security vulnerabilities. Examples are provided to show you step-by-step methods to use Nmap in your enterprise.

NOTE

Fyodor maintains an Nmap reference manual that is updated with each new version release located at http://insecure.org/nmap/man/. This chapter refers to the manual and builds upon it by providing more usage examples and output.

Starting Nmap Scanning

Traditionally, Nmap is run from a UNIX shell or Windows command prompt as a command-line interface. Nmap is easily executed with a variety of command-line options and parameters, and also easily scripted. You must have administrator or root privileges to use all of Nmap's features. After you have followed the installation instruction for your OS in Chapter 3, Getting and Installing Nmap, start running Nmap by typing **nmap** and pressing **Enter**. You must ensure that the directory that contains the nmap binary or Windows executable is in your $PATH or that you are in the directory where Nmap is installed. Running nmap with no parameters causes the following usage information to display on the screen:

```
# nmap
Nmap 4.50 (http://insecure.org)
Usage: nmap [Scan Type(s)] [Options] {target specification}
TARGET SPECIFICATION:
  Can pass hostnames, IP addresses, networks, etc.
  Ex: scanme.nmap.org, microsoft.com/24, 192.168.0.1; 10.0.0-255.1-254
```

```
  -iL <inputfilename>: Input from list of hosts/networks
  -iR <num hosts>: Choose random targets
  --exclude <host1[,host2][,host3],...>: Exclude hosts/networks
  --excludefile <exclude_file>: Exclude list from file
HOST DISCOVERY:
  -sL: List Scan - simply list targets to scan
  -sP: Ping Scan - go no further than determining if host is online
  -PN: Treat all hosts as online -- skip host discovery
  -PS/PA/PU [portlist]: TCP SYN/ACK or UDP discovery to given ports
  -PE/PP/PM: ICMP echo, timestamp, and netmask request discovery probes
  -PO [protocol list]: IP Protocol Ping
  -n/-R: Never do DNS resolution/Always resolve [default: sometimes]
  --dns-servers <serv1[,serv2],...>: Specify custom DNS servers
  --system-dns: Use OS's DNS resolver
SCAN TECHNIQUES:
  -sS/sT/sA/sW/sM: TCP SYN/Connect()/ACK/Window/Maimon scans
  -sU: UDP Scan
  -sN/sF/sX: TCP Null, FIN, and Xmas scans
  --scanflags <flags>: Customize TCP scan flags
  -sI <zombie host[:probeport]>: Idle scan
  -sO: IP protocol scan
  -b <FTP relay host>: FTP bounce scan
  --traceroute: Trace hop path to each host
  --reason: Display the reason a port is in a particular state
PORT SPECIFICATION AND SCAN ORDER:
  -p <port ranges>: Only scan specified ports
   Ex: -p22; -p1-65535; -p U:53,111,137,T:21-25,80,139,8080
  -F: Fast mode - Scan fewer ports than the default scan
  -r: Scan ports consecutively - don't randomize
SERVICE/VERSION DETECTION:
  -sV: Probe open ports to determine service/version info
  --version-intensity <level>: Set from 0 (light) to 9 (try all probes)
  --version-light: Limit to most likely probes (intensity 2)
  --version-all: Try every single probe (intensity 9)
  --version-trace: Show detailed version scan activity (for debugging)
SCRIPT SCAN:
  -sC: equivalent to --script=safe,intrusive
  --script=<Lua scripts>: <Lua scripts> is a comma separated list of
     directories, script-files or script-categories
  --script-args=<n1=v1,[n2=v2,...]>: provide arguments to scripts
```

```
  --script-trace: Show all data sent and received
  --script-updatedb: Update the script database.
OS DETECTION:
  -O: Enable OS detection
  --osscan-limit: Limit OS detection to promising targets
  --osscan-guess: Guess OS more aggressively
TIMING AND PERFORMANCE:
  Options which take <time> are in milliseconds, unless you append 's'
  (seconds), 'm' (minutes), or 'h' (hours) to the value (e.g. 30m).
  -T[0-5]: Set timing template (higher is faster)
  --min-hostgroup/max-hostgroup <size>: Parallel host scan group sizes
  --min-parallelism/max-parallelism <time>: Probe parallelization
  --min-rtt-timeout/max-rtt-timeout/initial-rtt-timeout <time>: Specifies
    probe round trip time.
  --max-retries <tries>: Caps number of port scan probe retransmissions.
  --host-timeout <time>: Give up on target after this long
  --scan-delay/--max-scan-delay <time>: Adjust delay between probes
FIREWALL/IDS EVASION AND SPOOFING:
  -f; --mtu <val>: fragment packets (optionally w/given MTU)
  -D <decoy1,decoy2[,ME],...>: Cloak a scan with decoys
  -S <IP_Address>: Spoof source address
  -e <iface>: Use specified interface
  -g/--source-port <portnum>: Use given port number
  --data-length <num>: Append random data to sent packets
  --ip-options <options>: Send packets with specified ip options
  --ttl <val>: Set IP time-to-live field
  --spoof-mac <mac address/prefix/vendor name>: Spoof your MAC address
  --badsum: Send packets with a bogus TCP/UDP checksum
OUTPUT:
  -oN/-oX/-oS/-oG <file>: Output scan in normal, XML, s|<rIpt kIddi3, and Grepable
format, respectively, to the given filename.
  -oA <basename>: Output in the three major formats at once
  -v: Increase verbosity level (use twice for more effect)
  -d[level]: Set or increase debugging level (Up to 9 is meaningful)
  --open: Only show open (or possibly open) ports
  --packet-trace: Show all packets sent and received
  --iflist: Print host interfaces and routes (for debugging)
  --log-errors: Log errors/warnings to the normal-format output file
  --append-output: Append to rather than clobber specified output files
  --resume <filename>: Resume an aborted scan
  --stylesheet <path/URL>: XSL stylesheet to transform XML output to HTML
```

```
  --webxml: Reference stylesheet from Insecure.Org for more portable XML
  --no-stylesheet: Prevent associating of XSL stylesheet w/XML output
MISC:
  -6: Enable IPv6 scanning
  -A: Enables OS detection and Version detection, Script scanning and Traceroute
  --datadir <dirname>: Specify custom Nmap data file location
  --send-eth/--send-ip: Send using raw ethernet frames or IP packets
  --privileged: Assume that the user is fully privileged
  --unprivileged: Assume the user lacks raw socket privileges
  -V: Print version number
  -h: Print this help summary page.
EXAMPLES:
  nmap -v -A scanme.nmap.org
  nmap -v -sP 192.168.0.0/16 10.0.0.0/8
  nmap -v -iR 10000 -PN -p 80
SEE THE MAN PAGE FOR MANY MORE OPTIONS, DESCRIPTIONS, AND EXAMPLES
```

The usage output is a quick, handy command reference, but it doesn't include all of Nmap features and options. To make use of Nmap features, use the following syntax to execute an Nmap command:

```
nmap [Scan Type(s)] [Options] {target specification}
```

NOTE

This chapter uses a variety of unroutable Internet Protocol (IP) addresses for examples and testing. Fyodor has granted users permission to scan scanme.nmap.org. The permission includes only scanning via Nmap, not exploit testing or Denial of Service (DoS) attacks. Fyodor requests that you limit your scanning to no more than a dozen scans per day. See http://insecure.org/nmap/man/man-examples.htmlfor more information.

A simple Nmap scan that scans a single target and uses the default options is the following:

```
# nmap 192.168.100.2
Starting Nmap 4.50 (http://insecure.org) at 2007-12-22 09:56 EST
Interesting ports on 192.168.100.2:
Not shown: 1705 closed ports
PORT      STATE    SERVICE
135/tcp   open     msrpc
```

```
139/tcp     open        netbios-ssn
3389/tcp    open        ms-term-serv
6346/tcp    filtered    gnutella
6347/tcp    filtered    gnutella2
8081/tcp    open        blackice-icecap
MAC Address: 00:12:F0:D3:BF:74 (Intel Corporate)
Nmap done: 1 IP address (1 host up) scanned in 4.837 seconds
```

NOTE

By default, when no other options are given, Nmap performs host discovery and then performs a SYN port scan against each active target. Nmap also performs ARP discovery by default against targets on the local Ethernet network.

The Nmap output includes a timestamp indicating the time the scan is started, a list of interesting ports, and the seconds that elapsed until the scan was completed. The interesting ports table lists the state of each port, its protocol, and the service name. Depending on the options used, Nmap can also show additional information such as the OS type and application versions:

```
# nmap -A 192.168.2.3
Starting Nmap 4.50 (http://insecure.org) at 2007-12-28 11:45 EST
Interesting ports on 192.168.2.3:
Not shown: 1705 closed ports
PORT        STATE       SERVICE         VERSION
135/tcp     open        msrpc           Microsoft Windows RPC
139/tcp     open        netbios-ssn
3389/tcp    open        microsoft-rdp   Microsoft Terminal Service
6346/tcp    filtered    gnutella
6347/tcp    filtered    gnutella2
8081/tcp    open        http            Network Associates ePolicy Orchestrator
(Computername: LT-A020479 Version: 3.6.0.453)
|_ HTML title: Site doesn't have a title.
Service Info: OS: Windows
Host script results:
|_ NBSTAT: NetBIOS name: LT-A020479, NetBIOS MAC: 00:11:25:D6:DA:43
Service detection performed. Please report any incorrect results at
http://insecure.org/nmap/submit/.
Nmap done: 1 IP address (1 host up) scanned in 1710.661 seconds
```

The *-A* command-line option performs OS and version detection, script scanning, and tracerouting, all in addition to default port scanning. As you can see, this is a lot of useful information. To really take advantage of the power of Nmap and its benefit to the enterprise, you must become familiar with the various scan types and command-line options, all of which are covered in this chapter.

TIP

Windows does not allow you to scan your own IP address, 127.0.0.1 loopback, or localhost. You must use the *-sT* and *-PN* command-line options to scan your own Windows system.

Target Specification

Nmap is designed to scan a variety of target types, from a single host to large networks. Nmap supports Classless Inter-Domain Routing (CIDR) notation, octet ranges, Domain Name Server (DNS) names, IPv6 addressing, random targets, and exclude lists directly on the command line. You can also use combinations of target specification methods on the same command line. For example, to scan the entire 192.168.1.0 Class C network using CIDR notation, along with selected systems from 192.168.100.0 using octet ranges, and a single host using the DNS name *myhost.xyz.com*, you could use the following command:

```
nmap 192.168.1.0/24 192.168.100.10-25 myhost.xyz.com
```

You can also specify selected octet ranges using a comma-separated list, for example to scan the following hosts:

- 192.168.5.10
- 192.168.5.20
- 192.168.10.10
- 192.168.10.20
- 192.168.15.10
- 192.168.15.20
- 192.168.16.10
- 192.168.16.20

you would use the command:

```
nmap 192.168.5,10,15-16.10,20
```

Another great Nmap feature is the exclude list. If you are interested in scanning your public-facing subnet or demilitarized zone (DMZ), to look for rogue hosts, but you don't want to scan your known Web, DNS, and mail servers, you could use the following command:

```
nmap -sP --exclude web.xyz.com,dns.xyz.com,mail.xyz.com 192.168.100.0/24
```

Nmap also supports target specification from an input file and excluded targets from an exclude file. The targets must be tab, space, or newline delimited. To perform a software version inventory of your Windows servers use the following command:

```
nmap -sV -iL windows_servers.txt
```

The file *windows_servers.txt* has a list of your known Windows servers from your asset database. A good way to audit a network for rogue hosts is to use an exclude file of known IP addresses from your asset database. For example:

```
nmap --excludefile asset_database.txt 192.168.0.0/16
```

Another good input file (or exclude file, depending on your purpose) to use for asset management is your list of currently leased Dynamic Host Configuration Protocol (DHCP) addresses.

A less used, but still interesting target specification option is the ability to scan random targets using the *-iR* command-line option. The option accepts a value for the number of target addresses to generate. For example, to scan 10 random targets for a Hypertext Transfer Protocol Secure (HTTPS) service, use the following command:

```
nmap -p 443 -iR 10
```

A value of 0 supplied to the random option produces an infinite scan.

Table 4.1 summarizes the target specification command-line options. As you can see already, Nmap is very flexible at handling input on the command line and from a file. This flexibility offers you a lot of control over the targets that are scanned or not scanned. It also offers the flexibility to use exported host data from other enterprise applications as input to Nmap.

Table 4.1 Target Specification Command-Line Options

Option	Description
-iL <filename>	Specify an input file with a list of tab-, space-, or newline-delimited targets.
-iR <number of targets>	Scan a specified number of random targets.
--exlude <host1[,host2][,host3],...>	Specify comma-separated targets to not scan
--excludefile <filename>	Specify an input file with a list of tab-, space-, or newline-delimited targets to not scan.

Discovering Hosts

Host discovery in the enterprise is a great way to create and maintain your asset database and to discover rogue devices on the network. Nmap uses a variety of techniques to determine if a host is active by attempting to solicit a response from a host. The simplest way to perform host discovery is to perform a ping scan:

```
# nmap -sP 192.168.2.0/24
Starting Nmap 4.50 (http://insecure.org) at 2007-12-28 11:40 EST
Host 192.168.2.1 appears to be up.
Host 192.168.2.3 appears to be up.
Host 192.168.2.4 appears to be up.
Nmap done: 256 IP addresses (3 hosts up) scanned in 1.281 seconds
```

The ping scan sends and Internet Control Message Protocol (ICMP) echo request packet and a Transmission Control Protocol (TCP) acknowledge (ACK) packet to port 80 (TCP SYN packet if executed by an unprivileged user) to all specified targets and prints out information on the hosts that responded. If the active target is on the same local Ethernet network, Nmap includes the Media Access Control (MAC) address and the associated manufacturer according to the Organizationally Unique Identifier (OUI). This is because Nmap uses the ARP scan (*-PR*) by default on the local Ethernet network. ARP scans are disabled by using the *--send-ip* command-line option. The ping scan does not scan ports or perform any other scan techniques. The ping scan can be used to create a network inventory, manage the asset database, and monitor system availability.

NOTE

Nmap OUI information is contained in the *nmap-mac-prefixes* file.

Nmap allows you to specify a variety of ICMP ping types. The ICMP type 8 echo request (*-PE*) expects an ICMP type 0 echo reply from an active host. The ICMP type 13 timestamp request (*-PP*) expects a type 14 timestamp reply from an active host and the ICMP type 17 address mask request (*-PM*) expects a type 18 address mask reply from an active host. Firewalls can be obstacles to ICMP discovery methods, as responses are often dropped. If you are scanning through a firewall, using one of the advanced host discovery techniques may offer better results.

Nmap offers several advanced methods to solicit replies from active hosts including the TCP SYN ping, TCP ACK ping, and the User Datagram Protocol (UDP) ping. The advanced methods can be combined (and also used with the (*-sP*) or used individually. The TCP SYN ping (*-PS*) creates a packet with the SYN flag set and sends it to specified ports on the target. By default, Nmap uses port 80, but you can specify a single port or multiple ports. If the specified port is closed the device will reply with an RST packet; if it is open it will reply with a SYN/ACK. Either response is acceptable for host discovery, because they both indicate that a device is active and responding. If no response is received, the target is either not active or the responses are being blocked by a firewall. The following shows the command-line options and output of a TCP SYN ping to port 80:

```
# nmap -sP -PS --reason 192.168.2.1-4
Starting Nmap 4.50 (http://insecure.org) at 2007-12-28 12:02 Eastern
StandardTime
Host 192.168.2.1 appears to be up, received syn-ack.
Host 192.168.2.3 appears to be up, received reset.
Nmap done: 4 IP addresses (2 hosts up) scanned in 13.309 seconds
```

This example uses the *--reason* command-line option to show more detail on the response from the target hosts. In this case, we see that we received a SYN/ACK from 192.168.2.1 in response to our SYN packet, indicating that both the host and the port are active and responding. Host 192.168.2.3 replied with a RST packet, indicating that the port is closed, but still revealing that the host is active and responding. The other two hosts in the target range, 192.168.2.2 and 192.168.2.4, did not respond, indicating that the host is either inactive or blocked by a firewall.

The TCP ACK (*-PA*) ping works the same way, except Nmap creates and sends a packet with the ACK flag set. If the target responds with a RST packet it is active. The UDP ping (*-PU*) is similar to the TCP SYN and ACK pings, but in this case Nmap creates and sends a UDP packet. By default, Nmap uses UDP port 31338 because it is unlikely to be open. If a UDP packet is sent to a closed port, an active host will respond with an ICMP port unreachable packet. Other ICMP error messages and no response may indicate that the host is not active. However, if a UDP port is open, the host will ignore the packet and not return any response. This is why you want to attempt to solicit the ICMP port unreachable response from a closed port to confirm the host is active.

TIP

Use both the *-PS* and *-PA* host discovery methods to try to detect hosts behind both stateless and stateful firewalls. Many of the Nmap host discovery options can be combined to scan through firewalls and evade intrusion detection systems.

The IP ping (*-PO*) is another way to solicit a reply from an active target. Nmap creates IP packets with the specified protocol numbers in the protocol field of the IP header. If no protocols are specified, Nmap uses protocols 1, 2, and 4 (ICMP, Internet Group Management Protocol [IGMP], and IP, respectively) by default. Active hosts will respond with a packet using the same protocol as the probes or with an ICMP Protocol Unreachable message. The following example uses protocol 1, ICMP, to solicit a reply, once again we used the *--reason* command-line option to see more detail on the response packet:

```
# nmap -sP -PO1 --reason 192.168.2.1-4
Starting Nmap 4.50 (http://insecure.org) at 2007-12-28 12:10 Eastern Standard Time
Host 192.168.2.1 appears to be up, received echo-reply.
Host 192.168.2.3 appears to be up, received echo-reply.
Nmap done: 4 IP addresses (2 hosts up) scanned in 13.299 seconds
```

NOTE

Don't confuse the *-PO* command with the former *-P0* (zero) that was used to disable ping scanning. *-P0* has been renamed *-PN* to avoid confusion.

Host discovery can be disabled with the *-PN* option. When this option is used, all other scanning options (either default or those provided on the command line) are performed against every target specified, whether it is known to be active or not.

The *-sL* Nmap option prints a list of potential targets and their DNS names. This option is passive since it does not send any packets to the targets, but it does perform DNS name lookups for each host. If you only want to generate an IP address list without names you can use the *-n* option to disable DNS lookups. The following is an example of a list scan. It is truncated for brevity since the actual output continued to 192.168.100.255 (including all 256 potential hosts in the 192.168.100.0/24 target range):

```
# nmap -sL 192.168.100.0/24
Starting Nmap 4.50 (http://insecure.org) at 2007-12-22 11:53 EST
Host 192.168.100.0 not scanned
Host router.home.com (192.168.100.1) not scanned
Host systemA.home.com (192.168.100.2) not scanned
Host systemB.home.com (192.168.100.3) not scanned
Host server.home.com (192.168.100.4) not scanned
Host 192.168.100.5 not scanned
Host 192.168.100.6 not scanned
Host 192.168.100.7 not scanned
Host 192.168.100.8 not scanned
Host 192.168.100.9 not scanned
Host 192.168.100.10 not scanned
```

You could then use this list as an input file for further scanning. You can send this output to a grepable file using the *-oG <filename>* command-line option:

```
# nmap -sL -n -oG host_list 192.168.100.0/24
```

Then you can use the cut command to create a list with just the IP addresses:

```
# cut -d" " -f2 host_list > IPs_only
```

The cut command uses the space to delimit the fields and then extracts the second field, which is the IP address. You must remove the first and last lines of the file either before or after the cut, since these lines contain Nmap status information, not IP addresses. You can perform similar file parsing to extract just the host names by omitting the *-n* command-line option.

Table 4.2 summarizes the host discovery command-line options. Host discovery techniques can be combined with the target specification methods for greater flexibility. Now you are ready to move on to port scanning. While you don't need to have a discovered hosts list or asset inventory to perform port scanning (since Nmap can perform both at the same time), having one makes scanning quicker and more efficient.

Table 4.2 Host Discovery Command-line Options

Option	Description
-sL	Print a list of targets and their DNS names
-sP	Perform a ping scan
-sN	Disable host discovery (this option used to be *-P0*)
-PS/PA/PU[portlist]	Advanced host discovery techniques using TCP SYN, TCP ACK, or UDP packets
-PE/PP/PM	ICMP host discovery techniques using echo request, timestamp request, and address mask request
-PO[protocol list]	Perform an IP protocol ping
-PR	Perform an ARP ping
-n	Disables DNS name resolution (also increased scan speed)
-R	Enables DNS name resolution on all targets, even non-active targets
--dns-servers <serv1[,serve2],...>	Specify DNS servers for Nmap to use
--system-dns	Use the system DNS resolver instead of Nmap to perform DNS lookups (slower and rarely needed)
--send-ip	Disables the default ARP ping for local Ethernet networks

Port Scanning

Nmap's real power is its ability to efficiently scan ports. Nmap offers a variety of port scan techniques, each with their own specific use and expected results. It is important to apply the proper scan technique to the environment and targets being scanned. Port scanning is effective in the enterprise for a number of activities including security auditing, asset management, and compliance. You may be interested in locating systems with file sharing ports or unauthorized File Transfer Protocol (FTP) servers or printers. Open ports reveal potential security weaknesses, provide application and services inventory, and validate compliance with approved software policies. Closed ports are useful for host discovery and OS detection. Remember that port scan results may not always be accurate. Issues such as firewalls and non-RFC compliant hosts and applications can give misleading results. In addition, packet filtering that drops responses to scans slows down the scan significantly as Nmap performs several retries.

Notes from the Underground...

Nmap Port States

At first glance, you may think that a port can have two states: open and closed. While this is true from the operating system's point of view, Nmap can detect other occurrences effecting state. Nmap detects the following six port states:

- **Open** Open ports have an active application accepting TCP connections or UDP packets.
- **Closed** Closed ports are accessible, but they do not have a listening application.
- **Filtered** Responses are blocked by a packet filter, therefore Nmap cannot determine if the port is open.
- **Unfiltered** Unfiltered ports are accessible, but Nmap is unable to determine if they are open or closed. (ACK scan only)
- **Open|filtered** Nmap is unable to determine if the port is open or filtered for scan types where open ports do not respond. (UDP, IP Proto, FIN, Null, Xmas scans)
- **Closed|filtered** Nmap is unable to determine if a port is closed or filtered. (IP ID idle scan only)

Basic Port Scanning

By default, Nmap performs a TCP SYN scan (*-sS*) against the specified target, when run with root or administrator privileges. SYN scanning is quick and provides reliable results for open, closed, and filtered ports. SYN scanning was once considered a stealthy scan method, however, most host- and network-based intrusion detection systems can now detect SYN scans. Ports are considered open if the port responds to the SYN packet with a SYN/ACK packet, and ports are closed if the system responds with a RST packet. A filtered port indicates an ICMP unreachable error or no response was received. Although Nmap performs a SYN scan by default, you can also perform it with the following command-line option:

```
# nmap -sS 192.168.2.3
Starting Nmap 4.50 (http://insecure.org) at 2007-12-28 09:46 Eastern
Standard Time
Interesting ports on 192.168.2.3:
Not shown: 1707 closed ports
PORT          STATE        SERVICE
135/tcp       open         msrpc
139/tcp       open         netbios-ssn
3389/tcp      open         ms-term-serv
8081/tcp      open         blackice-icecap
Nmap done: 1 IP address (1 host up) scanned in 26.248 seconds
```

What we are interested in here is the ports table, which includes the port number and protocol, the state, and the service. Unless you are using version detection, the service that is displayed is just a guess since it is pulled from the *nmap-services* file, a list of well know services and the ports they run on.

If a user doesn't have root or administrator privileges, Nmap will perform the TCP connect scan (*-sT*) by default. This is because Nmap uses the underlying OS to establish a connection with the target instead of using its built-in ability to create and send raw packets. This scan method tends to be less efficient since Nmap has less control than it does when creating raw packets. TCP connect scans are more likely to be logged since they complete a full TCP connection. System administrators should monitor logs for a large number of connection attempts to multiple ports, since this activity may indicate a port scan. TCP connect scans can also cause unwanted effects, such as causing DoS conditions for systems that do not efficiently close TCP connections. In our example, running a TCP connect scan against the same target detects additional open ports:

```
# nmap -sT 192.168.2.3
Starting Nmap 4.50 (http://insecure.org) at 2007-12-28 09:52 Eastern
Standard Time
Interesting ports on 192.168.2.3:
Not shown: 1704 closed ports
PORT          STATE       SERVICE
21/tcp        open        ftp
25/tcp        open        smtp
110/tcp       open        pop3
135/tcp       open        msrpc
139/tcp       open        netbios-ssn
3389/tcp      open        ms-term-serv
8081/tcp      open        blackice-icecap
Nmap done: 1 IP address (1 host up) scanned in 365.014 seconds
```

This may be because the target host is running a host-based firewall that may have been interfering with the results of the SYN scan method.

Many notable exploits (SQL slammer worm) have occurred because of security weaknesses on UDP services. UDP is used by many popular services including DNS, Simple Network Management Protocol (SNMP), Trivial File Transfer Protocol (TFTP), NFS, DHCP, Kerberos, and Syslog. The Nmap UDP scan (*-sU*) sends an empty UDP header to the target port. The target responds with an ICMP port unreachable error if the port is closed. Other ICMP errors indicate that the port is blocked by a packet filter. UDP services on open ports will respond with a UDP packet, however, some UDP services will not send a response. Because of this lack of response, Nmap performs several retries, which makes UDP scanning very slow. If Nmap cannot determine if the port is blocked by a packet filter it will indicate open|filtered for the port status. In this case, try performing a version scan (*-sV*) to gather additional information to determine if the port is actually open. The following is an example of a UDP scan and associated output:

```
# nmap -sU 192.168.2.3
Starting Nmap 4.50 (http://insecure.org) at 2007-12-28 10:04 Eastern Standard
Time
All 1488 scanned ports on 192.168.2.3 are open|filtered (1334) or closed (154)
Nmap done: 1 IP address (1 host up) scanned in 20.670 seconds
```

In this case, the UDP port scan may be filtered by the host-based firewall, or there may not be any open UDP ports. Let's scan another target and view the results:

```
# nmap -sU 192.168.100.4
Starting Nmap 4.50 (http://insecure.org) at 2007-12-28 10:15 Eastern
Standard Time
Interesting ports on 192.168.100.4:
Not shown: 1483 closed ports
PORT          STATE              SERVICE
123/udp       open|filtered      ntp
259/udp       open|filtered      firewall1-rdp
427/udp       open|filtered      svrloc
631/udp       open|filtered      unknown
5353/udp      open|filtered      zeroconf
MAC Address: 00:30:65:0D:28:32 (Apple Computer)
Nmap done: 1 IP address (1 host up) scanned in 56.742 seconds
```

This is more of what we are looking for. There are five UDP services that may be open on this target. You need to perform additional testing, with the version detection

(-*sV*) and other manual tests, to determine actual open services and versions. Version detection is covered later in this chapter.

NOTE

Only one port scan method may be used at a time, with the exception of the UDP scan (-*sU*), which can be used with any TCP scan method.

Nmap provides the ability to analyze IP protocols with the IP protocol scan (-*sO*). This isn't technically a port scan, however, it does use the same underlying port scan engine and reports its results in the port table. The IP protocol scan allows you to see which IP protocols are supported by the target system. The response to this scan is an ICMP protocol unreachable for unsupported protocols. Other ICMP responses cause the protocol to be reported as filtered, and no response is reported as open|filtered. The following is an example of an IP protocol scan and associated output:

```
# nmap -sO 192.168.2.3
Starting Nmap 4.50 (http://insecure.org) at 2007-12-28 12:24 EST
Interesting protocols on 192.168.2.3:
Not shown: 250 closed protocols
PROTOCOL     STATE            SERVICE
1            open             icmp
2            open|filtered    igmp
6            open|filtered    tcp
17           open             udp
47           open|filtered    gre
50           open|filtered    esp
MAC Address: 00:11:25:D6:DA:C7 (IBM)
Nmap done: 1 IP address (1 host up) scanned in 1.649 seconds
```

Advanced Port Scanning

Nmap includes several advanced port scanning options that manipulate the raw packet in a variety of ways to solicit responses from the target. According to the TCP Request For Comment (RFC), any packet not containing a SYN, RST, or ACK flag will result in a returned RST if the port is closed and no response if the port is open (reported as open|filtered). Nmap includes the following three scan options to take advantage of this characteristic:

- **TCP Null scan** The TCP Null scan (*-sN*) does not set any flag bits in the TCP header.
- **TCP FIN scan** The TCP FIN scan (*-sF*) sets only the FIN flag.
- **Xmas scan** The Xmas scan (*-sX*) sets the FIN, PSH, and URG flags.

If Nmap receives an ICMP unreachable error it will report the port as filtered. These advanced port scanning options are stealthy and may bypass firewalls and other security controls. However, most host- and network-based intrusion detection systems (IDSes) will detect this type of scan activity. Keep in mind that OSes that don't follow the TCP RFC may send misleading responses.

Nmap includes an advanced port scan option that is used to scan firewalls to determine their connection state and rulesets. The TCP ACK scan (*-sA*) creates and sends a packet to the target with only the ACK flag set. Unfiltered systems will respond with a RST packet for both open and closed ports. If an ICMP error message or no response is received, the port is considered filtered by a firewall.

A similar technique to the TCP ACK scan is the TCP Window scan (*-sW*). The Window scan sends a packet with only the ACK flag set, but also analyzes the TCP Window field in the RST response to determine if the port is open or closed. The TCP window size is an implementation detail of a few types of systems. Some systems will use a positive window size if the port is open, and a zero window size if the port is closed.

The Maimon scan (*-sM*), named after the discoverer Uriel Maimon, sets the FIN and ACK flags in the port scan packet. The target system will generate a RST packet for a port that is open or closed. More information on this scan technique can be found in Phrack Magazine issue #49 (November 1996), www.phrack.org/issues.html?issue =49&id=15 - article.

Another advanced port scanning technique is the Idle scan (*-sI*). The idle allows you to specify another system to use in the scanning, known as a *zombie host*. The zombie host is used to mask your IP address and to analyze IP fragmentation ID sequence generation to determine open ports on the target. The idle scan is a very stealthy, blind TCP port scan. A blind scan spoofs your real IP address as another host, so your scanning system will not see any responses from the target, since they are sent to the spoofed host. The trick is to analyze the spoofed host to conclude responses from the target. Fyodor has a great write up on the idle scan including examples at http://insecure.org/nmap/idlescan.html. The idle scan uses TCP port 80 by default if no ports are specified.

Another stealthy scan method is the FTP bounce scan (*-b*). The FTP bounce scan uses the FTP proxy feature on an FTP server to scan a target from the FTP server instead of your system. The FTP proxy feature allows you to log into an FTP server and request a file to be sent to another system. By sending files to a target system and port you can determine whether a port is open or closed. Most FTP servers no longer support this functionality, but some are still available. The FTP bounce scan can be used to bypass firewalls by scanning from an organization's FTP server, which may be on an internal network, or allowed to the internal network by the firewall rules.

To have even more control over packet creation, Nmap provides the *--scanflags* command-line option to allow you to specify TCP flags to set in the packet. This allows you to solicit a variety of responses from targets, as well as evade IDSes. You can use numerical flag values or symbolic names in any order. For example, to set the URG and PSH flags you would use the following option:

```
--scanflags URGPSH
```

You can provide a TCP scan type to tell Nmap how to interpret the results. For example, supplying the *-sA* command-line option along with the *--scanflags* tells Nmap to use the specified flags but to interpret the results the same way an ACK scan would. By default, Nmap uses the SYN scan for result interpretation.

Nmap has two other less used port scanning command-line options that provide valuable information. The *--traceroute* command-line option is performed after the scan and works with all scan types except the TCP connect scan (*-sT*) and idle scan (*-sI*). It uses Nmap's own traceroute algorithm and timing characteristics to determine the mostly likely port and protocol to reach the target. The *--reason* command-line option shows more detail about the responses from the target host, including the type of packet that was received in response to the probe. This option is also automatically enabled by the nmap debug (*-d*) command-line option.

Specifying Ports

Now that we have covered all of the port scanning techniques, let's take a look at how you can specify the ports to scan. By default, Nmap scans ports 1 through 1024 and those listed in the *nmap-services* file for the protocol being scanned (TCP or UDP).

Its worth taking a look at the *nmap-services* file to see the ports, especially the higher numbered ports, that Nmap includes. Nmap also allows you to specify the ports to scan and whether to scan them sequentially or randomized. By default, Nmap randomizes the order of ports scanned. You can scan sequentially by using the *-r* command-line option. To specify ports, use the *-p <port range>* command-line option. The port range parameter can be a single port or a range of ports. To scan for hosts with port 80 you could use the following:

```
nmap -p 80 192.168.100.0/24
Starting Nmap 4.50 (http://insecure.org) at 2007-12-28 12:58 Eastern
Standard Time
Interesting ports on 192.168.100.1:
PORT   STATE  SERVICE
80/tcp open   http
MAC Address: 00:14:6C:19:F8:45 (Netgear)

Interesting ports on 192.168.100.2:
PORT   STATE  SERVICE
80/tcp closed http
MAC Address: 00:30:65:0D:28:29 (Apple Computer)
Nmap done: 256 IP addresses (3 hosts up) scanned in 28.291 seconds
```

You can also specify a range of ports to scan. The following only scans ports 130 to 140 (since no scan methods are included, Nmap uses the SYN scan by default):

```
# nmap -p 130-140 192.168.2.3
Starting Nmap 4.50 (http://insecure.org) at 2007-12-28 13:05 EST
Interesting ports on 192.168.2.3:
PORT      STATE     SERVICE
130/tcp   closed    cisco-fna
131/tcp   closed    cisco-tna
132/tcp   closed    cisco-sys
133/tcp   closed    statsrv
134/tcp   closed    ingres-net
135/tcp   open      msrpc
136/tcp   closed    profile
137/tcp   closed    netbios-ns
138/tcp   closed    netbios-dgm
139/tcp   open      netbios-ssn
140/tcp   closed    emfis-data
MAC Address: 00:11:25:D6:DA:65 (IBM)
Nmap done: 1 IP address (1 host up) scanned in 0.158 seconds
```

Nmap also includes notation to scan from port 1 to a specified port. The following example scans from port 1 to port 100:

```
nmap -p -100 192.168.100.0/24
```

Keeping in similar syntax, Nmap can scan from a specified port to port 65535. The following example scans from port 60000 to port 65535:

```
nmap -p 60000- 192.168.100.0/24
```

Combining syntax allows you to scan all 65535 ports by using the following:

```
nmap -p- 192.168.100.0/24
```

If you are performing both TCP and UDP scans, you may want to specify different ports for each protocol. The following example shows the syntax to do just that:

```
nmap -sU -sS -p U:53,T:80,134-139 192.168.100.0/24
```

This Nmap command will perform a UDP scan on port 53, and a TCP SYN scan on ports 80 and 134 to 139. You can also specify port names instead of numbers. Make sure you use the port names included in the *nmap-services* file. Nmap also supports wildcards (* and ?) in port names. The following scans the FTP port and all HTTP ports:

```
nmap -p ftp,http* 192.168.100.0/24
```

By viewing the *nmap-services* file, you can see that this scan includes the following ports:

```
ftp             21/tcp      # File Transfer [Control]
http            80/tcp      # World Wide Web HTTP
http-mgmt       280/tcp     #
https           443/tcp     # secure http (SSL)
http-alt        591/tcp     # FileMaker, Inc. - HTTP Alternate
http-rpc-epmap  593/tcp     # HTTP RPC Ep Map
http-alt        8000/tcp    # A common alternative http port
http-proxy      8080/tcp    # Common HTTP proxy/second web server port
https-alt       8443/tcp    # Common alternative https port
```

Nmap also provides syntax to scan port ranges in the *nmap-services* file. For example, you can scan all ports that are included in the *nmap-services* file between port 6000 and port 6100:

```
nmap -p [6000-6100] 192.168.100.0/24
```

By viewing the *nmap-services* file, you can see that this scan includes the following ports:

```
X11             6000/tcp    # X Window server
X11:1           6001/tcp    # X Window server
X11:2           6002/tcp    # X Window server
X11:3           6003/tcp    # X Window server
X11:4           6004/tcp    # X Window server
```

```
X11:5           6005/tcp        # X Window server
X11:6           6006/tcp        # X Window server
X11:7           6007/tcp        # X Window server
X11:8           6008/tcp        # X Window server
X11:9           6009/tcp        # X Window server
xmail-ctrl      6017/tcp        # XMail CTRL server
arcserve        6050/tcp        # ARCserve agent
```

The port specification command-line option is also used with the IP scan technique to specify the protocol numbers (0–255) to scan. The following example shows the use of the IP protocol scan with the TCP protocol:

```
# nmap -sO -p 6 192.168.100.0/24
Starting Nmap 4.50 (http://insecure.org) at 2007-12-28 13:34 Eastern
StandardTime
Interesting protocols on 192.168.100.1:
PROTOCOL      STATE              SERVICE
6             open|filtered      tcp
MAC Address: 00:14:6C:19:F8:65 (Netgear)

Interesting protocols on 192.168.100.4:
PROTOCOL      STATE              SERVICE
6             open|filtered      tcp
MAC Address: 00:30:65:0D:28:34 (Apple Computer)
Nmap done: 256 IP addresses (3 hosts up) scanned in 39.747 seconds
```

NOTE

Nmap protocol information is contained in the *nmap-protocols* file.

Another port specification command-line option is the fast scan (*-F*), which scans only for ports listed in the *nmap-services* file. To make this option even more efficient, you can specify your own customized nmap-services file using the *–servicedb* command-line option, for example:

```
nmap --servicedb /home/me/my-services 192.168.100.0/24
```

Table 4.3 summarizes the port scanning command-line options. We are really starting to see the power and versatility of the Nmap scanner. One thing to keep in mind in terms of port scanning is that Nmap uses its built in *nmap-services* file to correlate ports and services to output in the results. Most of the time, these are actually the services running on these ports, however, in some cases it may be a different service or even a Trojan application. Luckily, Nmap also has the ability to probe active services for more information. The next two sections show you how to perform Nmap OS detection, and service and application version detection.

TIP

To speed up slow scans, scan hosts in parallel, scan just the most popular ports, and perform scanning behind the firewall.

Table 4.3 Port Scanning Command-Line Options

Option	Description
-sS	TCP SYN scan
-sT	TCP connect scan
-sU	UDP port scan
-sN	TCP null scan
-sF	TCP FIN scan
-sX	TCP Xmas scan
-sA	TCP ACK scan
-sW	TCP Window scan
-sM	TCP Maimon scan
-sI <zombie host[:probeport]>	TCP Idle scan
-sO	IP Protocol scan
-b <FTP relay host>	FTP Bounce scan
--scanflags <flags>	Set the TCP flags of your choice
--traceroute	Trace the path to the target host
--reason	Provide host and port state reasons
-p <port range>	Specify ports to scan
-F	Fast scan
-r	Don't randomize ports
--servicedb <filename>	Specify a file to use other than the default *nmap-services* file

Detecting Operating Systems

A really nice feature of Nmap is the ability to remotely detect OS versions. This is particularly useful for network asset inventory and OS patch management. For example, you may use Nmap OS detection to identify outdated or unauthorized systems on your networks. Nmap performs OS detection by probing the target host and analyzing the responses. Probes include TCP and UDP packets that examine OS specifics such as initial sequence numbers (ISN), TCP options, IP identifier (ID) numbers, timestamps, explicit congestion notification (ECN), and window sizes. Each OS has distinctive responses to the probes, which identify the OS and result in an OS fingerprint. The probes and response matches are located in the *nmap-os-db* file. Nmap will attempt to identify the following parameters:

- **Vendor Name** The vendor of the OS such as Microsoft or Sun.
- **Operating System** The underlying OS such as Windows, Mac OS X, Solaris.
- **OS Generation** The version of the OS such as Vista, XP, 2003, 10.5, or 10.
- **Device Type** The type of device such as general purpose, print server, media, router, WAP, or power device.

In addition to these parameters, OS detection also provides useful information on system uptime and TCP Sequence Predictability Classification, which is the measure of the difficulty to forge a TCP connection against the remote host. To enable OS detection with your port scan use the *-O* command-line option. For example:

```
# nmap -O 192.168.100.2
Starting Nmap 4.50 (http://insecure.org) at 2008-01-03 21:40 EST
Interesting ports on 192.168.100.2:
Not shown: 1709 closed ports
PORT        STATE    SERVICE
631/tcp     open     ipp
1033/tcp    open     netinfo
Device type: general purpose
Running: Apple Mac OS X 10.4.X
OS details: Apple Mac OS X 10.4.8 - 10.4.10 (Tiger) (Darwin 8.8.0 - 8.10.2)
Network Distance: 0 hops
OS detection performed. Please report any incorrect results at http://insecure.
org/nmap/submit/.
Nmap done: 1 IP address (1 host up) scanned in 11.844 seconds
```

This command will use Nmap's default SYN scan for port detection, but the OS detection option can be combined with any of the port detection techniques.

Nmap includes several command-line options to configure the OS detection engine. To limit OS detection to targets with at least one open port and one closed port, thus increasing your chances of a successful identification, you can use the *--osscan-limit* command-line option. If Nmap can't make a perfect match for an OS it will guess something that is close, but not exact. To make Nmap guess more aggressively, you can use the *--osscan-guess* command-line option. Lastly, to make OS detection quicker you can lower the *--max-os-retries* command-line option. By default, Nmap will retry OS detection five times, and two times when conditions aren't favorable. Setting the *--max-os-retries* to a lower value such as 1 will speed up the detection process, but detection may not be as reliable.

This section provided a basic introduction to Nmap's OS detection usage. Table 4.4 summarizes the OS detection command-line options. Nmap's OS detection features are covered in more detail in Chapter 6.

NOTE

For detailed information on OS detection, including usage and customization, check out http://insecure.org/nmap/osdetect.

Table 4.4 Operating System Detection Command-Line Options

Option	Description
-O	Enable OS detection
--osscan-limit	Only perform OS detection against targets with at least one open and one closed port
--osscan-guess	Guess near-matches aggressively
--max-retries <number>	Sets the number of OS detection retries

Detecting Service and Application Versions

By default, Nmap identifies open ports on the target host and correlates those port numbers with common services associated with those ports, located in the *nmap-services* file. But is it really a Web server running on port 80? When you are managing your network assets and performing security auditing, Nmap can go one step further to probe the open ports to attempt to identify the application or service running on it. For asset management, you are interested in the version of services and applications, not only for inventory reasons, but also for policy compliance. You may find systems running unauthorized servers, so you will want to identify the unauthorized services and applications that are running. For security auditing, you are interested in service and application versions from a vulnerability and patch management perspective.

Nmap can perform version detection to assist in gathering more detail on the services and applications running on the identified open ports. Version detection uses a variety of probes, located in the *nmap-services-probe*s file, to solicit responses from the services and applications. Nmap queries the target host with the probe information and analyzes the response, comparing it against known responses for a variety of services, applications, and versions. Nmap will attempt to identify the following parameters:

- **Service Protocol** The service running on the open port, such as FTP, Hypertext Transfer Protocol (HTTP), or Simple Mail Transfer Protocol (SMTP).
- **Application Name** The specific application for the service, such as WU-FTPD, Microsoft IIS, or Sendmail.
- **Version Number** The version of the application.
- **Hostname** The hostname of the target host. (This may be for an internal network and different than the DNS response).
- **Device Type** The type of device such as a print server, media, router, WAP, or power device.
- **Operating System Family** The underlying OS such as Windows, HP-UX, Cisco IOS, or Linux. (This could be different than what the Nmap OS detection reports if the system uses network address translator (NAT) and forwarding for the application).
- **Miscellaneous Details** Other details such as kernel information, serial numbers, firmware versions, user names, and password information.
- **Port State** Version detection also attempts to gain more information about UDP and TCP ports that were reported as open|filtered to determine the correct state of the port.

NOTE

If Nmap was compiled with OpenSSL support, it can attempt to discover listening services behind Secure Sockets Layer (SSL) encryption. By default, Nmap will look for OpenSSL libraries during install and include this capability. OpenSSL support is not available on the Windows version of Nmap.

To enable version detection with your port scan use the *-sV* command-line option. For example:

```
# nmap -sV 192.168.2.3
Starting Nmap 4.50 (http://insecure.org) at 2008-01-03 21:44 EST
Interesting ports on 192.168.2.3:
Not shown: 1705 closed ports
PORT        STATE      SERVICE         VERSION
135/tcp     open       msrpc           Microsoft Windows RPC
139/tcp     open       netbios-ssn
3389/tcp    open       microsoft-rdp   Microsoft Terminal Service
6346/tcp    filtered   gnutella
6347/tcp    filtered   gnutella2
8081/tcp    open       http            Network Associates ePolicy Orchestrator
(Computername: LT-A030443 Version: 3.6.0.453)
Service Info: OS: Windows
Service detection performed. Please report any incorrect results at
http://insecure.org/nmap/submit/.
Nmap done: 1 IP address (1 host up) scanned in 11.317 seconds
```

This command will use Nmap's default SYN scan for port detection, but the version detection option can be combined with any of the port detection techniques.

Nmap includes several command-line options to configure the version detection engine. The *nmap-service-probes* file excludes probing certain ports (e.g., printer ports will print anything that is sent to it). To enable all ports for version detection, use the *--allports* command-line option. You can also control the version scanning intensity with the -*--version-intensity* command-line option. By default, Nmap uses an intensity of 7 (out of 0–9). The intensity level controls the probes that are used in version detection; the higher intensity means that more probes are used. Probes are classified with a rarity value between 1 and 9, with 1 being very common and highly useful, and 9 being rare and less useful. Higher intensity scans take longer since they use more of the rare probes, but you are more likely to have services and versions correctly detected.

If you want quick but less reliable version detection, you can also use the *--version-light* command-line option, which is equal to a version intensity level of 2. If you want comprehensive and reliable version detection by executing every probe, you can also use the *--version-all* command-line option, which is equal to a version intensity level of 9. You can also get detailed information during the version detection process by using the *--version-trace* command-line option. You can specify a customized service probe file, instead of the default *nmap-service-probes*, by using the *--versiondb* command-line option.

NOTE

The *-A* command-line option enables version detection, OS detection, script scanning, and traceroute.

Nmap version detection also includes Remote Procedure Call (RPC)-specific probes to discover the RPC program and version. These are enabled by default when version detection discovers RPC services, but it can also be enabled separately outside of version detection by using the *-sR* command-line option. The RPC probes can gather the same type of information as executing the **rpcinfo -p** UNIX command, even if the target host's portmapper is behind a firewall.

Table 4.5 summarizes the service and application version detection command-line options. Version detection is a growing and evolving feature of Nmap, with numerous enterprise capabilities.

Notes from the Underground...

OS and Version Detection Community Contribution

The Nmap OS and version detection probe databases grow by contributions from its users. When Nmap receives responses to probes but it still can't identify the OS or application version, it will display a special fingerprint and a Uniform Resource Locator (URL) to submit the signature. OS detection relies on at least one open port and one closed port on the target host to print a reliable fingerprint.

> If you are sure what OS or application and version is running on a port, please submit this fingerprint to help grow the database of signatures. If Nmap didn't receive any responses for version detection and does not print a fingerprint, this means that there isn't a probe for this service. You can also contribute to Nmap by writing and submitting version detection probes. This takes longer than simply submitting a fingerprint, but if you have time it is a great way to support the open source community! For detailed information on service and application version detection, including usage and developing probes, check out http://insecure.org/nmap/vscan.

Table 4.5 Service and Application Version Detection Command-Line Options

Option	Description
-sV	Enable version detection for services and application
-sR	Enable RPC version detection (enabled by default with *-sV* option)
--allports	Don't exclude any ports from version detection
--version-intensity <intensity>	Set version scan intensity from 0 to 9
--version-light	Set version intensity to level 2 for quick version scanning
--version-all	Set version intensity to level 9 to attempt all probes
--version-trace	Print debugging information during version detection
--versiondb <service probes file>	Specify a customized services probes file

Other Scanning Options

Nmap has a variety of other command-line options to assist with network mapping and port scanning. These command-line options include scripting, performance and optimization, output logging, and evasion and spoofing. You have seen the power of Nmap in its ability to perform robust port scanning and detect OSes and service and application versions. These scanning options demonstrate Nmap's unrivaled flexibility and features that allow you to customize Nmap scanning to your needs.

Nmap Scripting Engine

The Nmap Scripting Engine (NSE) extends Nmap's capabilities to enable it to perform a variety of tasks and report the results along with Nmap's normal output. Some examples of NSE scripts include:

- **Enhanced Network Discovery** Perform whois lookups, perform additional protocol queries, and act as a client for the listening service to collect information such as available network shares.
- **Enhanced Version Detection** Perform complex version probes and attempt service brute-force cracking.
- **Vulnerability Detection** Execute probes to check for specific vulnerabilities.
- **Malware Detection** Execute probes to discover Trojan and worm backdoors.
- **Vulnerability Exploitation** Execute scripts to exploit a detected vulnerability.

NOTE

By default, version scanning (*-sV*) also executes all NSE scripts in the version category. The *-A* command-line option executes the *-sC* command-line option (safe and intrusive categories).

NSE scripts are written in the Lua scripting language and named with the extension *.nse*. They are stored in the *scripts* subdirectory of the main Nmap directory. The *script.db* file is also located in the main Nmap directory, and it contains the list of all NSE scripts and their associated categories (safe, intrusive, malware, backdoor, version, discovery, vulnerability). The NSE script will first determine whether it should be run against the target host (does the target host meet certain criteria such as an open port or running service), by analyzing Nmap's scan output before it executes the actions of the script. The quickest way to start using NSE is to use the *-sC* command-line option:

```
nmap -sC 192.168.100.0/24
```

This option will perform a script scan of all safe and intrusive scripts. You can use the *--script* option to have more granular control over the specific scripts and categories that are executed. For example, to execute all scripts in the vulnerability category you can use the following:

```
nmap --script=vulnerability 192.168.100.3
```

This will perform a lightweight vulnerability scan of the specified target. To execute a single script you can use the following:

```
nmap --script=promiscuous.nse 192.168.100.0/24
```

This will execute the *promiscuous.nse* script to look for Ethernet cards in promiscuous mode. In the enterprise, this is something worth investigating for security auditing, because it will discover systems that are running sniffers. Sniffers may be running on legitimate network analyzer systems, or employees may have installed them, or they may be running on a system compromised by an attacker. This security auditing can also be coupled with policy compliance checking to determine if unauthorized individuals are running sniffers. You may have a certain subset of NSE scripts that you would like to execute. You can run these by specifying the directory where they are located:

```
nmap --script=/my-scripts 192.168.100.0/24
```

This will execute all NSE scripts in the *my-scripts* directory. Use the *all* parameter to execute all NSE scripts that are included with Nmap:

```
# nmap --script=all 192.168.100.4
Starting Nmap 4.50 (http://insecure.org) at 2008-01-03 21:55 EST
Interesting ports on server.home.com (192.168.100.4):
Not shown: 1705 closed ports
PORT        STATE       SERVICE
135/tcp     open        msrpc
139/tcp     open        netbios-ssn
445/tcp     open        microsoft-ds
2000/tcp    open        callbook
6346/tcp    filtered    gnutella
6347/tcp    filtered    gnutella2
MAC Address: 00:11:F5:92:26:65 (Askey Computer)
Host script results:
|_ NBSTAT: NetBIOS name: MYLAPTOP, NetBIOS MAC: 00:11:F5:92:26:65
|_ Promiscuous detection: Win98/Win2K/WinXP with pcap installed. I'm unsure
if they're sniffing. (tests: "1_1_____1_")
Nmap done: 1 IP address (1 host up) scanned in 6.343 seconds
```

Notice the **Host script results** in the output. The scripts detected the NetBIOS name and that WinPcap is installed. NSE includes a few advanced NSE command-line arguments, mostly for script developers and debugging. These include the ability to pass arguments to scripts to override script values, running a trace for a script, and updating the script database. Table 4.6 summarizes the NSE command-line options. We should see a lot more NSE scripts in the future, since NSE is a new and evolving Nmap feature with lots of expansion capabilities.

NOTE

For detailed information on NSE, including usage and script development, check out http://insecure.org/nmap/nse.

Table 4.6 Scripting Command-Line Options

Option	Description
-sC	Execute safe and intrusive scripts
--script <script-categoriesldirectoryl filenamelall>	Execute specified scripts and categories
--script-args=<n1=v1[,n2=v2,...]>	Provide arguments to override script values
--script-trace	Print all incoming and outgoing script communication
--script-updatedb	Update the script database name/category mapping

Performance and Optimization

When using Nmap in the enterprise to scan large networks, performance and optimization is a high priority. Nmap has several features to enhance the timing and performance, including advanced algorithms and executing tasks in parallel. You can also control various timing and performance features with Nmap's command-line options. You can use various parameters to scope your scan to obtain specific information and eliminate unnecessary tests. Throughout this chapter we provide examples on scoping the Nmap scan by using various command-line options and parameters. This section provides information on using timing options for performance and optimization.

NOTE

The time parameter is specified in milliseconds by default, however, you can also specify *s*, *m*, or *h* to indicate seconds, minutes, and hours. For example, 1 h, 60 m, 3600 s, and 3600000 all equal the same.

Nmap timing options are addressed in the following categories:

- **Timing Template** Nmap offers six timing templates to control the speed of the Nmap scan. Timing templates may be specified by their name or numerical value. The timing templates are paranoid (0), sneaky (1), polite (2), normal (3), aggressive (4), and insane (5). By default, Nmap scans with a the normal template (-T3). The slower templates lower the impact on the network and systems and are used for Intrusion Detection System (IDS) evasion. The faster templates are used on very fast networks, and although they are very fast, they may be less accurate. Some example uses of Nmap timing templates include the following:

  ```
  nmap -T4 192.168.100.0/24
  nmap -Tparanoid 192.168.100.0/24
  ```

  Keep in mind that the paranoid template scans only one port at a time, and waits five minutes between each probe. This can take a very long time!

- **Parallelism** Nmap makes good use of parallelism for performance optimization. Nmap divides the target IP addresses into groups and scans one group at a time. You can control the group sizes with the *--min-hostgroup* and *--max-hostgroup* command-line options. Specifying a large minimum group size increases the scanning speed. Nmap also executes probes in parallel. Nmap can dynamically adjust the number of parallel probes based on network performance. You can control the probe parallelism with the *--min-parallelism* and *--max-parallelism* command-line options. Since Nmap dynamically controls parallelism, these command-line options are rarely used. Some people do set the *--max-paralellism* to small values, such as 1, to limit the number of probes sent to a host at a time (e.g., scanning critical production systems).

- **Timouts** Nmap dynamically adjusts the timeout value to wait for a probe response based on the response time of previous probes. You can specify a minimum timeout value and a maximum timeout value as well as the initial timeout value using the *--min-rtt-timeout*, *--max-rtt-timeout*, and *--initial-rtt-timeout* command-line options. Most people only use the maximum and initial timeout values to lower them to decrease scan times, especially on filtered networks. The *--scan-delay* and *--max-scan-delay* command-line options allow you to specify the amount of time to wait between each probe. This is useful for systems that rate limit responses. By default, Nmap dynamically adjusts scan delay when it detects rate limiting. Scan delay may also be used to evade intrusion detection and prevention devices. Some systems will also rate limit RST packets, which can slow down scans. You can use the *--defeat-rst-ratelimit* command-line option to ignore this type of rate limiting. For example, if you are running a SYN scan, RST packets indicate a closed port, but if you are only interested in open ports, you don't care about the RST packets. You can also specify the maximum amount of time to spend scanning a target so that you don't waste a lot of time on very slow responding hosts. For example, you can set the value to 15m to move on to the next target if the scan on the current host isn't completed in 15 minutes.

- **Retries** When Nmap doesn't receive a response to a probe it will retransmit it. You can specify the maximum number of retries to increase scan speed by using the *--max-retries* command-line option. You can set the value to 0 to prevent any retransmissions, but this is not recommended due to poor network reliability and other factors.

Table 4.7 summarizes the timing and performance command-line options. As you can see there is a lot of configurability in terms of timing parameters. In general, unless you are an advanced user you can leave these parameters to Nmap to adjust dynamically (with the exception of the timing templates). If you are an advanced user with special scanning needs you may find the other options beneficial to your scanning performance.

Table 4.7 Timing and Performance Command-Line Options

Option	Description
-T <paranoidlsneakylpolitel normallaggressivelinsane> Or -T <0–5>	Sets the timing template
--min-hostgroup/max-hostgroup <size>	Specify the parallel scan group size

Continued

Table 4.7 Continued. Timing and Performance Command-Line Options

Option	Description
--min-parallelism/max-parallelism <time>	Specify the number of probes to execute in parallel
--min-rtt-timeout/max-rtt-timeout/ initial-rtt-timeout <time>	Specify the probe round trip timeout before giving up or retransmitting a probe
--scan-delay/–max-scan-delay <time>	Specify the delay between probes
--max-retries <tries>	Specify the number of probe retransmissions
--host-timeout <time>	Specify a maximum amount of time to spend scanning a host before moving on to the next target
--defeat-rst-ratelimit	Ignore RST rate limiting

Evasion and Spoofing

As we have mentioned throughout this chapter, security controls such as packet filters, router access control lists, and firewalls will limit the results of your Nmap scanning. Nmap scans are also easily detected by intrusion detection and prevention systems (IDPS). In the enterprise, this may not be a concern since you may have physical access to internal networks behind the security controls and you are not concerned with being detected. However, Nmap does include several options to attempt to evade firewalls and IDPSes. You may be interested in using these features to test the robustness of your security controls and their susceptibility to evasion techniques. You may also wish to use these techniques as part of a full security audit or penetration test to attempt to defeat security controls using the same methods as attackers. For example, evasion techniques are often used to verify that firewall filters are operating properly. We have already mentioned some evasion techniques in the "Port Scanning" section, such as the Idle scan and FTP bounce. We also mentioned some evasion techniques that use timing parameters in the "Performance and Optimization" section. In this section, we will take a closer look at evasion methods that use fragmentation, spoofing, and packet manipulation techniques.

NOTE

Security control evasion is an art and skill that goes well beyond the functionality that Nmap offers, and beyond the scope of this book. A great starting point for more information is the paper titled *Insertion, Evasion, and Denial of Service:Eluding Network Intrusion Detection* located at www.snort.org/docs/idspaper/. While this paper is old, published in 1998, it is a classic paper on the theory behind evasion techniques.

Packet fragmentation is an old and common evasion technique that splits the packet header across many small packets. This will sometimes break up distinguishing characteristics across packets and evade pattern matching detection techniques. You can fragment your Nmap packets by using the *-f* command-line option. This will break the packets into a maximum of 8 bytes after the IP header. If you use this option twice, Nmap will break the packets into a maximum of 16 bytes after the IP header. You can use the *--mtu* command-line option (instead of the *-f* option) to specify your own packet size for fragmentation in multiples of 8. For example, the following command-line options perform the same fragmentation:

```
nmap -f -f 192.168.100.0/24
nmap --mtu 16 192.168.100.0/24
```

Fragmentation doesn't always evade security controls these days, because controls have built-in techniques to detect and handle fragmentation. However, sometimes controls don't have this feature enabled for performance and routing reasons.

Spoofing is another evasion technique where you mask your IP address by pretending to be another system on the Internet. We saw this with both the Idle and FTP bounce scans. The Nmap decoy scan (*-D*) combines spoofing and confusion to attempt to evade detection. By specifying decoys, you are making it appear that other hosts are also scanning the target in hopes that you won't be detected or singled out. You can specify multiple decoys as a comma-separated command-line parameter. You can also specify *ME* in the list to represent the position for your actual system, otherwise Nmap will position your system randomly. Positioning your system further down the list increases the chances that you will not be detected. Attackers often use real IP addresses of active hosts on the Internet, but for enterprise auditing this may not be necessary, and may get you into trouble if the owners of the active systems take action. For security testing purposes, you can specify other IP addresses in your network, maybe even ones set up in a development or lab environment for this purpose. An example of a decoy scan includes the following:

```
nmap -D <192.168.100.1,192.168.100.4,192.168.100.20,192.168.100.3,192.168.100.55,19
2.168.100.100,ME,192.168.100.29,192.168.100.57> 192.168.2.0/24
```

This example uses 8 decoys with the real scanning system at position 7. Although this isn't "traditional" spoofing since your address will still show up as scanning the target, it can add enough confusion to the mix to evade detection.

NOTE

Decoys don't work with Nmap's connect scanning or version detection, but it does work with the other scanning options and OS fingerprinting.

If you want to use traditional spoofing to make your system appear as another system, use the *-S* command-line option. However, you won't get responses back from the target since they will go to the spoofed system. This option is also used to specify the IP address of the interface on your system that you will use to send packets when Nmap can't determine your actual IP address. You can also use the -e command-line option to specify an interface to use in this case. You can use the *--spoof-mac* command-line option to specify a MAC address to be included in the Nmap packets. If you specify a 0 as the option parameter, Nmap will choose a random MAC address for you. You can also specify a full MAC address, or a vendor prefix or name, in which case Nmap fills in the rest for you with random values. However the vendor name must be included in the *nmap-mac-prefixes* file. Some examples of MAC spoofing include the following:

```
nmap --spoof-mac 0 192.168.100.0/24
nmap --spoof-mac 11:22:33:44:55:66 192.168.100.0/24
nmap --spoof-mac 000D93 192.168.100.0/24
nmap --spoof-mac D-Link 192.168.100.0/24
```

Nmap will then report the MAC address that it is using. The last example provided the following output:

```
Spoofing MAC address 00:05:5D:DA:32:64 (D-Link Systems)
```

In addition to source IP and MAC addresses, you can also specify source ports to use for scanning. Specifying a popular source port that is often allowed through firewalls (such as DNS port 53) is a common way to evade firewalls. Nmap includes two equivalent command-line options to specify a source port: *-g* and *--source-port*. For example, the following uses perform the same scanning, using a source port of 53:

```
nmap -g 53 192.168.100.0/24
nmap --source-port 53 192.168.100.0/24
```

Nmap offers several packet manipulation techniques that may be used for evasion. You can use the *--date-length* command-line option to append a specified number of random bytes to the packets Nmap sends during scans. This may avoid Nmap detection signatures and other detection techniques. You can also specify IP options to include in the packet by using the *--ip-options* command-line option. You can specify record route (*R*), record timestamps (*T*), record timestamps and route (*U*), loose source routing (*L*), or strict source routing (*S*). To have more granular control than these built-in parameters, you can also use hex notation to specify IP options as long as they are each preceded by an \x. IP options may evade security controls by specifying routes to take to the target.

NOTE

For details and examples of the various uses of Nmap *–ip-options* see http://seclists.org/nmap-dev/2006/q3/0052.html.

You can set the time to live (TTL) field to a given value with the *--ttl* command-line option. This may be effective at evading some security controls. Another method to avoid detection is to randomize the target hosts that are being scanned by using the *--randomize-hosts* command-line option. You can have Nmap use an invalid TCP or UDP checksum with the *--badsum* command-line option. Most hosts will drop packets with bad checksums, so if you receive responses to these scans, they are probably coming from security controls, such as firewalls, that don't verify checksums.

Table 4.8 summarizes the evasion and spoofing command-line options. Nmap just scratches the surface of possible evasion and spoofing techniques. There are a variety of advanced tools available to go beyond what has been presented here. The features that Nmap does provide for evasion and spoofing are more than adequate for typical enterprise scanning.

Table 4.8 Evasion and Spoofing Command-Line Options

<table>
<tr><th>Option</th><th>Description</th></tr>
<tr><td>-f</td><td>Fragment packets to a maximum of 8 bytes (can be used twice for 16 bytes)</td></tr>
<tr><td>--mtu <value></td><td>Specify the maximum packet size in multiples of 8 for packet fragmentation</td></tr>
<tr><td>-D <decoy1,decoy2[,ME],...></td><td>Specify decoys to perform scanning in conjunction with your system</td></tr>
<tr><td>-S <IP address></td><td>Specify a source IP address, either your own or another system</td></tr>
<tr><td>-e <iface></td><td>Specify an interface to use for scanning</td></tr>
<tr><td>-g/–source-port <portnum></td><td>Specify a source port to use for scanning</td></tr>
<tr><td>--data-length <num></td><td>Specify a number of bytes of random data to append to packets</td></tr>
<tr><td>--ip-options <R|T|U|S [IP IP2...] |L [IP IP2 ...] >
Or
--ip-options <hex string></td><td>Specify IP options to include in packets</td></tr>
<tr><td>--ttl <val></td><td>Specify a TTL value</td></tr>
<tr><td>--randomize-hosts</td><td>Randomize the target hosts list before scanning</td></tr>
<tr><td>--spoof-mac <mac address/prefix/ vendor name></td><td>Specify a MAC address to use for scanning</td></tr>
<tr><td>--badsum</td><td>Send packets with bad TCP or UDP checksums</td></tr>
</table>

Output Logging

Nmap output goes well beyond the on screen reporting shown in the examples so far. Nmap offers a variety of output formats for standard output and file-based formats, such as XML, for interoperability with other software programs. Nmap output also offers various levels of verbosity and debugging messages. Nmap offers the following output formats:

- **Interactive** By default, Nmap reports results to standard output, on the screen, to be analyzed interactively. This format is always displayed, even when other output options are used, unless you use the hypen (-) to disable interactive output.

- **Normal** The results are also sent to standard output, but with less runtime information and warnings. To report results in normal output format use the *-oN <filename>* command-line option.
- **XML** The results are reported in XML format that can be converted to HTML and parsed by other software programs. To report results in XML format, use the *-oX <filename>* command-line option. The XML document type definition file is located at http://insecure.org/nmap/data/nmap.dtd. It includes the Nmap XML formatting specifics. You can download the file and view it with a text viewer. Besides using XML for software interoperability, you can also view the XML output in a Web browser, as shown in Figure 4.1.
- **Grepable** Output that can be easily parsed by scripts and other software programs. To report output in grepable format, use the *-oG <filename>* command-line option. Grepable output is considered depreciated in favor of XML output, but grepable output is still highly used because it is a much easier format to use for quick scripting. UNIX tools such as grep, sed, awk, and cut are all used with grepable output. Perl is also a great language to use to parse grepable output. More information on grepable output format can be found at www.unspecific.com/nmap-oG-output.
- **s|<rIpt kIddi3** The output is written in Leetspeak, which uses symbols and numbers to replace alphabet characters. Leet has been used among hackers and script kiddies since the 1980s. Nmap incorporates Leet to mock script kiddies, but to also demonstrate how output can be modified in arbitrary ways, as mentioned at http://seclists.org/nmap-hackers/2000/0005.html. To report results in s|<rIpt kIddi3 (script kiddie) format use the *-oS <filename>* command-line option.

Figure 4.1 XML Output

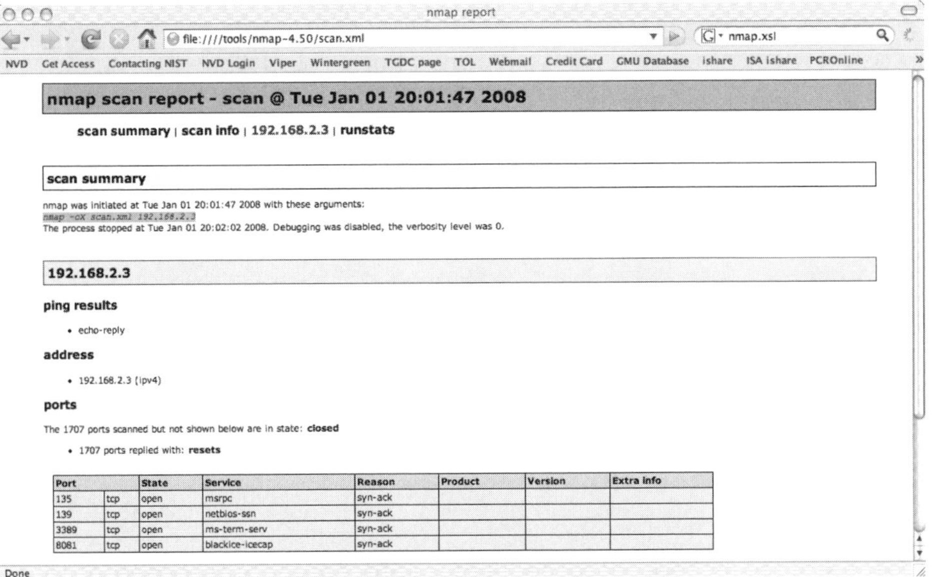

Notes from the Underground...

Runtime Interaction

When running Nmap in interactive mode, there are some commands that you can use to toggle the verbosity, debugging, and packet tracing:

- Typing a lower case **v** will increase the verbosity level; an uppercase **V** will decrease the verbosity level
- Typing a lower case **d** will increase the debugging level; an uppercase **D** will decrease the debugging level
- Typing a lower case **p** will enable packet tracing; an uppercase **P** will disable packet tracing

You can press any other key to have Nmap display a status message that includes elapsed time, completed hosts, scan percentage completed, and the estimated completion time. For example:

```
Stats: 0:00:03 elapsed; 0 hosts completed (1 up), 1 undergoing Connect Scan
Connect Scan Timing: About 61.43% done; ETC: 20:15 (0:00:02 remaining)
```

The following example logs Nmap results in grepable format:

```
# nmap -oG myscan.gnmap 192.168.100.3
```

Grepable output contains commas, colons, and forward slashes to facilitate use of UNIX commands and programming languages for parsing the output:

```
# nmap 4.50 scan initiated Sat Jan 5 18:12:34 2008 as: nmap -oG myscan.gnmap
192.168.100.3
Host: 192.168.100.3 (systemB.home.com)    Ports: 135/open/tcp//msrpc///, 139/open/
tcp//netbios-ssn///, 3389/open/tcp//ms-term-serv///, 6346/filtered/tcp//gnutella///,
6347/filtered/tcp//gnutella2///, 8081/open/tcp//blackice-icecap///
# Nmap done at Sat Jan 5 18:12:38 2008 - 1 IP address (1 host up) scanned in
3.810 seconds
```

The output formats can be combined, but you can only specify each format once. For example, you can send results to both normal and XML format by using the following command:

```
nmap -oN scan.nmap -oX scan.xml 192.168.100.0/24
```

You can also use the *-oA <filename>* command-line option to output results in normal, XML, and grepable formats at once:

```
nmap -oA myscan 192.168.100.0/24
```

The files are stored as *myscan.nmap*, *myscan.xml*, and *myscan.gnmap*. As noted earlier, interactive output is always displayed unless it is disabled as in the following example:

```
nmap -oN - 192.168.100.0/24
```

Nmap allows users to control the verbosity and debugging features with a variety of command-line options. The most commonly used option is the verbose (*-v*) option, which provides additional information such as completion time estimates, and displays open ports as they are discovered. The verbose option can be provided twice for greater verbosity. For example:

```
# nmap -v -v 192.168.2.3
Starting Nmap 4.50 (http://insecure.org) at 2008-01-01 18:40 Eastern
Standard Time
Initiating Ping Scan at 18:40
Scanning 192.168.2.3 [2 ports]
Completed Ping Scan at 18:40, 0.12s elapsed (1 total hosts)
Initiating Parallel DNS resolution of 1 host. at 18:40
Completed Parallel DNS resolution of 1 host. at 18:40, 11.06s elapsed
Initiating SYN Stealth Scan at 18:40
```

```
Scanning 192.168.2.3 [1711 ports]
Discovered open port 3389/tcp on 192.168.2.3
Discovered open port 135/tcp on 192.168.2.3
Discovered open port 8081/tcp on 192.168.2.3
Discovered open port 139/tcp on 192.168.2.3
Completed SYN Stealth Scan at 18:40, 4.75s elapsed (1711 total ports)
Host 192.168.2.3 appears to be up ... good.
Interesting ports on 192.168.2.3:
Not shown: 1707 closed ports
PORT          STATE     SERVICE
135/tcp       open      msrpc
139/tcp       open      netbios-ssn
3389/tcp      open      ms-term-serv
8081/tcp      open      blackice-icecap
Read data files from: C:\Program Files\Nmap
Nmap done: 1 IP address (1 host up) scanned in 19.729 seconds
           Raw packets sent: 1746 (76.804KB) | Rcvd: 1712 (68.484KB)
```

You can get even more output information by using Nmap's debugging option (*-d*). Nmap debugging accepts a numerical level up to a value of 9. With debugging you can gain insight into the very details of what Nmap is doing during the scan, and you also get a substantially large amount of information to sift through. Another method of debugging is to use the *--packet-trace* command-line option. This option will print every packet sent and received during the Nmap scan, just like a packet sniffer. The *--iflist* command-line option is used for debugging, because it displays a list of the scanning system's interfaces and network routes. This is a status option only and does not perform a scan, so it can be specified without a target host. Another useful debugging feature is error logging. Although errors are displayed on the screen as part of interactive output, you can log them to a file with the *--log-errors* command-line option. The errors get displayed in the normal output file so you must also use the *-oN* (or *-oA*) command-line option:

```
nmap -oN myoutput.nmap -log-errors 192.168.100.0/24
```

A way to customize Nmap output is to use the *--open* command-line option to show only open, open|filtered, and unfiltered ports. Another nice feature is the ability to append to existing output files instead of overwriting them, which is what Nmap will do by default. You can use the *--append-output* command-line option to add your new results to an existing output file. Existing output files are also useful to resume scans that have been canceled or interrupted. If you are logging out to normal or grepable format, you can use the *--resume* command-line option to have Nmap continue the scanning and append the new results to the existing output file:

```
nmap --resume scanoutput.nmap
```

Nmap also includes a few command-line options for configuring XML output. To view XML output as Hypertext Markup Language (HTML), you must have the XSL stylesheet (*nmap.xsl*) installed on the same system. This file installs by default in the Nmap directory. If you are viewing the XML file on another system, it won't be displayable if Nmap isn't installed. You can use the *--stylesheet* command-line option to specify a path or URL to an *nmap.xsl* stylesheet, but even easier you can use the *--webxml* command-line option to retrieve the latest version of the stylesheet from *insecure.org*. You can also use the *--no_stylesheet* command-line option to omit a stylesheet altogether.

NOTE

A good way to organize your output files is to date and timestamp them. Nmap supports two options, *%D* and *%T*, to do this for you automatically. For example, the command *-oN myscan-%D-%T.nmap* will name the output file in the format of *myscan-010108-112927.nmap*.

Table 4.9 summarizes the output logging command-line options. Nmap allows users to display a variety of levels of output information and formats. This configurability allows Nmap to be viewed interactively, scripted, or integrated with other output parsers.

Table 4.9 Output Logging Command-line Options

Option	Description
-oN/-oX/-oS/-oG <file name>	Report output to normal, XML, sl<rlpt kIddi3, and grepable format respectively to the supplied file name
-oA <file name>	Report output to normal, XML, and grepable format all at once
-v	Specify a verbosity level for more information

Continued

Table 4.9 Continued. Output Logging Command-line Options

Option	Description
or	
-vv	
-d[level]	Specify a debugging level for even more information
--packet-trace	Show all packets sent and received
--open	Display only open, openlfiltered, and unfiltered ports
--iflist	Display scanning host interfaces and network routes
--log-errors	Logs errors to normal output
--append-output	Append instead of overwrite output files
--resume <filename>	Resume an aborted scan
--stylesheet <path/URL>	Specify a stylesheet path or URL
--webxml	Reference the latest stylesheet at Insecure.org
--no-stylesheet	Don't use an XLS stylesheet

Miscellaneous

Nmap has several other usage options that don't fit into any of the above categories. Many networks are moving to IPv6, so Nmap offers support for most of its main features. You can use the *-6* command-line option to enable IPv6 scanning. All other command syntax and output is the same as IPv4 scanning. The *-A* command-line option is a handy option that combines OS detection (*-O*), version detection (*-sV*), script scanning (*-sC*), and traceroute (*–traceroute*) all into one simple option. We have mentioned several data files that Nmap uses for scanning, such as *nmap-services*, *nmap-protocols*, and so forth. By default, these are located in the directory where Nmap is installed. If they are in another location you can use the *--datadir* command-line option to specify where the files are located. Nmap can determine the best layer to use to send raw packets for the platform it is running on. You can also use the *--send-ip* and *--send-eth* command-line options to force Nmap to use raw sockets at the IP layer or raw Ethernet at the data link layer. You can also toggle the way Nmap views user privileges at run time by using the *--privileged* and *--unprivileged* command-line options.

These are useful for debugging purposes. Lastly, two informational command-line options are *-V*, which prints the Nmap version number, and *-h*, which prints the Nmap usage help (just like executing nmap without any command-line options). Table 4.10 summarizes the miscellaneous command-line options.

Table 4.10 Miscellaneous Command-Line Options

Option	Description
-6	Enable IPv6 scanning
-A	Enable OS detection, version detection, script scanning, and traceroute
--datadir <dirname>	Specify a location that contains Nmap data files
--send-ip	Send data using packets at the IP layer
--send-eth	Send data using raw Ethernet frames at the data link layer
--privileged	Assume that the user is fully privileged
--unprivileged	Assume that the user is not a privileged user
-V	Print the Nmap version number
-h	Print the Nmap usage

NOTE

A great resource is the nmap-hackers mailing list. It is used for announcements about Nmap, Insecure.org, and related projects. You can also subscribe to the nmap-dev mailing list, which discusses Nmap development, patches and suggestions. You can find both mailing lists at: http://cgi.insecure.org/mailman/listinfo/.

Summary

This chapter covered basic Nmap usage to assist you with enterprise activities such as network inventory, asset management, policy compliance, and security auditing. In this chapter, you learned how to use Nmap to discover hosts, port status, OSes, services and applications, and more.

You should now be able to use Nmap to gather a variety of information for your asset database, including active host IP addresses and host names, open ports, installed applications and versions, and the OS version. You should also be able to use Nmap for policy compliance to scan for unauthorized services and applications, unauthorized servers, and unauthorized sniffers. In addition to policy compliance, this information will also assist you with vulnerability and patch management. This chapter showed you how to optimized Nmap's performance for scanning enterprise networks. You can now output your Nmap results in a variety of formats for later analysis, scripting, and software interoperability.

Now that you are familiar with Nmap's usage and features, you can continue on to the next chapter to learn about Zenmap and its advanced scan management features.

Solutions Fast Track

Starting Nmap Scanning

☑ Nmap can be run from the command line or Zenmap GUI.

☑ You must have administrator or root privileges to use all of Nmap's features.

☑ Running Nmap with no options displays the usage information.

☑ Nmap supports a variety of ways to specify scanning targets.

Discovering Hosts

☑ Nmap can discover available hosts by using ping scanning and other ICMP requests, TCP SYN pings, TCP ACK pings, UDP pings, and IP Protocol pings.

☑ TCP SYN and TCP ACK pings are often used to detect hosts behind firewalls.

☑ You can disable host discovery during your Nmap scan.

Port Scanning

- ☑ Nmap offers a variety of port scanning techniques.
- ☑ Nmap reports port status as one of six possible states.
- ☑ Nmap performs SYN scanning by default.
- ☑ If a user doesn't have root or administrator privileges, Nmap will perform the TCP connect scan (*-sT*) by default.
- ☑ Nmap offers several stealthy port scanning techniques such as idle scanning and FTP bounce scanning.
- ☑ Nmap offers a variety of ways to specify ports to scan.

Detecting Operating Systems

- ☑ Nmap performs OS detection by probing the target host and analyzing the responses.
- ☑ Each OS has distinctive responses to the probes which identify the OS and result in an OS fingerprint.
- ☑ Nmap includes several command-line options to configure the OS detection engine.

Detecting Service and Application Versions

- ☑ Nmap can perform version detection to gather more detail on the services and applications running on the identified open ports.
- ☑ Nmap needs OpenSSL to discover listening services behind SSL encryption.
- ☑ The OS and version detection probe databases are continually growing from contributions from the user community.

Other Scanning Options

- ☑ The NSE performs a variety of advanced techniques such as vulnerability and malware detection and exploitation.
- ☑ Nmap has several features to enhance timing and performance, including advanced algorithms and executing tasks in parallel.

- ☑ Nmap timing options include timing templates, parallelism, timeouts, and retries.
- ☑ Nmap includes evasion methods that use fragmentation, spoofing, and packet manipulation techniques.
- ☑ Nmap reports scanning results to standard output, known as interactive output.
- ☑ Nmap can log results in normal, XML, grepable, and s|<rIpt kIddi3 format.
- ☑ You can get more information by using Nmap's verbosity and debugging levels.
- ☑ Nmap supports IPv6 scanning.

Frequently Asked Questions

Q: What if I am having problems using Nmap?

A: First, make sure you are using the latest version of Nmap. You can also perform a Web search on the problem you are having. If you are getting an error message, search on the exact message. You can also browse or post to the Nmap development (nmap-dev) list. If you are going to post a question about a problem, make sure you include the Nmap version number, platform you are running, and describe the problem including error messages.

Q: Will Nmap scanning crash a system or network?

A: Although it is rare, sometimes Nmap scanning can crash a system or network device. Some devices may crash in response to perceiving a ping flood or SYN flood.

Q: Can I save my commonly used Nmap commands for repeated use?

A: Nmap doesn't have a built-in way to save commands, so you should store them in a text file. Zenmap does have the ability to save Nmap commands as profiles for repeat use.

Q: How can I see what Nmap is doing while it performs the scan?

A: There are several ways to view more information while Nmap is scanning, including using increased verbosity levels, debugging, and packet tracing.

Q: Can I craft packets with Nmap?

A: Nmap has some packet-crafting features, such as the ability to specify source and destination IP addresses and ports, TCP flag combinations, IP options, TTL, and append random data to the packet. However, to have full control over packet creation, you should use a packet-crafting tool such as Nemesis.

Chapter 5

Using Zenmap

Solutions in this chapter:

- Running Zenmap
- Managing Zenmap Scans
- Building Commands with the Zenmap Command Wizard
- Managing Zenmap Profiles
- Managing Zenmap Results

☑ Summary

☑ Solutions Fast Track

☑ Frequently Asked Questions

Introduction

Zenmap is a multi-platform, user-friendly, front-end GUI for Nmap. Like Nmap, Zenmap is free and open source. Zenmap allows you to perform all of the same usage options as in the command line version of Nmap, and it has the following additional features:

- **Command wizard**. An interactive method to create Nmap commands.
- **Profile creation**. Zenmap includes several default profiles for common scan configurations. You can also save your own scans as profiles so you can run them repeatedly.
- **Scan tabs**. Zenmap allows you to run and display more than one scan at a time by using scan tabs.
- **Scan results saving**. Scan results can be saved to a file and viewed later.
- **Results comparison**. Saved scan results can be compared with each other to look for differences.
- **Searchable database**. Scan results are stored in a searchable database.

In this chapter you will learn how to use the Zenmap GUI and its various features for robust scanning management in the enterprise.

NOTE

Nmap has been selected as part of the Google Summer of Code in 2005, 2006, and 2007. These programs provide stipends to university students to create or enhance open source software over their summer breaks. As part of these programs Andriano Monteiro Marques created a front-end GUI for Nmap called Umit, which later became integrated into Nmap in 2007 as Zenmap.

Running Zenmap

You can start Zenmap by typing **zenmap** on the command line or by clicking on the Zenmap desktop icon. The main Zenmap window opens with a default setting for an intense scan. To start using Zenmap you can enter a target address in the Target field and click on the **Scan** button. The Zenmap Target field supports the same target specification methods as Nmap. You can use the Target drop down box to select previously scanned targets. You can also choose from one of the default profiles as shown in Figure. 5.1. The Nmap command line option is displayed in the Command field for each profile. You can also edit the parameters in the Command field directly. This allows you to edit default profile options and to create a new command with customized options.

NOTE

A detailed Zenmap usage manual is located at http://insecure.org/nmap/zenmapguide.

Figure 5.1 Zenmap Profile Options

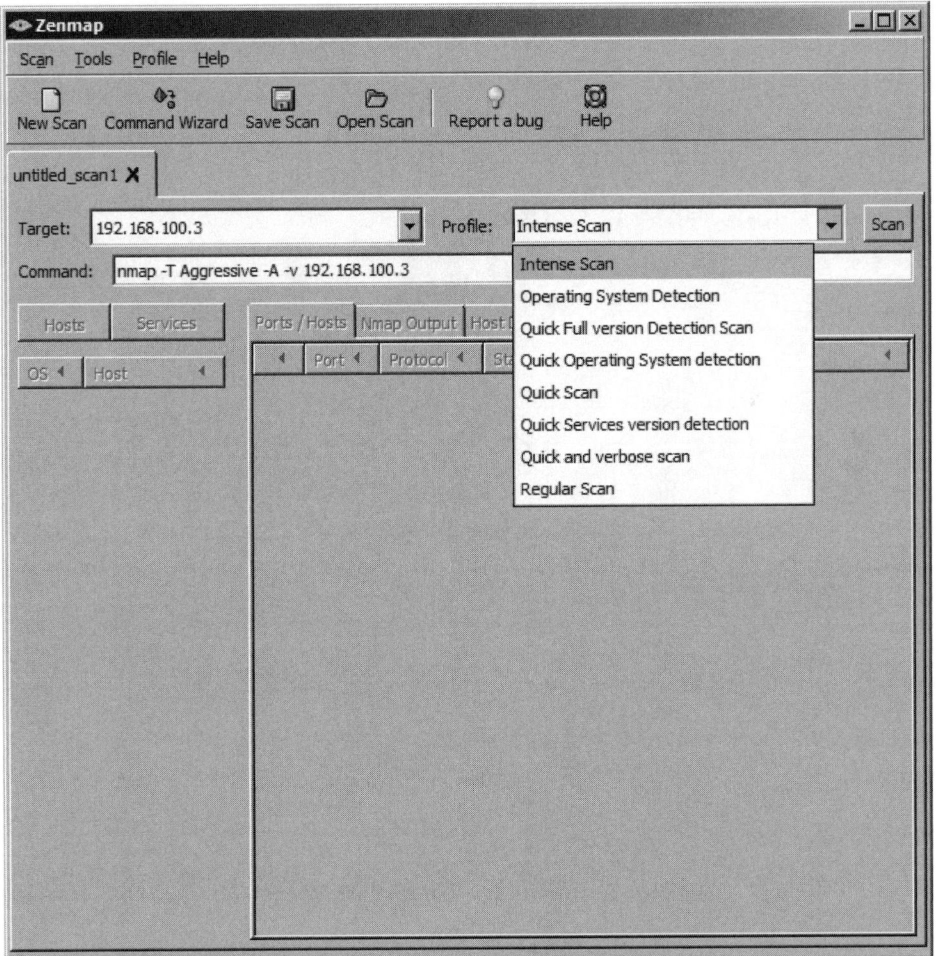

Like Nmap's interactive mode, Zenmap displays output as the scan is running and when it completes. You will see the Scanning status in the left window pane and results displayed in the Nmap Output tab. When the scan completes, the left window pane will display the target hosts scanned. Zenmap displays the same output as Nmap, in an aggregated and easily readable format. The results are arranged into four tabbed pages: Ports/Hosts, Nmap Output, Host Details, and Scan Details.

- **Ports/Hosts**. You can toggle the Ports and Hosts output by clicking on either the Hosts or Services buttons in the left hand window pane. Clicking the Hosts button displays a list of all hosts that were scanned. Hosts can be sorted by OS or IP address by clicking on the headers above the list. If you click on a host the Ports/Host pane shows the ports and version information for the selected host (Figure 5.2). Clicking the Services button displays a list of ports/services that are open, filtered, or open|filtered on any of the scanned hosts. The list can be sorted in regular or reverse alphabetical order by clicking on the header above the list. If you click on a service, the Ports/Host pane shows the hosts that have the selected port open or filtered (Figure 5.3).

Figure 5.2 Ports/Hosts Tab with Hosts Results

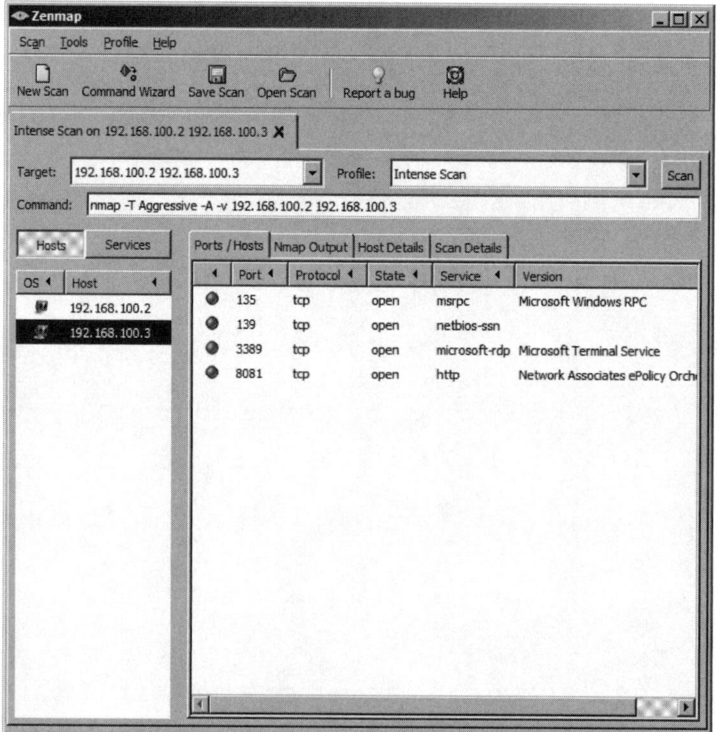

Figure 5.3 Ports/Hosts Tab with Services Result

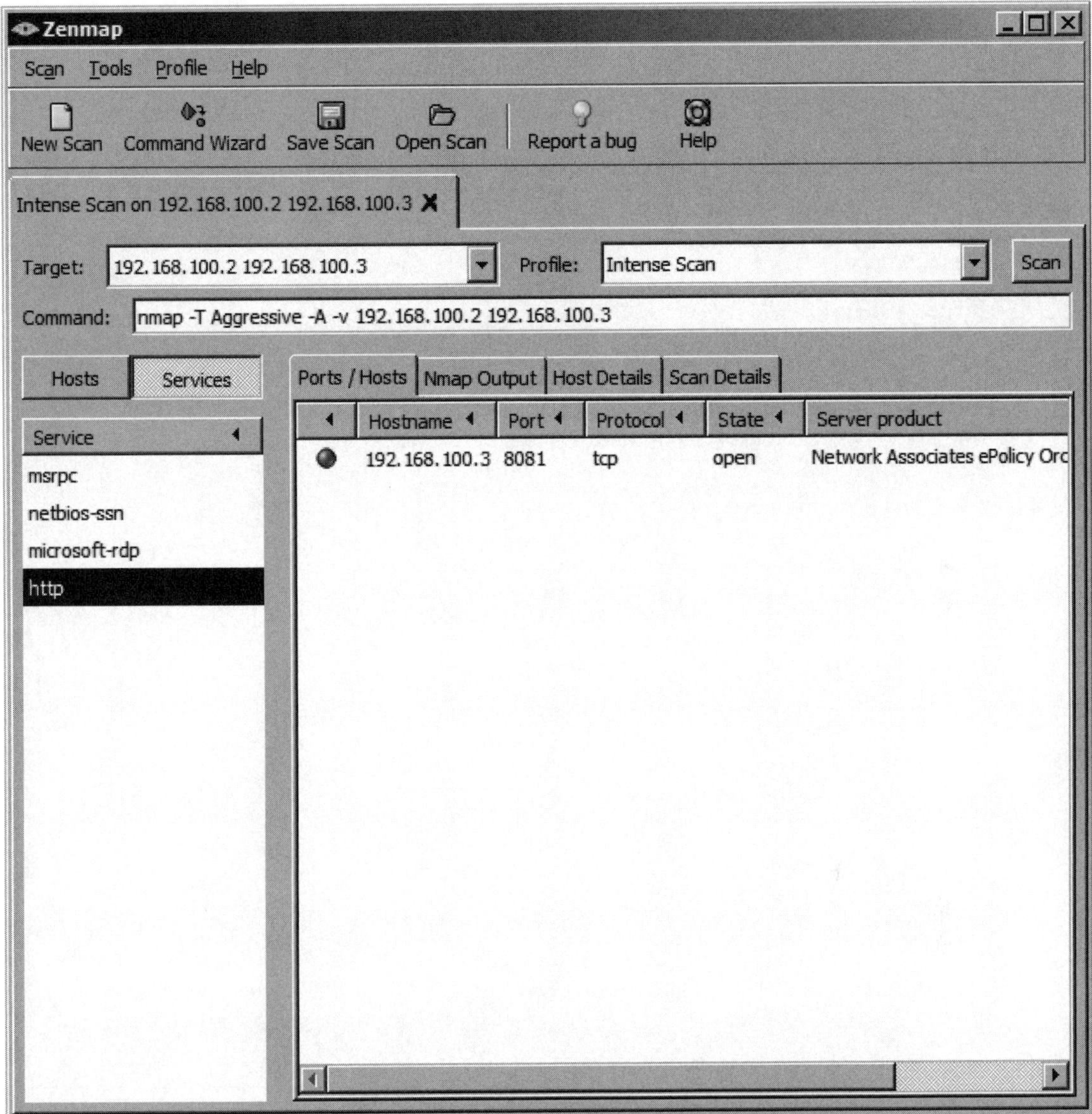

- **Nmap Output**. The Nmap Output tab displays the same interactive output that Nmap displays to standard out. This tab is displayed by default when a scan starts. Figure 5.4 shows the Nmap Output tab with example results. You can enable highlighting by clicking on the "Enable Nmap output highlight" at the bottom of the tab. You can view and change the highlighting options by clicking on the **Preferences** button at the bottom of the tab, shown in Figure 5.5.

Figure 5.4 Nmap Output Tab with Results

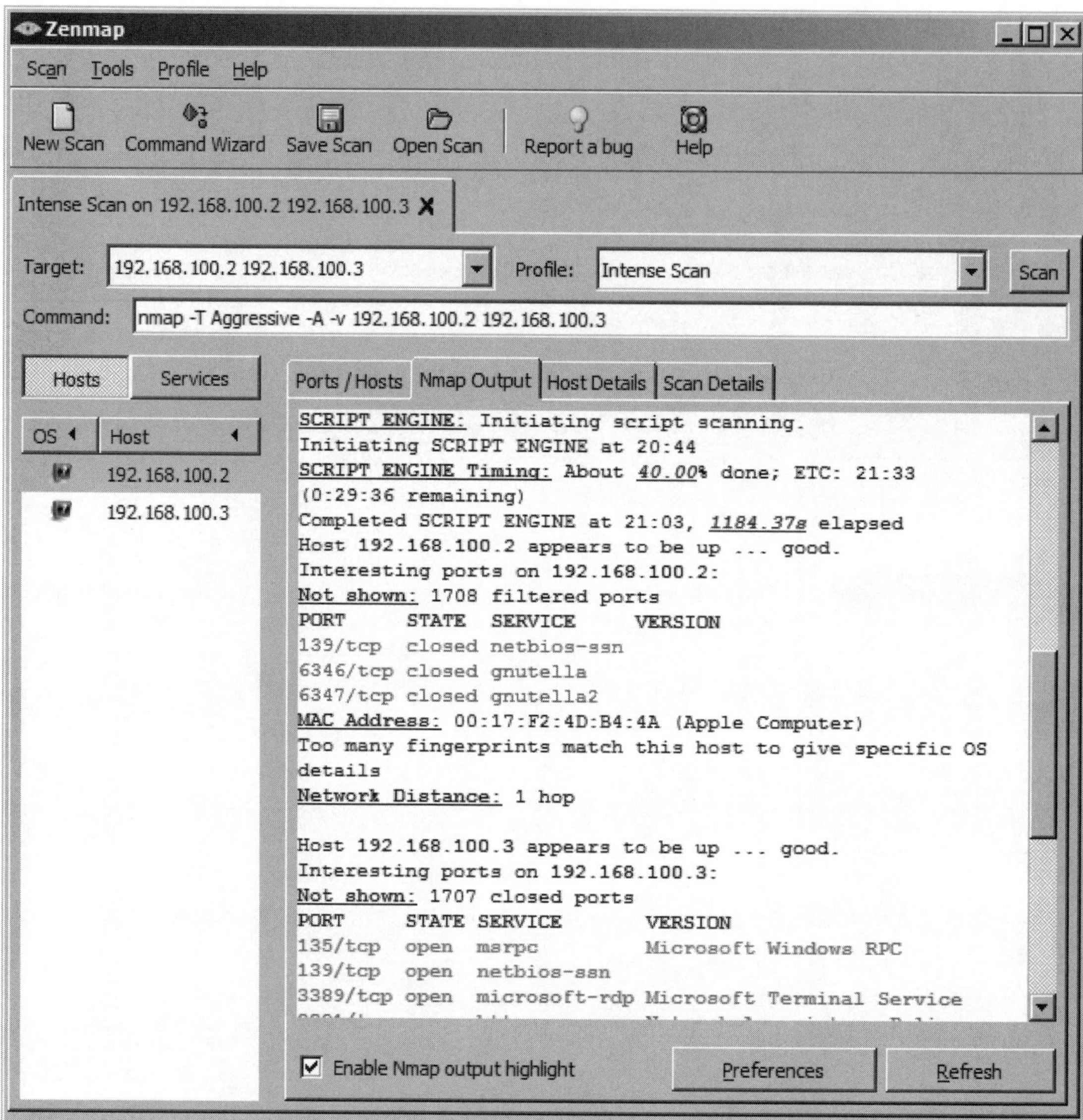

Figure 5.5 Highlight Definitions

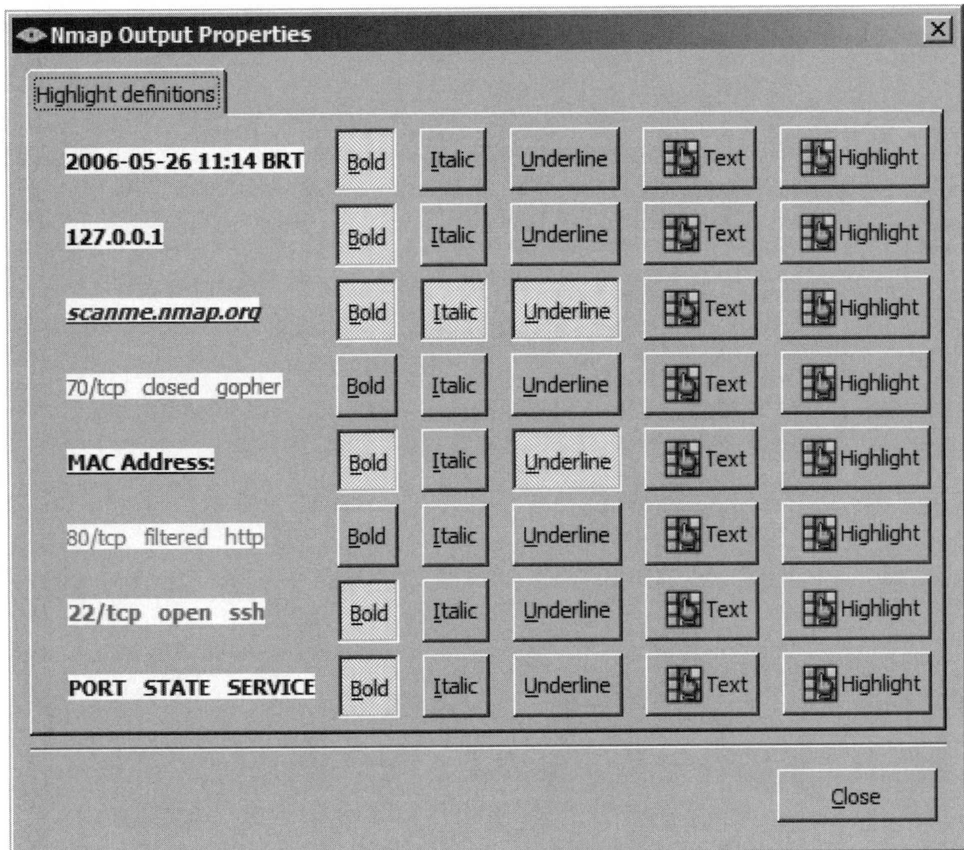

- **Host Details**. The Host Details tab displays host information, such as addresses, host names, state, port information, operating system, and uptime, in a hierarchical format. The output also shows a vulnerability icon based on the number of open ports. You can also enter remarks in the Comment field, which are saved when the scan results are saved to a file. Figure 5.6 shows the Host Details tab with example results.

Figure 5.6 Host Details Tab

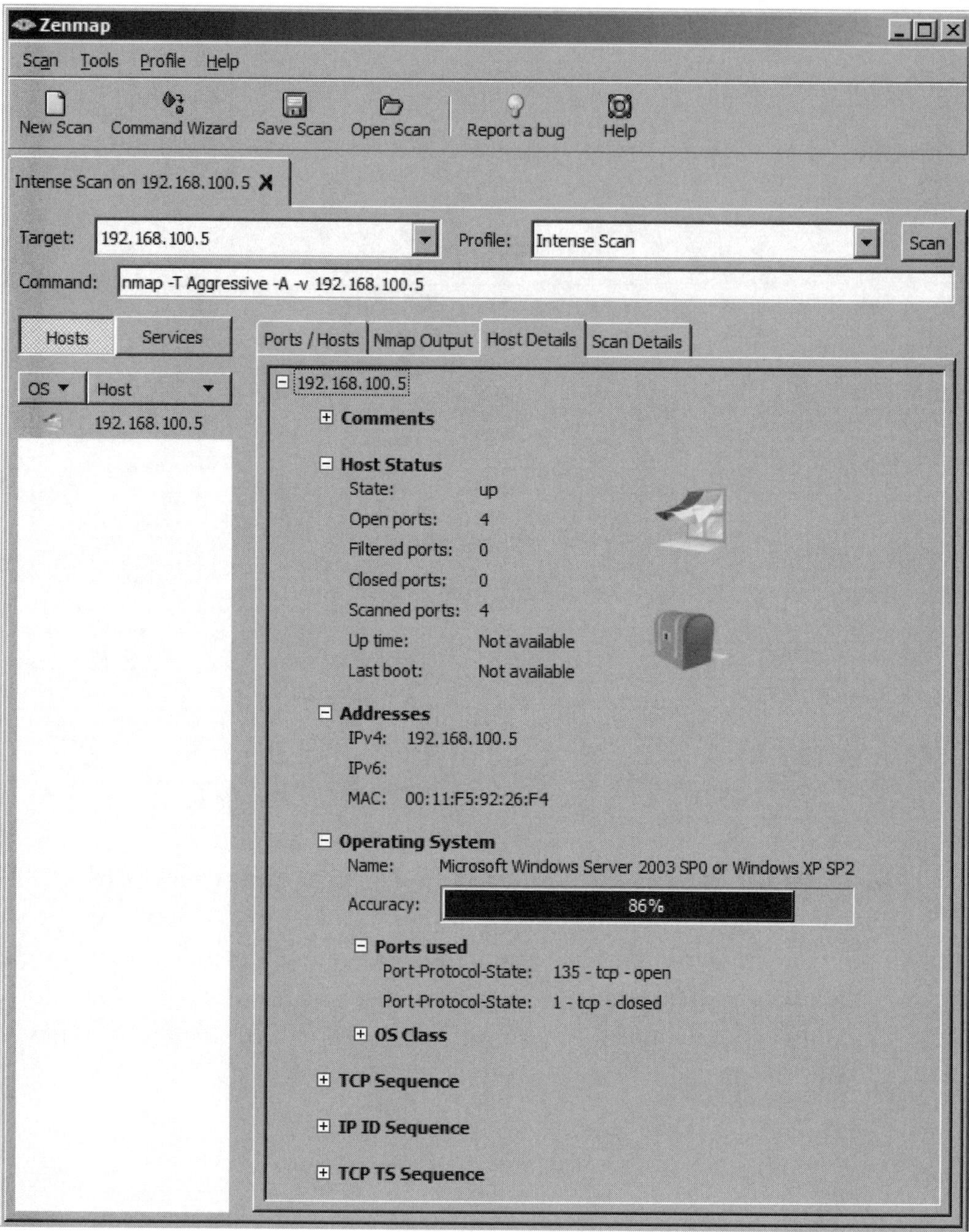

Table 5.1 shows the types of icons used for various operating systems based on their representative mascots or logos.

Table 5.1 Operating System Icons

Icon	Operating System
	OS detection not performed or no matches were made
	FreeBSD
	Irix
	Linux
	Mac OS
	OpenBSD

Continued

Table 5.1 Continued. Operating System Icons

Icon	Operating System
	Red Hat Linux
	Solaris or OpenSolaris
	Ubuntu Linux
	Microsoft Windows
	Other

Table 5.2 shows the list of icons which represent the number of ports open on the target system.

Table 5.2 Vulnerability Icons

Icon	Open Ports
	0–3 open ports
	4–5 open ports
	6–7 open ports
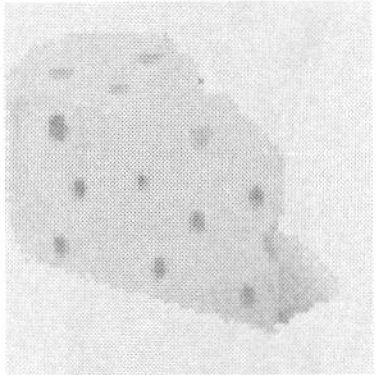	8–9 open ports
	10 or more open ports

- **Scan Details**. The Scan Details tab lists miscellaneous information about the scan itself, such as the Nmap command that was executed, Nmap version, verbosity and debug level, scan start and finish times, host and port information, and scan type information. Figure 5.7 shows the Scan Details tab with example results.

Figure 5.7 Scan Details Tab with Results

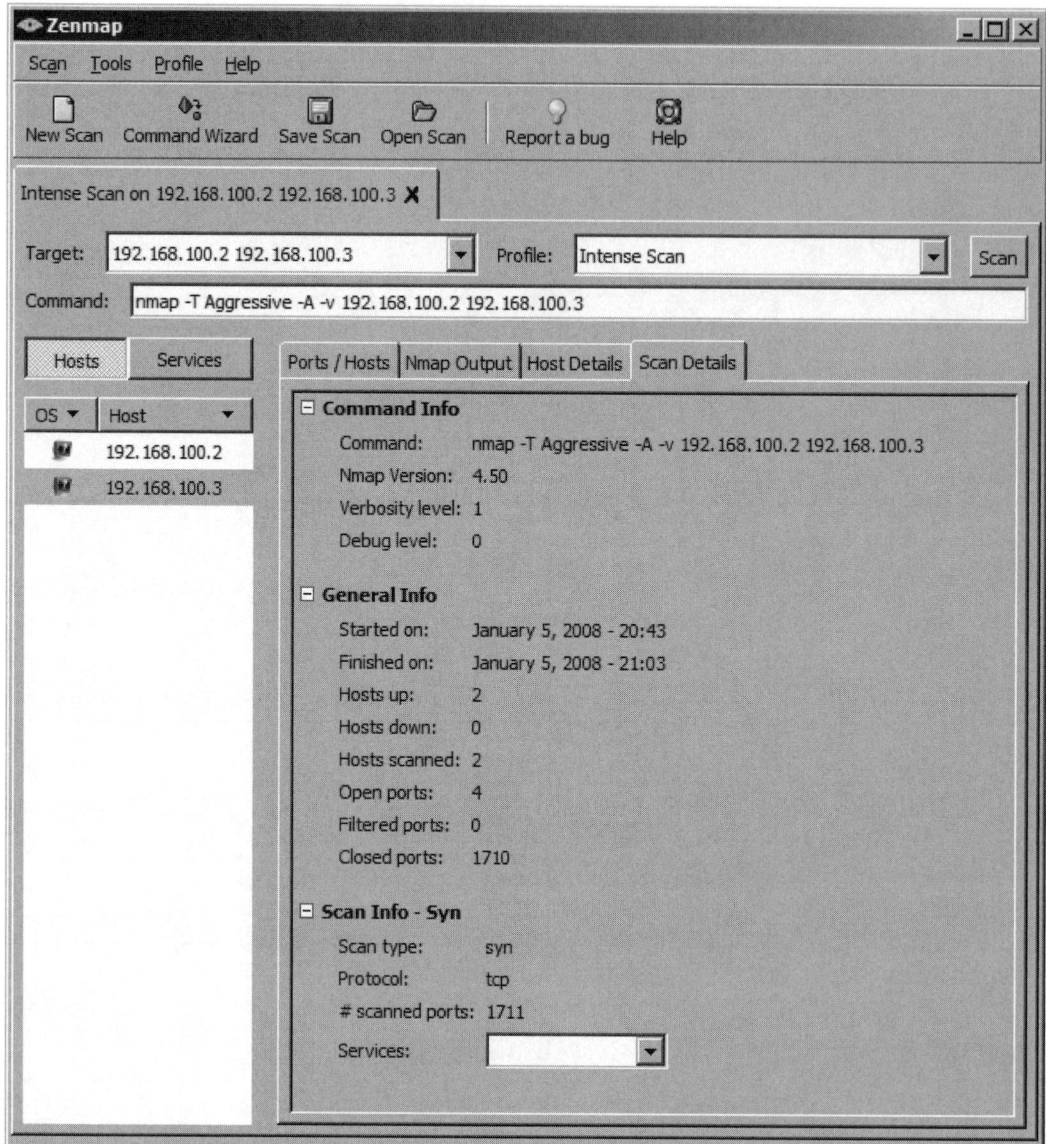

Managing Zenmap Scans

Zenmap allows you to run and view results for multiple scans using the scan tabs. The following features are available to manage Zenmap scans:

- **Create a new scan**. To open a new scan tab, choose "New Scan" from the toolbar icon or **Scan** menu.

- **Close a scan**. To close a scan, choose "Close Scan" from the **Scan** menu or click on the X on the tab.
- **Save a scan**. You can save scan results by clicking on the scan tab you would like to save and choosing "Save Scan" from the toolbar icon or **Scan** menu. The results are saved in Umit Scan Results (.usr) format.
- **Open a scan**. To open saved scan results, choose "Open Scan" from the toolbar icon or **Scan** menu. Zenmap can open Umit Scan Results (.usr) files and Nmap XML (.xml) files.

NOTE

Closing a scan is the only way to stop a scan. Unfortunately you will lose any results displayed on the tab output.

Building Commands with the Zenmap Command Wizard

You don't have to remember all of those Nmap command line options when using Zenmap, it comes with a built-in command wizard to assist you in constructing Nmap commands. The following steps walk you through the command constructor wizard:

1. You can start the Nmap command constructor wizard by choosing the Command Wizard from the toolbar icon or **Tools** menu.
2. You are first presented with the option to construct the profile as a Novice or Expert user. The Expert user option opens the Profile Editor, discussed in the following section. Choose **Novice** and click **Forward**.
3. Next you have the option of just creating a command or creating a profile for the command. Creating a profile is recommended if you intend to repeatedly run the scan. If you select to create a profile you will be prompted to enter a profile name and optional description information. If you don't wish to create a profile, choose the Command option and enter a target. The target can be in any of the target specification formats discussed in Chapter 4. Once you

have created a profile or selected a target you can click **Forward** and begin selecting your command options.

4. The next screen presents three drop down menus to allow you to select your TCP scan type (ACK, FIN, Null, SYN, Connect, Window, Xmas), special scan (IP protocols, List, and Ping scanning), and one of the seven timing options (None, Paranoid, Sneaky, Polite, Normal, Aggressive, Insane). You also have the option of performing service version detection and operating system detection by clicking the check boxes. Each selection you make automatically updates the Nmap command in the Command field. Once you have selected your parameters, click **Forward** to continue.
5. The next screen presents you with a variety of Ping options. You can choose to disable pinging, or select one of the other ICMP, TCP, or UDP options. Once you have selected your parameters, click **Forward** to continue.
6. The next screen allows you to select specific target options, such as hosts or network to exclude and ports to scan. You must enter excluded hosts and ports to scan according to the syntax discussed in Chapter 4. You can also select the check box to only scan ports listed in the Nmap service file. Once you have selected your parameters, click **Forward** to continue.
7. The next screen allows you to select limited evasion techniques, such as specifying decoys, a source IP address, and source port address. Once you have selected your parameters, click **Forward** to continue.
8. The next screen presents a variety of miscellaneous options, such as TTL value, fragmentation, verbosity, debugging, and packet tracing. It also includes a field for other user defined options. Once you have selected your parameters, click **Forward** to continue.
9. The next screen allows you to create your profile or command. If you chose to create a command it will run immediately. If you chose to create a profile, it will be available in the Profile drop down menu to use when needed.

NOTE

At any time during the command constructor wizard, you can modify the command by typing in the Command field.

Managing Zenmap Profiles

Zenmap includes several default profiles of commonly used commands. When you select a profile, the Nmap command line option is displayed in the Command field. As you saw during the Command Wizard, you have the option to create a new profile for a command. Command profiles allow you to save Nmap commands and run them repeatedly. You can create, edit, and remove profiles by using the options on the **Profile** menu.

To create a new profile, select **New Profile** from the **Profile** menu. You will be presented with the Profile Editor, as shown in Figure 5.8. The Profile Editor allows you to create your profile name and associated Nmap command through a series of tabs. The tabs include similar options as the Command Wizard, with some advanced options as well. As you select scan options, the command displayed in the Command field will automatically update. Once you have created your profile it will be displayed along with the default profiles in the Profile drop down menu.

NOTE

You don't specify a target when creating a profile because you specify it when you run a scan using the associated profile.

Figure 5.8 Profile Editor

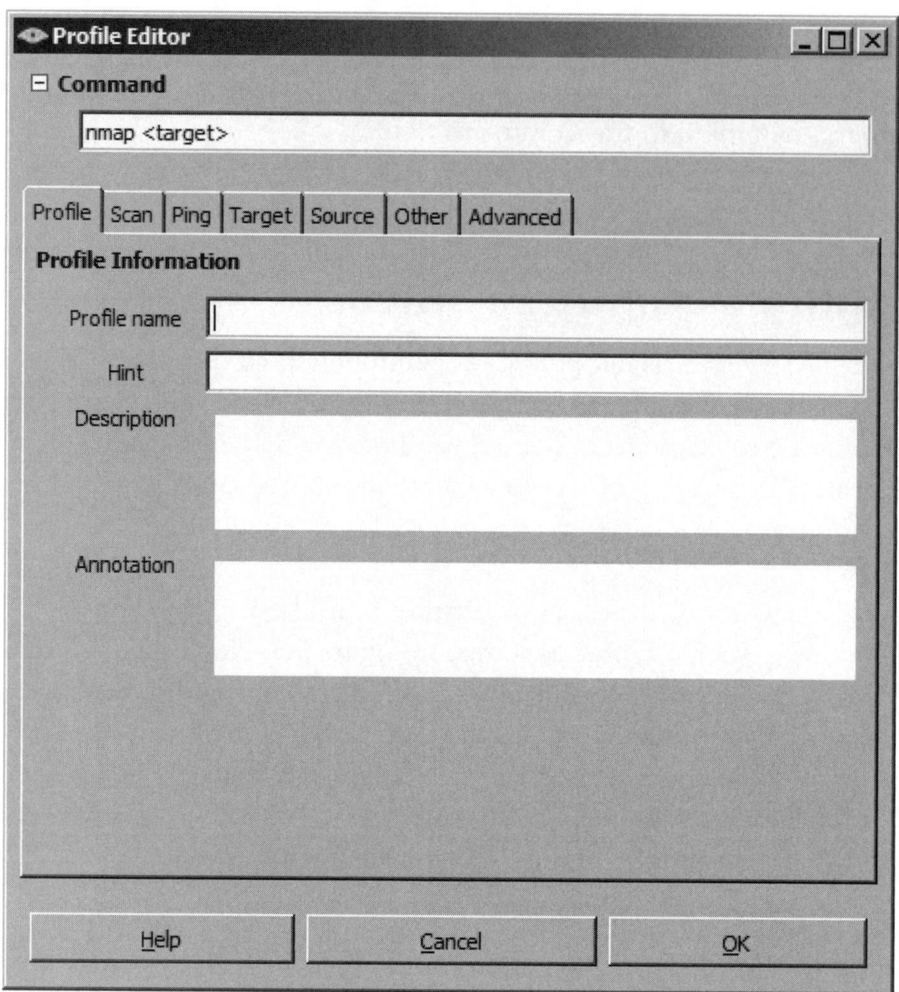

You can edit current profiles by selecting the profile from the Profile field drop down menu in the scan tab, then choosing **Edit Selected Profile** from the **Profile** menu. The Profile Editor appears with the information for the selected profile. Once you make a change to a profile you can not undo the change. If you wish to delete the profile click the **Cancel** button in the Profile Editor. You will be prompted to make sure you really want to delete the profile. Clicking Cancel even after you have made changes to the profile, prompts you to delete the profile, so once again, there is no way to undo changes.

Instead of editing a profile directly, you may want to make a copy of it to edit and test. You can do this by creating a new profile using a selected profile as a template. First, select the profile you would like to copy from the Profile field drop down menu in the scan tab. Next, choose **New Profile with Selected** from the **Profile** menu. This will open the Profile Editor with the same Nmap command line options as the selected profile, but with a blank profile name. You can choose a name for the profile, make modifications and click **OK** when you are done.

Managing Zenmap Results

Zenmap scan results are saved in a searchable database, named zenmap.db, for 60 days. You can also save your scan results to a file in Umit Scan Results (.usr) format. Both of these formats are searchable by the Zenmap search feature. You can open the Search Window, by choosing **Search Scan Results** from the **Tools** menu. Figure 5.9 shows the Zenmap Search Window. You can search on a variety of criteria by clicking on the various tabs. For example you could search by target IP or MAC address, port number and state, OS class, or general keyword. The Search Options tab allows you to specify the search location. By default, Zenmap only searches scans in open scan tabs and the scan database. If you want to search saved scan files, you must specify a directory that contains the files. You can search both Zenmap and Nmap file types by specifying them in semicolon delimited format, for example: `usr;nmap;gnmap;xml`. The Search Options tab also allows you to modify the Zenmap database options including enabling and disabling database storage and database searching, and modifying how long scans are stored in the database.

Once you have entered your search criteria, click on **Find** button to start the search. Search results will appear in the Results window pane on the right. You can open a found scan in the Results window by selecting it and clicking on the **Open** button.

NOTE

Text matches are case sensitive, except for those against the profile, OS, or service version.

Figure 5.9 Zenmap Search Window

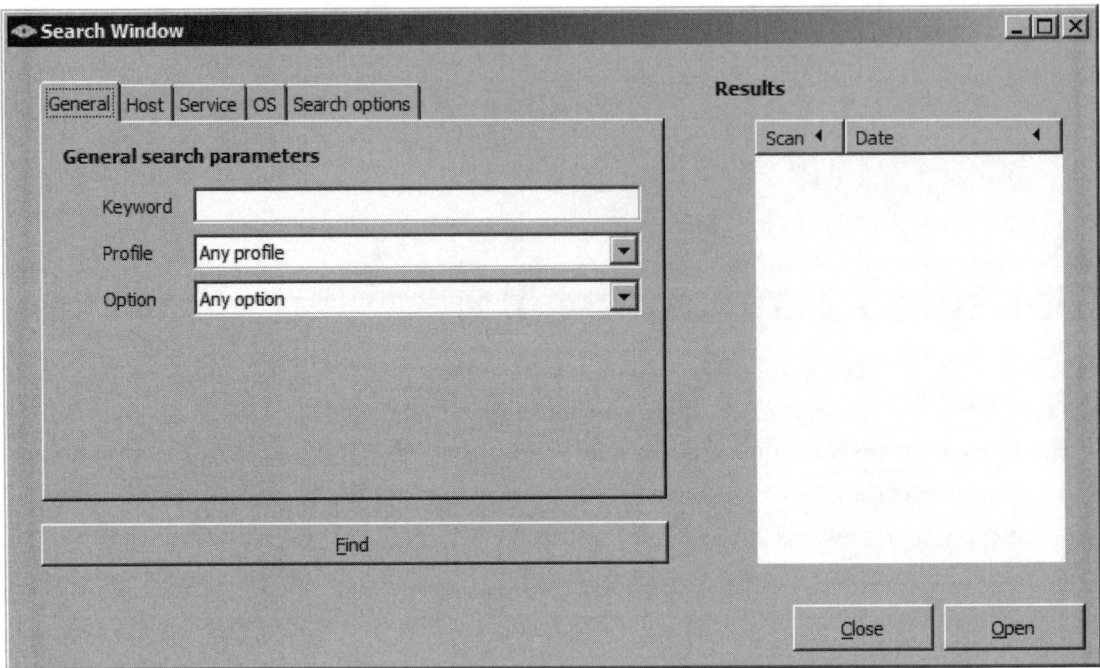

When performing scanning in the enterprise, there are often times you want to run the same scan more than once and compare results. For example, you may be interested in running Nmap before and after you install a patch or new software to a system, make a firewall or router access control list change, or make a configuration change. You may also be interested in comparing the results of a scan of two different systems to see how they differ, or compare the results of scans that used different scanning options. In addition to the ability to save your Nmap command to make it easy to run it repeatedly, Zenmap also has the ability to compare the results of multiple scans.

You can open the Compare Results window, by choosing **Compare Results** from the **Tools** menu. Zenmap allows you to compare the results of two scans at a time. You can use the drop down box for each Scan Result field to open a current scan results tab, or you can click on the Open button to open a saved scan result. Make sure you take into consideration which scans you open as Scan Result 1 and Scan Result 2 because this will impact your comparison. Comparisons are made to show how Scan Result 2 differs from Scan Result 1. Comparison automatically starts once you choose your two scans to compare.

Figure 5.10 shows the Zenmap Compare Results window with the graphical comparison of two scans that use different Nmap options to scan the same system. The graphical results are depicted with colors that represent how the second scan differs from the first. For example, was this aspect of the scan unchanged, added, modified, or not present in the second scan? You can change the color mapping by clicking the **Color Descriptions** button and choosing alternate colors. If you don't want to see the graphical results, you can change the comparison mode by clicking on the **Text Mode** button. Text mode still uses colors to represent changes, but the results can easily be copied and pasted into a file.

Figure 5.10 Zenmap Compare Results Window

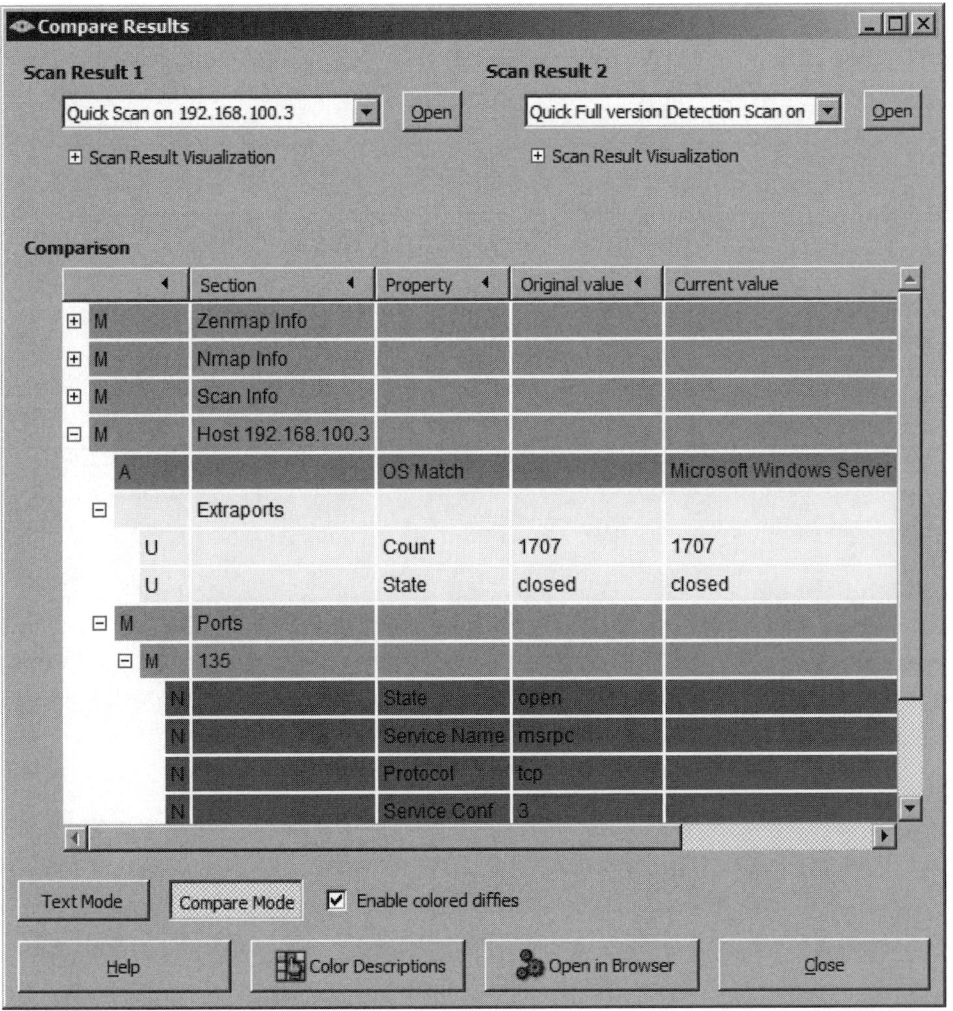

Text mode results use special characters to indicate the meaning of a line. Table 5.3 shows the special characters and their meanings. Lastly, you can click on the **Open in Browser** button to view the results in HTML format.

NOTE

You can compare results of scans from the scan database by first opening them using the search window. This will open the results into a scan tab.

Table 5.3 Text Mode Characters

Character	Meaning
Space	The line is identical in both scans
+	The line was added in the second scan
–	The line was removed in the second scan
?	^, +, – characters on the line indicate which characters were modified, added, or removed, in the line above

Summary

This chapter showed you the enterprise capabilities of the Zenmap GUI in terms of building and running Nmap commands and managing scan profiles and results. In this chapter, you learned about the major features of the Zenmap GUI and how to use them. You should now be able to run Zenmap scans and analyze the results. You are also equipped to create and edit scanning profiles, save scan results, and search and compare scan results. You can also use the Zenmap Command Wizard to build complex Nmap commands. The Zenmap GUI is great to use in the enterprise for full-scale Nmap capabilities wrapped up into a scan management platform.

Solutions Fast Track

Running Zenmap

☑ Zenmap is a GUI front-end for Nmap that was originally named UMIT.

☑ Zenmap has all of the Nmap capabilities, plus scan management features.

☑ Zenmap scan results are arranged into four tabbed pages: Ports/Hosts, Nmap Output, Host Details, and Scan Details.

☑ Zenmap includes graphical icon representations for vulnerability severity.

Managing Zenmap Scans

☑ Zenmap allows you to run and view results for multiple scans using the scan tabs.

☑ You can create new scans, open scans, and save scans.

☑ Scans are saved in Umit Scan Results (.usr) format.

Building Commands with the Zenmap Command Wizard

☑ The Command Wizards walks you through creating an Nmap command by allowing you to check boxes and choose from pull down lists.

☑ You can create a command or a profile to save a command.

☑ The Expert user option opens the profile editor for access to advanced features.

Managing Zenmap Profiles

☑ Zenmap includes several default profiles of commonly used commands.

☑ Command profiles allow you to save Nmap commands and run them repeatedly.

☑ You can create, edit, and remove profiles.

☑ You can easily create copies of current profiles.

Managing Zenmap Results

☑ You can use Zenmap's search feature to search results saved in the database and files.

☑ You can search on a variety of criteria including target IP or MAC address, port number and state, OS class, general keyword, and others.

☑ Zenmap also has the ability to compare the results of multiple scans.

☑ Comparison results are displayed in color coded graphical or text formats.

Frequently Asked Questions

Q: Zenmap has several configuration files; do I need to make changes to them?

A: You do not need to change anything in the configuration files manually. When you make changes to profiles, etc. in the GUI, these files are automatically updated. Extreme care should be used if you are going to edit the files directly.

Q: I am an experienced UNIX system administrator that prefers the command line over GUIs, what advantages do I have running Zenmap instead of Nmap?

A: The biggest advantage to running Zenmap is its scan management features such as profile creation and built in results searching and comparison. Otherwise, Zenmap includes all of the same capabilities as Nmap.

Q: Can I save my results in other formats besides the .usr format?

A: Zenmap can only save results in Umit Scan Results (.usr) format.

Q: I am using the Command Wizard to create an Nmap command, but some of the options I need are not there, where do I find them?

A: You can use the Profile Editor to create commands with advanced features.

Chapter 6

Nmap OS Fingerprinting

Solutions in this chapter:

- What is OS Fingerprinting?
- The Mechanics of Nmap OS Fingerprinting
- Nmap OS Fingerprint Scan as an Administrative Tool
- Detecting and Evading the OS Fingerprint Scan

☑ Summary

☑ Solutions Fast Track

☑ Frequently Asked Questions

Introduction

Nmap OS fingerprinting can cover a wide range of topics pertaining to an enterprise environment. As an administrator, you can use Nmap for asset management, security audits, documenting equipment inventory, and as a crisis management tool. Aside from the positive uses of this tool, some have also been known to capitalize on its power for malicious deeds. Unfortunately, attacks against our enterprise infrastructures and computing environments are happening on an hourly basis. It is the way of the digital world today. Knowing this and knowing what an attacker can do with Nmap OS fingerprinting, and employing a few simple techniques of your own can help to secure your infrastructure. In the world of information security, we can often find positives from areas of negative influence; the important part is being aware in your environment. Nmap's OS fingerprinting can be a very powerful tool in the realm of enterprise awareness.

In this chapter we will work through the mechanics of Nmap OS fingerprinting, how it can be used as a proactive tool by systems administrators, how nefarious individuals tend to use it as a weapon in their arsenal, and how you can defend against those techniques.

What is OS fingerprinting?

Operating system fingerprinting is so named because of its similarity to taking a person's fingerprints in order to determine their identification. The unique characteristics of a person can be translated from the person's fingertips to an object simply by touching it. As with OS fingerprinting, a rather innocuous session can be conducted between two computers where one acquires, via probes, a unique set of *impressions* or response data, relating to the destination machine. This process of analyzing the impressions of the destination machine is known as OS fingerprinting.

Notes from the Underground...

Why conduct OS fingerprint scans?

Aside from the positive aspects gained by systems administrators, the OS fingerprint scan can yield a wealth of information for a hacker to use against you. A person conducting reconnaissance of your network will have an invaluable set of data if they successfully obtain results from even just one target. Knowing exactly what OS and available corresponding services are running can make it much simpler to attack at will; especially if your company does not stay on top of security patches, application and server hardening! One simple OS scan can paint an alarmingly clear picture of any potential footholds attackers might use to gain access to your resources.

The Mechanics of Nmap OS Fingerprinting

OS fingerprinting can be done passively or actively as follows:

- **Passive** OS fingerprinting involves sniffing network traffic at any given collection point and matching known patterns that pass to a table of pre-established OS identities. No traffic is sent with passive fingerprinting.
- **Active** OS fingerprinting requires the use of a set of specialized probes that are sent to the system in question. System responses from this active probing give insight into what type of OS might be installed.

Nmap does not use a passive style of fingerprinting. Instead it performs its Operating System Fingerprinting Scan (OSFS) via active methodologies. The active process that Nmap applies in order to conduct its fingerprinting scan involves a set of as many as 15 probes. These powerful probes are designed to utilize TCP, UDP, and ICMP protocols. The probes are gentle manipulations of packet structure designed to reveal subtle nuances in response.

NOTE

Nmap's variations on packet structure include queries designed to gather information using variations of: window size, window field, IP DF (Don't Fragment) bit, timestamp, explicit congestion notification control flags, sequence numbers, as well as other nuances like TTL (time to live). Although these probes are simple in their structure, they are used in sophisticated ways to generate responses that are then analyzed for their differences to determine a potential hit on OS identification. There is a careful science behind the fingerprinting methods employed by Nmap: crafting the probes themselves, determining how the mutated packets impact individual OS response, and matching responses to entries found in the continually-updated OS database.

Ultimately, the information gathered via these specialized probes is used to generate the unique fingerprint that is compared in a database of known operating systems characteristics. These unique sets of OS traits are kept in the *nmap-os-db* file. Nmap uses this comparison to try to determine an OS fingerprint match. Thus, in the end, Nmap can take a very intelligent guess at just what OS the remote computer is running by conducting a rather low signature set of probes. Released in 2006, the *nmap-os-db* file is part of the second generation of OS fingerprinting featured in Nmap. In prior versions of Nmap, if you wanted to utilize the original style of OS fingerprinting, you had the option of invoking it by using an `-O1` flag. This `-O1` flag told Nmap to use the file *nmap-os-fingerprints* instead of the new standard. The current generation of OS fingerprinting simply uses the `-O` (letter O, not the number 0) flag. Accordingly, the base OS scan command with minimum ports is simply:

```
#nmap -F -O <ip address>
```

This performs the most basic OS fingerprint scan. Although you can employ advanced flag settings in an OS scan command, it's not really necessary. Nmap's base OS fingerprinting methodology has a very low network resource overhead. The reason for its small footprint is its streamline use of the probes. All of the probes are very lightweight, but pack a powerful punch in yielded information. Aside from a small network presence, it is also easy on local system resources.

Figure 6.1 System Resources Utilized, Prior to Nmap Application Launch

```
root@localhost:~
File  Edit  View  Terminal  Tabs  Help
top - 02:37:32 up 12:35,  2 users,  load average: 0.18, 0.14, 0.05
Tasks: 124 total,   1 running, 122 sleeping,   0 stopped,   1 zombie
Cpu(s):  0.2%us,  0.8%sy,  0.0%ni, 99.0%id,  0.0%wa,  0.0%hi,  0.0%si,  0.0%st
Mem:    515244k total,   503912k used,    11332k free,    23592k buffers
Swap:  1048568k total,       36k used,  1048532k free,   206628k cached

  PID USER      PR  NI  VIRT  RES  SHR S %CPU %MEM    TIME+  COMMAND
 2704 root      15   0  181m  60m  22m S    1 12.0   3:37.50 firefox-bin
 2375 root      15   0 47572  21m 7344 S    1  4.2   1:39.97 Xorg
 2169 root      34  19  109m  99m 5664 S    0 19.7   1:42.95 yum-updatesd
 2514 root      18   0 39912  13m 7172 S    0  2.8   0:03.85 gnome-settings-
    1 root      15   0  2136  596  520 S    0  0.1   0:02.71 init
    2 root      RT   0     0    0    0 S    0  0.0   0:03.73 migration/0
    3 root      34  19     0    0    0 S    0  0.0   0:00.05 ksoftirqd/0
    4 root      RT   0     0    0    0 S    0  0.0   0:00.00 watchdog/0
    5 root      RT   0     0    0    0 S    0  0.0   0:02.96 migration/1
    6 root      34  19     0    0    0 S    0  0.0   0:00.02 ksoftirqd/1
    7 root      RT   0     0    0    0 S    0  0.0   0:00.00 watchdog/1
    8 root      10  -5     0    0    0 S    0  0.0   0:01.82 events/0
    9 root      10  -5     0    0    0 S    0  0.0   0:01.60 events/1
   10 root      10  -5     0    0    0 S    0  0.0   0:00.01 khelper
   11 root      10  -5     0    0    0 S    0  0.0   0:00.01 kthread
   51 root      10  -5     0    0    0 S    0  0.0   0:00.50 kblockd/0
   52 root      10  -5     0    0    0 S    0  0.0   0:00.26 kblockd/1
```

The screenshot in Figure 6.1 represents resource utilization prior to the launch of the Nmap scan. Contrast this with Figure 6.2; notice how the Firefox session is consuming 3 times the system resources as an Nmap OSFS during its peak. Nmap does a very good job of using only minimal resources, both local and network, to achieve fantastic results. This OSFS example only consumed 4.2% of local system memory to conduct the scan for this particular example. Incidentally, this was also being run from within a small virtual machine ... not bad.

Figure 6.2 System Resources Utilized, after Nmap Launch

```
root@localhost:~
File  Edit  View  Terminal  Tabs  Help
top - 02:39:32 up 12:37,  2 users,  load average: 0.09, 0.13, 0.06
Tasks: 125 total,   1 running, 123 sleeping,   0 stopped,   1 zombie
Cpu(s):  0.2%us,  1.0%sy,  0.0%ni, 98.7%id,  0.0%wa,  0.2%hi,  0.0%si,  0.0%st
Mem:    515244k total,   494624k used,    20620k free,    18016k buffers
Swap:  1048568k total,       36k used,  1048532k free,   181672k cached

  PID USER      PR  NI  VIRT  RES  SHR S %CPU %MEM    TIME+  COMMAND
 2704 root      15   0  181m  60m  22m S    1 12.0   3:39.18 firefox-bin
28919 root      15   0  2200 1020  792 R    0  0.2   0:00.49 top
28932 root      15   0 25984  21m 1784 S    0  4.2   0:02.11 nmap
    1 root      15   0  2136  596  520 S    0  0.1   0:02.71 init
    2 root      RT   0     0    0    0 S    0  0.0   0:03.73 migration/0
    3 root      34  19     0    0    0 S    0  0.0   0:00.05 ksoftirqd/0
    4 root      RT   0     0    0    0 S    0  0.0   0:00.00 watchdog/0
    5 root      RT   0     0    0    0 S    0  0.0   0:02.96 migration/1
    6 root      34  19     0    0    0 S    0  0.0   0:00.02 ksoftirqd/1
    7 root      RT   0     0    0    0 S    0  0.0   0:00.00 watchdog/1
    8 root      10  -5     0    0    0 S    0  0.0   0:01.82 events/0
    9 root      10  -5     0    0    0 S    0  0.0   0:01.61 events/1
   10 root      10  -5     0    0    0 S    0  0.0   0:00.01 khelper
   11 root      10  -5     0    0    0 S    0  0.0   0:00.01 kthread
   51 root      16  -5     0    0    0 S    0  0.0   0:00.50 kblockd/0
   52 root      10  -5     0    0    0 S    0  0.0   0:00.26 kblockd/1
   53 root      14  -5     0    0    0 S    0  0.0   0:00.00 kacpid
```

NOTE

The base OS scan is nice in its simple elegance, but unleashing the power of advanced Nmap options provides greater flexibility. Of course, as you work with incorporating progressive Nmap options, you also incur more overhead during your scan. As well, attackers will divulge more and more aspects of themselves as they further utilize options in the Nmap toolkit. The more in-depth that an attacker probes, the longer and more risky is it that he exposes himself to the systems being probed. Aside from the length of exposure to the target network, the attacker also is more likely to be caught by protective systems, such as IPS/IDS typically employed on enterprise networks. The more ports an attacker touches and the more varied the scan or ping, then all the more likely they are to be discovered and potentially caught. A security conscious administrator is well advised to utilize some sort of honey pot on their network. A well placed and configured honey pot can draw in and occupy an attacker while reverse reconnaissance is performed on them. If you are not familiar with honey pot technology, you can get a quick overview at http://en.wikipedia.org/wiki/Honeypot_(computing).

Nmap OS Fingerprint Scan as an Administrative Tool

For an administrator, Nmap is not only cost effective, but it can also save you an enormous amount of time and labor. It can even save you money by keeping your license information to date. The operating system fingerprint scan gives all of these benefits to us in the `-o` flag. Something as simple as:

```
#nmap --O <ip subnet>
```

Or even a happy median for a typical system administrator performing an inventory scan or security audit might be something along the lines of:

```
#nmap --fuzzy -sV -F <ip address or subnet>
```

The `--fuzzy` flag tells Nmap to take its best guess at determining the type of operating system running. The `--fuzzy` flag is comparable to another liberal guessing algorithm that can be utilized by issuing the `--osscan_guess` flag in your commands. The `–sV` flag tells Nmap to try to determine service version information as well. Version detection is dependant upon the OS fingerprint scan finding an open TCP or UDP port. After port discovery, version detection takes over and starts its process of probing for information regarding what is open and running on the target. This portion of the scan can be the key to an easy attack in the hands of would be hackers. For example, imagine how simple it might be to find a HP-UX system running an unpatched, older version of BIND. Imagine further still, how easy an attack would be given the added luxury of knowing the BIND service version number. This, indeed, would narrow the time needed for an attacker to infiltrate the system and potentially gain root access. A smaller attack footprint equals a lesser chance you have to detect the attacker before the damage is done. All too often, administrators come in well after an intrusion has occurred and are left with a shadowy trail leading back to an unknown, foreign system that makes it impossible to pursue any viable prosecution avenues. This is why proactive administrators should fully understand Nmap and put into place methods to protect themselves from it, by using its assets to their own advantage. With this understanding comes protection and the ability to use Nmap as a very powerful tool in your organization.

And now, back to our scan. Version scanning has its place, but a wealth of information alone can be obtained about a system by simply utilizing Nmap's OS fingerprinting facilities with the option to allow Nmap to take its best guess at the OS if its not exactly matched using the `--osscan_guess` flag.

Here we see the return on the scan of a Cisco Linksys Wireless G router using such tactics:

```
#nmap -F -O --osscan_guess 192.168.10.24
...
Interesting ports on 192.168.10.24:
Not shown: 1254 closed ports
PORT STATE SERVICE
80/tcp open http
443/tcp open https
MAC Address: 00:12:17:34:XX:XX (Cisco-Linksys)
Aggressive OS guesses: Linux 2.4.22 (Fedora Core 1, x86) (90%), Ipcop V1.4.11
firewall (Linux 2.4.31) (90%), Xerox WorkCentre Pro 265 multifunction printer (89%),
Linux 2.4.20 - 2.4.32, Linux-based embedded device (Linksys WRT54GL WAP, Buffalo
AirStation WLA-G54 WAP, Maxtor Shared Storage Drive, or Asus Wireless Storage
Router) (89%), Linux 2.4.18-10 (Red Hat 7.3) (87%), Netgear DG834 or DG834G
(wireless) DSL Router (86%), Aladdin eSafe security gateway (runs Linux 2.4.21)
(85%), D-Link DSL-G604T ADSL router WAP, runs Linux 2.4.17 (85%), Belkin Wireless
Pre-N Router (85%), Siemens Gigaset SE515dsl wireless broadband router (85%)
No exact OS matches for host (If you know what OS is running on it, see http://
insecure.org/nmap/submit/).
TCP/IP fingerprint:
OS:SCAN(V=4.50%D=11/18%OT=80%CT=1%CU=40873%PV=Y%DS=1%G=Y%M=001217%TM=4740A1
OS:A8%P=i686-pc-linux-gnu)SEQ(SP=D0%GCD=1%ISR=CC%TI=Z%II=I%TS=7)OPS(O1=M5B4
OS:ST11NW0%O2=M5B4ST11NW0%O3=M5B4NNT11NW0%O4=M5B4ST11NW0%O5=M5B4ST11NW0%O6=
OS:M5B4ST11)WIN(W1=16A0%W2=16A0%W3=16A0%W4=16A0%W5=16A0%W6=16A0)ECN(R=Y%DF=
OS:Y%T=40%W=16D0%O=M5B4NNSNW0%CC=N%Q=)T1(R=Y%DF=Y%T=40%S=O%A=S+%F=AS%RD=0%Q
OS:=)T2(R=N)T3(R=N)T4(R=N)T5(R=Y%DF=Y%T=40%W=0%S=Z%A=S+%F=AR%O=%RD=0%Q=)T6(
OS:R=N)T7(R=N)U1(R=Y%DF=N%T=40%TOS=C0%IPL=164%UN=0%RIPL=G%RID=G%RIPCK=G%RUC
OS:K=G%RUL=G%RUD=G)IE(R=Y%DFI=N%T=40%TOSI=S%CD=S%SI=S%DLI=S)
Uptime: 0.060 days (since Sun Nov 18 13:08:02 2007)
Network Distance: 1 hop
```

As it turns out, Nmap does not have an exact match for the operating system of this host. In this situation, Nmap prints out the TCP/IP fingerprint in hopes that the end-user ultimately verifies the OS of the targeted system and in turn, submits the fingerprint to help upgrade Nmap's fingerprint database. In order to more easily interpret the output, it is helpful to have some insight into how the fingerprint is formed. The block of text that we just saw is formatted for easy submittal to the insecure.org website for research and potential entry into the Nmap database. For our purposes in understanding the output, we'll reformat the block to better see the tests:

```
TCP/IP fingerprint:
SCAN(V=4.50%D=11/18%OT=80%CT=1%CU=40873%PV=Y%DS=1%G=Y%M=001217%TM=4740A1A8%P=
i686-pc-linux-gnu)
SEQ(SP=D0%GCD=1%ISR=CC%TI=Z%II=I%TS=7)
```

```
OPS(O1=M5B4ST11NW0%O2=M5B4ST11NW0%O3=M5B4NNT11NW0%O4=M5B4ST11NW0%O5=M5B4ST11NW0%O6=
M5B4ST11)
WIN(W1=16A0%W2=16A0%W3=16A0%W4=16A0%W5=16A0%W6=16A0)
ECN(R=Y%DF=Y%T=40%W=16D0%O=M5B4NNSNW0%CC=N%Q=)
T1(R=Y%DF=Y%T=40%S=O%A=S+%F=AS%RD=0%Q=)
T2(R=N)
T3(R=N)
T4(R=N)
T5(R=Y%DF=Y%T=40%W=0%S=Z%A=S+%F=AR%O=%RD=0%Q=)
T6(R=N)
T7(R=N)
U1(R=Y%DF=N%T=40%TOS=C0%IPL=164%UN=0%RIPL=G%RID=G%RIPCK=G%RUCK=G%RUL=G%RUD=G)
IE(R=Y%DFI=N%T=40%TOSI=S%CD=S%SI=S%DLI=S)
```

Here are a few more things we need to know in order to understand this output:

- Multiple sub-tests can be attempted for each main test: `SCAN`, `SEQ`, `OPS`, `WIN`, `ECN`, `T1-T7`, `U1` and `IE`.
- Sub-tests are separated by the `%` symbol. For example: `R=Y%DF=Y%T=40` describes the results of 3 sub-tests.
- Sub-test results may be empty in which case you will see a `%` or right-hand terminating parentheses. In this example, `RD=0%Q=)` the sub-test `RD` reported a result of `0`, whereas the `Q` sub-test did not report any result.
- In order for a fingerprint to match an entry in the database, the sub-test results must exactly match the fingerprint definition.
- `R=N` means that no result was returned for any tests of that main test.

What's going on in this OS fingerprint? Let's break down the block to see.

- The first line, `SCAN(V=4.50%D=11/18%OT=80%CT=1%CU=40873%PV=Y%DS=1%G=Y%M=001217%TM=4740A1A8%P=i686-pc-linux-gnu)`, is a record of Nmap version and other related local info pertaining to this scan. We can see the Nmap version (4.50) being utilized, in addition to some date, timestamp, and scanning operating system information:

`SCAN(V=4.50` **Describes the version of Nmap utilized.**

`D=12/13` **is the date the scan was run.**

`OT=80%CT=1` **describe the Open and Closed TCP ports that Nmap used during the fingerprinting process.**

CU=40873 **is the Closed UDP port utilized for the fingerprint test.**

PV=Y **this tells us that the IP address fingerprinted resides in Private (RFC-1918) IP address space.**

DS=1 **is the number of hops in network distance from the Nmap scanner to the scanned host.**

G=Y **this means that our fingerprint results are Good enough to submit to insecure.org, if we decide to do so.**

M=001217 **if DS=1, then Nmap is able to discern the MAC OID of the targeted system.**

TM=4740A1A8 **this is the time the scan was performed in Unix hexadecimal time format.**

P=i686-pc-linux-gnu) **Describes the platform the scan was conducted from.**

Next we'll check out the SEQ, OPS, WIN, and T1 variables. These results are derived from a set of 6 very precise probes that are sent to the open TCP port on the targeted host.

- The SEQ test, `SEQ(SP=D0%GCD=1%ISR=CC%TI=Z%II=I%TS=7)` returns information regarding sequence analysis:

SEQ(SP=D0 **Reports on TCP Initial Sequence Number (ISN) Predictability.**

GCD=1 **Greatest Common Denominator, this sub-test provides feedback about TCP ISN incrementation.**

ISR=CC **Describes the ISN sequence rates.**

TI=Z **Evaluates the TCP SEQ probe IP header ID field. In this example, Z means that all IP ids returned were set to 0.**

II=I **Evaluates the IP IDs based on the responses to the ICMP probes. A value of I reflects incremental ids.**

TS=7) **Returns information about the TCP timestamp attached to the responses. 7 reflects a 100Hz frequency in use by the target.**

- The OPS response, `OPS(O1=M5B4ST11NW0%O2=M5B4ST11NW0%O3=M5B4NNT11NW0%O4=M5B4ST11NW0%O5=M5B4ST11NW0%O6=M5B4ST11)` contains the TCP options received for each of the 6 probes.

OPS(O1=M5B4 **Test O1 reports a Maximum Segment Size (MSS) of 0x5B4.**

ST11 **provides information about a permitted Selective ACK and the timestamp of the packet.**

N **is a NOP or No Operation.**

W0 **reflects a Window scale size of 0.**

You can determine the makeup of the responses for the remaining responses of this test:

O2=M5B4 **Test O2 reports a MSS of 0x5B4**

ST11

N

W0

```
O3=M5B4 Test O3.
N
N
T11
N
W0
O4=M5B4 Test O4.
ST11
N
W0
O5=M5B4 Test O5.
ST11
N
W0
O6=M5B4ST11) Test O6.
```

- WIN, `WIN(W1=16A0%W2=16A0%W3=16A0%W4=16A0%W5=16A0%W6=16A0)` returns the TCP initial windows size information for each of the 6 probes.

```
WIN(W1=16A0
W2=16A0
W3=16A0
W4=16A0
W5=16A0
W6=16A0)
```

- Finally, we see the `ECN(R=Y%DF=Y%T=40%W=16D0%O=M5B4NNSNW0%CC=N%Q=)` or explicit congestion notification response.

```
ECN(R=Y indicates whether or not the target responded to our probe.
DF=Y evaluates whether the IP don't fragment bit is enabled or not.
T=40 The IP time-to-live value found in the response.
W=16D0 TCP initial window size information.
O=M5B4NNSNW0 TCP Options information.
CC=N Examines the Explicit Congestion Notification (congestion control) capability
of the target. N indicates the target does not support ECN.
Q=) Looks for any known quirks in the TCP stack of the target.
```

Next in the process, we see 6 TCP specific probes. This is part of the second wave of probes. By now you should have a feel for interpreting these test results. If any of the following sub-tests look unfamiliar, or if you are interested in even more information about these tests, you can also check out http://insecure.org/nmap/osdetect/osdetect-methods.html.

- This is the first of the TCP probes that are sent. This is the more intense of the TCP probes.

  ```
  T1(R=Y%DF=Y%T=40%S=O%A=S+%F=AS%RD=0%Q)
  ```

- T2 is a null packet sent with the IP DF bit set and a window field size of 128.

  ```
  T2(R=N)
  ```

- T3 is a TCP packet set with FIN, URG, PSH, and SYN flags all set and a window field size of 256.

  ```
  T3(R=N)
  ```

- T4 sends a TCP ACK packet with a window field of 1024 and IP DF bit set.

  ```
  T4(R=N)
  ```

- T5 sends a SYN packet with the ubiquitous and glorious prime 31337 as its window field size.

  ```
  T5(R=Y%DF=Y%T=40%W=0%S=Z%A=S+%F=AR%O=%RD=0%Q=)
  ```

- T6 is very similar to T4, just a larger window field size of 32768 and to a closed port, instead of open.

  ```
  T6(R=N)
  ```

- Here we finish up this set of TCP probes by sending a packet with FIN, URG, and PSH flags set. This probe goes to a closed port with a window field size of 65535.

  ```
  T7(R=N)
  ```

- This is the U1, UDP probe results. This probe goes to a closed port and the character 'C' is repeated 300 times in the data field.

  ```
  U1(R=Y%DF=N%T=40%TOS=C0%IPL=164%UN=0%RIPL=G%RID=G%RIPCK=G%RUCK=G%RUL=G%RUD=G
  ```

- The IE probe is based on the ICMP protocol. It is a two part probe, both being very similar in structure and comprised of such elements as: type-of-service (TOS), IP ID, sequence numbers, and data payloads consisting of the typical repeated character methodology used in other probes.

  ```
  IE(R=Y%DFI=N%T=40%TOSI=S%CD=S%SI=S%DLI=S)
  ```

One question you might ask at this point would be, "Yes, but how can this help me in my enterprise environment? How can I use this as a tool and in a proactive way in my environment?"

An Nmap OSFS will yield information on any live IP addresses found in the range specified at command issuance. This means that it can supply information regarding your switches, routers, storage appliances, servers of all types, and anything else alive on an IP address. As you get more comfortable running and interpreting the fingerprints for your enterprise, you will be able to take any fingerprint returned and unknown by Nmap, and modify the OS fingerprint database, *nmap-os-db*. All you need to do is clean up the returned unidentified OS fingerprint as we did above, and integrate it into the *nmap-os-db* to reflect the format of the current standard entries.

NOTE

Below, we see the block returned when we did our previous scan. The scan was performed on a Linksys Wireless Router, but Nmap was unsure about what it had found.

```
SEQ(SP=D0%GCD=1%ISR=CC%TI=Z%II=I%TS=7)OPS(O1=M5B4
OS:ST11NW0%O2=M5B4ST11NW0%O3=M5B4NNT11NW0%O4=M5B4ST11NW0%O5=M5B4ST11NW0%O6=
OS:M5B4ST11)WIN(W1=16A0%W2=16A0%W3=16A0%W4=16A0%W5=16A0%W6=16A0)ECN(R=Y%DF=
OS:Y%T=40%W=16D0%O=M5B4NNSNW0%CC=N%Q=)T1(R=Y%DF=Y%T=40%S=O%A=S+%F=AS%RD=0%Q
OS:=)T2(R=N)T3(R=N)T4(R=N)T5(R=Y%DF=Y%T=40%W=0%S=Z%A=S+%F=AR%O=%RD=0%Q=)T6(
OS:R=N)T7(R=N)U1(R=Y%DF=N%T=40%TOS=C0%IPL=164%UN=0%RIPL=G%RID=G%RIPCK=G%RUC
OS:K=G%RUL=G%RUD=G)IE(R=Y%DFI=N%T=40%TOSI=S%CD=S%SI=S%DLI=S)
```

By removing the OS prefix and correcting the wrapping at each terminating parenthesis, this raw fingerprint return would then be translated into the proper format reflected in the default database:

```
SEQ(SP=D0%GCD=1%ISR=CC%TI=Z%II=I%TS=7)
OPS(O1=M5B4ST11NW0%O2=M5B4ST11NW0%O3=M5B4NNT11NW0%O4=M5B4ST11NW0%O5=M5B4ST11NW0%O6=M5B4ST11)
WIN(W1=16A0%W2=16A0%W3=16A0%W4=16A0%W5=16A0%W6=16A0)
ECN(R=Y%DF=Y%T=40%W=16D0%O=M5B4NNSNW0%CC=N%Q=)
T1(R=Y%DF=Y%T=40%S=O%A=S+%F=AS%RD=0%Q=)
T2(R=N)
T3(R=N)
T4(R=N)
T5(R=Y%DF=Y%T=40%W=0%S=Z%A=S+%F=AR%O=%RD=0%Q=)
T6(R=N)
T7(R=N)
U1(R=Y%DF=N%T=40%TOS=C0%IPL=164%UN=0%RIPL=G%RID=G%RIPCK=G%RUCK=G%RUL=G%RUD=G)
IE(R=Y%DFI=N%T=40%TOSI=S%CD=S%SI=S%DLI=S)
```

By adding your own fingerprints into the database, you will build up your custom database with relevance to your particular infrastructure. This way, you have the power of expanding the functionality of Nmap in your environment, instead of waiting for your particular fingerprints to be incorporated into the next release by the Nmap development team. Of course, you also have the option of documenting it and sending the related information to Fyodor at http://insecure.org/nmap/submit/. Taking the time to submit your fingerprints to Nmap for their reference, you in turn aide the community in making Nmap a more powerful overall product. Every user is highly encouraged in this way to participate fully in the open source philosophy. Doing so, we all work together to further enhance products and make our networks even more secure.

The ability to modify your local OS fingerprinting database gives you a very powerful tool in the area of asset management and equipment inventory documentation. Of course, utilizing this capability will require that systems administrators be proactive and thorough in their execution and documentation.

Nmap to the Rescue! Tool for Crisis?

Nmap OSFS can be a useful tool for an administrator in more than a few ways. In addition to proactive usefulness, the information yielded by a well-planned and executed Nmap OS and version scan can aide an administrator in times of crisis.

For example, assume you have a computer on your LAN that's been infected with a trojan-carrying virus that in turn, has spawned an e-mail server. A fairly simple Nmap OS and version scan can tell you the computer, its related IP and MAC address information, the type of services it has running and their related ports. This can save a battle-weary administrator a midnight "suspicious system search" in the event of an outbreak such as this. One common problem that exacerbates this example is when the owner of that suspicious computer is on vacation during the outbreak or otherwise unavailable. This makes it even more difficult to locate the afflicted computer. System administrators have long relied on various ways of performing this type of task using widely-regarded commercial appliances and lots of manpower. However, you can also become intimately familiar with your environments and utilize the full potential of powerful open source applications such as Nmap. Ultimately, this philosophy could save your organization money and make you a very valuable asset.

Saving Hard Money with the Nmap OSFS

Nmap OS fingerprinting can also assist your IT budget by providing important details on operating systems in the enterprise and making it much easier to keep your licenses and related contracts in order.

For example, you may think you have 142 SQL servers on your network, when in reality; Bob's engineering team stopped using SQL databases 6 months ago. They did not inform you or your team of the changes. Their team previously accounted for 126 of those 142 total SQL databases. Lucky for you, you're not relying on Bob's good intentions to have your budgets and account payables in order. An Nmap OSFS of Bob's subnet tells you that they are actually only using 97 SQL databases now. That's a difference of 29 SQL databases and quite a savings when it comes down to the licensing. It is often quite difficult for the IT department to justify itself because of its inability to provide a positive cash flow for the organization. This method and approach to proactive savings will give you ability and credibility to justify your resource requirements and cost adjustments.

Another scenario that could be posed to the administrator is the task of finding all the computers across the network that are still using Windows 2000, and decommission them. At one point during the deployment of these systems, the organization had a restructure that required a few labs to switch around and expand or contract causing general mayhem in your otherwise well-documented and structured IT world. On top of it, two of the labs decided to trade some hardware with one another. All a savvy administrator needs to do in this situation is use Nmap and its OS fingerprinting capabilities. You can then take the results and parse them for IP addresses corresponding to the Windows 2000 signature. After you have your list of IP addresses, you can search through them against your network file to find their corresponding VLANs and subnets. This would then tell you the switch the machines are physically attached to, which should tell you a very close approximation to where they potentially sit.

Security Audits and Inventory

Nmap OS and version scanning can be an invaluable tool for recurring security audits. In the enterprise, we are frequently faced with mandatory security scans and audits for such federal regulations such as Sarbanes Oxley (SOX). This practice is something we should all strive to do, even if we do not have to satisfy SOX or other requirements.

Scanning with Nmap can yield information such as open services, ports, and versions known to have exploits or otherwise malicious repercussions if left untouched. You may find that you have a rather easily exploited version of BIND running in a lab somewhere that you were not informed of.

For example, every year we have annual inventory. This helps us keep track of assets and manage them in a more proactive and financially beneficial way. Staying on top of asset inventory will help lessen employee theft as well as help you keep an eye on assets that are coming to the end of their life cycle.

Aside from equipment such as servers, Nmap can also discover information regarding appliances on the network. One common application could include staying up on network attached storage and its firmware and OS versions. An administrator could scan storage networks for OS and version information and yield a list of filers that are susceptible to a bug that could cause major issues regarding valuable data. Protecting high-risk or critical data is every admin's number one goal. We should all strive to maintain a properly documented, patched, and protected network to house this valuable and sensitive information.

H4x0rz, Tigers and Bears…Oh MY!

Most security minded administrators keep abreast of the latest exploits being released that can affect systems in their networks. Upon hearing of a new exploit, a proactive administrator would start a scan across the network searching for versions of the potentially afflicted OS. Within a short period of time, a list could be generated and a targeted patching regiment could be initiated to get these machines back into a green state. Otherwise, if we do nothing, we leave ourselves open to a potentially crippling attack that could cost an organization untold amounts of money. Costs related to outages and data loss can easily be devastating to a business, not to mention the career of administrators asleep at the wheel.

Conversely an attacker can use Nmap and its OS fingerprinting and version detection against you in very devastating ways. If someone is allowed to scan even the most superficial areas of your network, they can ultimately gain the highest level of access and get at your information and intellectual property. Every enterprise environment of any scale is a constant target to the general hacking and malicious traffic going across the Internet at any given second. The bigger the enterprise and the more unique or valuable the data it houses, the more skilled hacker they attract. Keeping that in mind, know that even the least sophisticated hackers will use tools such as Nmap to do OS fingerprinting reconnaissance.

Information that was useful for you as a proactive admin is now a soft point for an attacker to work their way into your systems or otherwise deny them of services and impede your business flow. Aside from information regarding operating systems and exploits, an attacker could use the simple OS and version information derived from an Nmap fingerprinting attack to know the IP address of an externally facing router or wireless access point. For instance, an attacker could see a Linksys fingerprint, much like the one given as an example previously, and instantly have a foothold in attempting to gain further access to the network.

Detecting and Evading the OS Fingerprint Scan

One simple way to avoid a lot of these types of attacks is simply to stay patched and updated across the infrastructure. Unfortunately, patching and maintenance is not enough to deter a lot of hackers worth their salt. Some tactics you can use to hide from the dreaded Nmap fingerprinting scan are to employ firewalls and system-level virus protection and port stealthing. This will greatly increase your ability to remain invisible to Nmap. Other methods include the use of programs such as Morph and IP Personality. Another technique employs the use of strategically-placed honey pots. A few well placed and thought out honey pots can add a tremendous level of proactive security to your network, as well as allow you to more easily use Nmap on your network in a positive way. You simply need to exclude your honey pots in your fingerprinting scans, or take them offline while you conduct your security scans and audits.

Morph and IP Personality

One good way to avoid having Nmap successfully used against you by an attacker is to confuse the situation by presenting a false face. There are two ways to do this rather nicely. One is with a program called Morph and another called IP Personality.

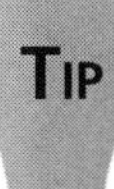

TIP

IP Personality currently can be found at http://ippersonality.sourceforge.net/. Morph can be downloaded by visiting www.synacklabs.net/projects/morph.

Morph is a neat little program for Linux that allows a user to select some other OS to emulate. In doing so, the TCP, ICMP and UDP responses and behaviors can be modified to represent some other OS when an attacker tries to perform their reconnaissance OSFS on your network resources.

IP Personality is another program for Linux used to change how Nmap sees you in its scan results. It allows you to manipulate TCP and UDP parameters via iptables rules. This affords you the ability to further disguise yourself when it comes to giving up information regarding what OS you're really running. The less valid information you provide to an attacker, the better.

Honey Pots

Honey pots stand as welcome hosts for would be attackers, crackers and other nefarious types. Bad guys are sucked in by the promise of an easy target and soon stuck in a sugarcoated death trap designed only in appearance to give them the soft target that they've been looking for. Depending on type and complexity of your honeypot setup, this technique can potentially thwart a number of mid-range hacker types that may know a thing or two, but aren't experienced enough to recognize a trap like this until it is too late. Honey pots are meant to give you time to respond to a situation. They occupy an intruder and allow you precious time to do your own reconnaissance about their attack types and targets of interest in your infrastructure.

A very good and well-used honey pot system is *honeyd*. This tiny daemon allows you to spoof hosts on your network with whatever OS you want to represent. You can download it from www.honeyd.org.

Summary

Knowing what you do now about operating system fingerprinting and how Nmap conducts its probes, you should have no problem thwarting unwarranted Nmap scans against your resources. By knowing how the probes are constructed, you can easily build access control lists (ACLs) or other rules to reject these packets. You can also run system level firewalls if you're a Windows desktop user. The built-in Windows firewall actually does a pretty good job at hiding itself from basic Nmap scans. Most security appliances used in corporate networks are also quite capable of detecting Nmap operating system fingerprinting activity. All it takes is a little creativity and a solid working knowledge of your environment, and for literally no money, you can protect yourself from a potentially deadly reconnaissance attack. It is only a matter of time before an asset under your management will be attacked or otherwise probed for information. Arm yourself first with Nmap.

In this chapter we've discussed just what an operating system fingerprint scan is, and how Nmap goes about identifying operating systems running on detected hosts. We've discovered that operating system fingerprint scans are weapons in the hands of attackers. Conversely, the operating system fingerprint scan used in the hands of a skilled administrator can yield many rewards. Some of the main enterprise benefits to be gained from operating system fingerprint scans by Nmap are detailed inventory across vast environments, compliance with today's security audit controls, and even the ability to save time and money.

The ability to modify the operating system fingerprint database gives administrators great flexibility in their environments. This feature makes it so that you can customize your database to reflect special operating system variances that may exist on only your network, and would be against non-disclosure agreements to send information regarding them to outside sources. Nmap recognizes this and puts the power in your hands with the option to submit the scan to the developers for further product enhancement for the community.

Ultimately, if hackers find their way to your network bandwidth and start to perform their OS fingerprint scans in their preliminary reconnaissance regarding your resources, the knowledge of how Nmap conducts its probes will give you the ability to properly defend your environment. Using such tactics as incorporating honey pots with Honeyd or manipulating return data with Morph or IP Personality will give you a solid start point for defending against such scans. Of course, with any good security model, you will need to apply multiple layers to be effective in thwarting would be attacks.

Solutions Fast Track

What is OS Fingerprinting?

☑ OS fingerprinting is the technique of identifying or intelligently guessing what operating system is running on a particular system by sending targeted probes or by passively listening on the network.

☑ Attackers will typically perform an OSFS on a target network as part of their information gathering process.

The Mechanics of Nmap OS Fingerprinting

☑ Nmap conducts its OS fingerprinting actively with a series of probes.

☑ TCP, UDP, and ICMP protocols are used by the probes.

☑ The probes consist of various structured packets.

☑ Some probes are very similar in nature, only varying slightly in composition. These subtle differences return values that are recorded as a fingerprint.

☑ Fingerprints are compared to a database of known signatures to attempt an OS guess.

Nmap OSFS as an Administrative Tool

☑ Nmap OSFS will yield information an administrator can use to conduct inventory scans of their environment.

☑ Compliance with typical security audits is made simpler by utilizing the Nmap OSFS.

☑ An administrator could use operating system fingerprinting to determine what machines need particular attention regarding patching or other matters.

☑ Nmap OSFS can save your organization money by helping administrators of vast networks establish efficient and detailed reports of particular systems or services that may or may not be running. This is beneficial because it allows you to fine tune your license agreements.

- ☑ Nmap gives you the ability to update its fingerprint database with your own custom entries. This ability will allow you to properly identify potentially sensitive information regarding systems on your network and make it a valid return on future operating system fingerprint scans.

Detecting and Evading the OS Fingerprinting Scan

- ☑ Firewalls, ACLs, and port masking are all ways to shield your network from Nmap OS scans.
- ☑ Morph and IP Personality are effective at sending deceptive and particular responses to Nmap probes.
- ☑ Honeypots are a great idea for giving desired returns to would be attackers to tie them up while you gain time to detect them.

Frequently Asked Questions

Q: Why would you want to edit the Nmap fingerprint database, instead of submitting it to Fyodor for addition to the official database?

A: For the most part, the proper thing to do is to enhance the community and the product and make your submission for the next official release. However there are many environments that have high security regarding internal information about operating systems and versions of software in use. For these enterprises, you are given the freedom to take the unrecognized signature generated by the OSFS, and enter it into your local Nmap database for a valid return on your next scan.

Q: I keep getting all these undetermined signatures when I scan. I really don't want to edit the database this much. Is there anything I can do to make my scans return better information?

A: Certainly, with the breadth of operating systems available and in use these days, there will be times between version releases that invalid matches will be returned to you via the reported signature. There are two very robust methods for making Nmap take the plunge and take a guess. One of these methods is to use the *--fuzzy* flag. This option will force Nmap to "maybe" take a guess at what it thinks is the proper match for running OS. Another equally comparable option is given to Nmap with the *--osscan_guess* option.

Q: What can I do at a system level to protect myself from hackers and attackers performing these types of scans?

A: If you can hide your server behind a system level software firewall you are doing a fair job already. Turning on your firewall is always a good idea, but not necessarily quite enough to shield yourself from such scans. As another step in your plan of action, you should also consider a port stealther to mask open ports. There are also applications, such as Morph and IP Personality, that will allow a person to disguise themselves if these probes manage to eventually touch the system.

Q: I understand that Nmap can detect operating systems running on computers. Will it also help me detect info regarding my WI-FI adapters, filers, or switches on the network?

A: This is the beauty of the Nmap OS scan, especially when coupled with the version detection option. Almost any device out there that is alive on a network with an IP address is susceptible to yielding valuable data regarding its running OS and other services alive on some port.

Chapter 7

Tooling Around with Nmap

Solutions in this chapter:

- Introduction to Nmap Add-on and Helper Tools
- NDiff–Nmap diff
- RNmap–Remote Nmap
- Bilbo
- Nmap-Parser

☑ Summary

☑ Solutions Fast Track

☑ Frequently Asked Questions

Introduction

Prior to this chapter, we learned a lot about Nmap and its scanning capabilities. We have seen examples of various types of scans and their respective enterprise usage. At this point, you are probably wondering about ways of further integrating Nmap into your infrastructure to make it even more useful. Luckily for us, plenty of administrators have also been down this same path and have already created some fantastic tools to give Nmap that extra enterprise-edge. The good news is that you don't have to be a developer to use these Nmap helper tools. However, anytime you start working with added functionality like this; it helps to have a healthy dose of patience! The level of necessary patience is always in direct correlation to the complexity of the add-on tool.

A great place to find all sorts of Nmap add-on tools is Packetstorm, which can be found at http://packetstormsecurity.org/UNIX/nmap/. Whenever you get ready to download and test out a new tool from a compilation site such as Packetstorm, it's helpful to double-check the original site of the tool as well, just in case newer versions have been released that are not included on Packetstorm yet.

NOTE

Sites like Packetstorm and SecurityFocus are well-known download repositories for security tools. Many users in the security industry rely on sites like this to learn about new tools that are available. Additionally, tools downloaded from these sites should be free from any malware. Regardless, you should always test new tools on a development system and preferably one that is connected to a lab-only network.

NDiff–Nmap Diff

NDiff is used to compare Nmap scan results. Much like the Linux tool of the same name, it does a file comparison; however, this particular version is focused solely on Nmap scans. This application can be very useful when performing large numbers of Nmap scans with a high degree of output.

If you are tasked with security for a large organization and have automated your scanning function for performing ongoing scans, then you can use NDiff to look for and report on any differences that might be found. For example, let's assume a web server you scanned months ago, that came back with a clean report at that time, has been recently misconfigured and is now serving as an open mail relay. NDiff can quickly spot this open port in the sea of Nmap results information. Another example from the attacker point of view is where a target has been potentially identified or is intriguing in some way. With NDiff, the attacker can continually monitor hosts or subnets and compare open ports to see if anything changes with their desired target.

Source and Install

NDiff, until recently, could be found at www.vinecorp.com/ndiff/. It may or may not be available at the time of this printing. However, multiple versions are available on http://packetstormsecurity.org and other security sites. According to the README included in the `NDiff-0.04` package, *NDiff requires Perl 5.005_03 or later and nmap 2.53 or later*. Our NDiff install is being performed on a SUSE 10 server, so after downloading the tar.gz file, we'll extract the contents to the hard drive by performing this command:

```
NDiff-server:/software/download # gzip -dc NDiff-0.04.tar.gz | tar -xvf -
```

In our example, this command will extract the contents of the NDiff tar.gz file to a sub-directory called `NDiff-0.04` in the `download` directory. Now we can see that the NDiff-0.04 directory includes two important files for us, the README and INSTALL file.

TIP

The majority of open-source software you install should come complete with files similar to the README and INSTALL files we discovered in the extracted contents of the NDiff-0.04 application. Anytime you are working with a new application, it is wise to look for these files and consult them before attempting any installation or configuration of your new program.

The INSTALL file for NDiff gives us some simple installation assistance:

```
# perl Makefile.PL
# make; make install
# man NDiff_Quickstart
```

Running these three commands is fairly simple, so let's get to it. After creating the Makefile and then installing it, our NDiff application is ready to perform. You can see the short help instructions for many applications by typing the tool name followed by a -h. NDiff provides us the following assistance:

```
NDiff-server:/software/download/NDiff-0.04 # ndiff -h

ndiff [-b|-baseline <file-or-:tag>] [-o|-observed <file-or-:tag>]
      [-op|-output-ports <ocufx>] [-of|-output-hosts <nmc>]
      [-fmt|-format <terse| minimal | verbose | machine | html | htmle>]
```

While that gives us some idea of what we can do to get started with NDiff, it's also a good idea in this case to review the man page that the developer, James D. Levine, supplied with the NDiff package. The man page has much more detail about other NDiff capabilities, like how to establish a picture of your "perfect" baseline network .nm file and subsequently incorporate it into an Nmap NDiff scan. This neat feature gives us a way to perform compliance scanning against our desired baseline. It also describes some tips for creating file names that include %-style substitutions to incorporate run-time or date specifics. The man page covers another advanced item concerning the use of data stores to help with results storage and retrieval in the case of automated scans. Finally, and luckily for us, it includes some great examples of how to easily and quickly get up and running with some sample scans.

Example Usage

NDiff uses the concept of a baseline scan for comparison purposes. The filename is output in an .nm format. NDiff compares the second scan to the baseline scan and then outputs to a third file which describes three different types of hosts: missing hosts, new hosts and changes to existing hosts. Results are obtained via comparison to the existing baseline.

Here's a simple example of a comparison to a baseline created against our 192.168.1.0/24 network. In this example usage, we are first creating our baseline .nm file and then coming back at a later point in time to run a comparison against our scan2.nm file. We'll also use a UNIX trick to redirect any erroneous output to the bit bucket, aka /dev/null. This will help with the readability of our output. NDiff provides some command syntax reminders concerning our request and then our results:

```
1. nmap -n -m baseline.nm 192.168.1.0/24 > /dev/null
2. nmap -n -m scan2.nm 192.168.1.0/24 > /dev/null

3. ndiff -b baseline.nm -o scan2.nm
ndiff run Oct 21 09:10:21 EST 2007
command line: -b first_scan.nm -o second_scan.nm
baseline: first_scan.nm
```

```
observed: second_scan.nm
- - - - - - - - - - - - - - - - - - - - - - - - - -
new hosts:
192.168.1.10
80/tcp      open

- - - - - - - - - - - - - - - - - - - - - - - - - -
missing hosts:

- - - - - - - - - - - - - - - - - - - - - - - - - -
changed hosts:
192.168.1.33
25/tcp      open
```

We utilized the `-n`, no DNS resolution, and `-m`, machine parseable, Nmap switches to perform two Nmap scans against an entire subnet. In the first command, we perform the actual baseline; then at a later time, we use command number two to run our follow-up scan of the subnet. Lastly, command number three instructs NDiff to perform the comparison of the two files. In the resulting NDiff output, we can see that a new host was found, with port 80 open and a host that was previously found now has changed and has port 25 open.

NOTE

If you are the curious type (like the authors!) and wondering where that *–m* option came from–you will be interested in this bit of information from the Nmap changelog, found at http://nmap.org/changelog.html.

Nmap 2.3BETA12

The -o and -m options have been deprecated. From now on, you should use -oN for normal (human readable) output and -oM for machine parseable output. At some point I might add -oH (HTML output) or -oSK (sKr|pt kiDdi3 0uTPut).

Then the option evolved to its current day usage with this version:

Nmap 2.54BETA6

Added XML output (-oX). Hopefully this will help those of you writing Nmap front ends and other tools that utilize Nmap. The "machine-readable" output has been renamed "grepable" (-oG) to emphasize that XML is now the preferred machine-readable output format. But don't worry if your tool uses -oM , that format (and the deprecated -oM flag) won't go away any time soon (if ever).

As it turns out, the *–m* option is a supported, carry-over option from the original days of Nmap.

RNmap–Remote Nmap

RNmap or Remote Nmap is a python-based client/server tool for creating a distributed scanning environment. The RNmap server performs user authentication of the RNmap clients as they connect in to perform Nmap scans.

Source and Install

RNmap is a UNIX-based application that will require other components in order to run. For the RNmap server and any clients, you will have to install the latest version of Python from www.python.org/download/. For our examples here, we are using the UNIX compressed source tarball version for our SUSE 10 RNmap manager and for our separate SUSE 10 client. You will also have to make sure the latest version of Nmap is installed on your RNmap server.

Installation for the tarballs is straightforward for current installations of the Linux platform. For example, for the Python "more compressed" UNIX tarball:

```
bzip2 -cd Python-2.5.1.tar.tar | tar xvf -
cd Python-2.5.1
./configure
make
su root
make install
```

For the Nmap tarball:

```
bzip2 -cd nmap-4.52.tar.bz2 | tar xvf -
cd nmap-4.52
./configure
make
su root
make install
```

At this point, you have one final package to install–RNmap. The gzip RNmap package is quite small, measuring in at less than 30 kilobytes. You can download the package from sourceforge here: http://sourceforge.net/projects/rnmap/. Installing it is also fairly easy: First you must extract the contents of the file:

```
gzip -dc rnmap_0.10.tar.gz | tar -xvf -
```

This will extract the file contents to a newly created `./rnmap` directory on your hard drive. Once created, you must navigate to the server directory: `/rnmap/server`. In order to get started, you have to run the python rnmap-adduser script and tell

RNmap the names and passwords of your remote users. In our example, we created a user 'Test1' with a password of 'test1'.

```
vmware1:/software/rnmap/server # python rnmap-adduser.py
Username: Test1
Password:
Retype password:
All done.
```

This creates a new file in the `/server` directory named `users.list`. The cool thing is that RNmap creates an *md5 hash* of your password and stores the hash so that your users' passwords aren't stored in clear text. Something else that is important to notice here is that RNmap also sets the UNIX permissions on the `users.list` file to 600 so that only the file owner has access. You do not want other users to be able to view or copy the file to download hashes for attempted cracking. Here is what our `users.list` file looks like after creating our Test1 user and affiliated password:

```
vmware1:/software/rnmap/server # more users.list
Test1:/jXrQhrwMhrbb7STyWp5Gw==
```

TIP

You can learn more about UNIX file permissions by reading the man page for `chmod`. It's easy to find many sites pertaining to this topic just by typing `man chmod` into the Google search bar. Understanding and properly using UNIX file permissions is integral to securing your files, users and applications.

At this point, we are ready to start the RNmap server and test our rnmap.py client from our SUSE client! RNmap does come with the capability of utilizing SSL to encrypt the channel between the clients and server and while this is certainly recommended, for the purposes of our test, we'll be calling it without SSL support. Firing up the RNmap server now is pretty straight-forward. First RNmap tells us we need to use the –nossl option:

```
vmware1:/software/rnmap/server # ./rnmapd
Can't find pyOpenSSL module. If you want to start non SSL Rnmap server
use '-nossl' command line option.
```

Retrying with this option, we are able to get the server started and then see it running by performing a quick grep for the service name in our process list:

```
vmware1:/software/rnmap/server # ./rnmapd -nossl
vmware1:/software/rnmap/server # ps -ef | grep rnmapd
root       8465      1 0 03:38 ?         00:00:00 python ./rnmapd -nossl
```

You can also run a quick netstat command to see if the RNmap port is showing up on its default TCP port of 3418:

```
vmware1:/software/rnmap/server # netstat -nap | grep 3418
tcp    0       0 0.0.0.0:3418        0.0.0.0:*      LISTEN 8465/python
```

Now it looks like we are in business on the server end. Let's copy the *rnmap.py* client and the RNmap `/lib` directory to our SUSE client workstation where we have already installed Python and try to connect back to the RNmap server. Again, for the purposes of our demo, we won't be using SSL and we made a quick-access RNmap directory and dropped the client and the lib files in our Python directory structure to keep things simple. Now, let's see if the client is going to work (Usage instructions edited for fit):

```
Vmware2:/Python/RNmap-lib # python rnmap.py -nossl

Rnmap cli client v. 0.10

Copyright (C) 2000-2003 Tuomo Makinen
Redistributable under the terms of the GNU General Public License

Usage:
    -s address       Rnmap server address
    -p port          Server port (default 3418)
    -f file          Filename to save the scanning result (no stdout)
    -n cmd           Nmap command
    -u user          Username
    -c file          Text file with Username, Password & Server:Port info
                     (Newline separated)
    -help            Prints this message
    -nossl           Turns SSL support off
    -mparseable      Use machine parseable log form
    -scriptkiddie    Use script kiddie log form
    -xml             Use xml log form

    -version         Show version of rnmap cli client

    example:
    # rnmap.py -s 192.168.1.78 -n "-sS -p 1-65535 192.168.1.10" -mparseable
```

Looks good! Now we'll move on to some usage examples in the next section and see if we can get some results.

Example Usage

For our first RNmap client/server test, we'll perform a simple scan of a Windows XP Pro laptop. Using the example from the RNmap usage instructions as our guide, let's test our setup and output the results to a text file:

```
Vmware2:/Python/RNmap-lib # python rnmap.py -nossl -s 10.1.0.195 -f TestResults.txt
-n "-sS -p 1-65535 10.1.0.194"
Username for 10.1.0.195: Test1
Password:
```

You won't see the password as you type it in, but keep in mind that we are using RNmap without SSL, so your password will be sent in clear-text across the network. Ultimately, you would want to integrate the SSL option in order to protect your users' passwords from casual network sniffing. Once our Nmap session completes, we can view the TestResults.txt file that was created:

```
Vmware2:/Python/RNmap-lib # more TestResults.txt
# Nmap 4.52 scan initiated Wed Jan 9 04:28:04 2008 as: /usr/bin/nmap
-sS -p 1-65535 -oN - 10.1.0.194
Interesting ports on 10.1.0.194:
Not shown: 65531 closed ports
PORT     STATE  SERVICE
135/tcp  open   msrpc
139/tcp  open   netbios-ssn
445/tcp  open   microsoft-ds
3389/tcp open   ms-term-serv
MAC Address: 00:12:3F:CB:43:12 (Dell)

# Nmap done at Wed Jan 9 04:28:26 2008 - 1 IP address (1 host up)
scanned in 22.656 seconds
```

It is important to think about where you end up placing the RNmap server in your infrastructure and how you control access to the service. The INSTALL and README files included with the package both talk about locking down access via the use of a *chrooted jail* and *SSL*, respectively. Once you extract the files from the RNmap package, you will find both of these files in your newly-created *rnmap* directory. By properly securing access to your new RNmap server, encrypting communication to it and properly storing the results information, you will reap the benefits of utilizing Nmap in this client/server relationship. As you grow your RNmap infrastructure, another security item to think about is logging for auditing of users and scans run.

Bilbo

Bilbo is a Perl script that can control and track Nmap scans by virtue of creating a reporting file that acts as a flat-file database for your scan information. All that is required is Nmap, the ability to execute a set of Perl instructions (the *bilbo* script), and a trivial amount of patience to get your first scan off the ground and running.

Source and Install

Bilbo can be found at http://doornenburg.homelinux.net/scripts/bilbo/. Once you download the package to your UNIX system, you will have to extract the contents of the package to a directory on your hard drive. You can also investigate the contents of the file, without extracting anything, by first using `tar` with the `-t` option:

```
Bilbo-server:/software/download # gzip -dc bilbo-0.12.tar.gz | tar -tvf -
-rwx------ bart/bart      12672 2005-09-24 13:28:27 bilbo
-rw------- bart/bart        281 2005-09-24 13:05:02 infile.example
```

This shows us the contents of the file. One thing to notice with this particular package is that the files are packaged in such a way that they will be extracted to whatever directory you happen to be in at the time, unless you specify your own directory. You can also see that the files were packaged under the user-permissions of the package creator, *bart*. When we extract these files, this is what happens:

```
Bilbo-server:/software/download # gzip -dc bilbo-0.12.tar.gz | tar -xvf -
bilbo
infile.example
```

Let's take a quick look at the user and group permissions assigned to the files. Remember, in the original package, both files were owned by 'Bart'.

```
Bilbo-server:/software/download # ls -alt
-rwx------   1     500    500    12672 Sep 24   2005 bilbo
-rw-------   1     500    500      281 Sep 24   2005 infile.example
```

We can see that our UNIX server interpreted bart's permissions with a new *UID* and *GID* of 500. For the purposes of this example, we are manipulating the files under the *root* user account, so this shouldn't impact us. However, in a production environment, you will want to investigate tightening permissions on both files and setting up either a *chroot*'d environment or a *sudo*-ers file for access.

TIP

Since we don't have a user named *bart* on our Bilbo-server, the system has automatically assigned a user numerical ID (*UID*) of 500 and a group numerical ID (*GID*) of 500 to each of the files. Depending on which Linux platform you are using, in addition to the *UID*s and *GID*s you already have established, your mileage may vary on what IDs actually get assigned. You will need to *chown* and *chmod* the permissions of both files. *Chown* will allow you assign the 2 files to a new owner on your OS and *chmod* will help you set the appropriate permissions on the files for the new owner.

Let's open `infile.example` to see what it looks like and get a feeling for what we are going to be setting up:

```
# Example inputfile for Bilbo.
# $id$
# Lines starting with a # are ignored.

# as empty lines too.
# Add ip-addresses:
1.2.3.4

# Or hostnames:
host.my.lan

# Or networks:
192.168.21.0/24

# Even change the behaviour of nmap on the flight:
<OPT> -sT -sU -PT80,443,25
my.new.host
```

This looks pretty straightforward. We can add in individual IP addresses, hostnames, or subnets to scan, in addition to manipulating the Nmap options. In the next section, we'll make a copy of the infile and tune it to run some test scans.

Are You Owned?

Checking File Integrity

Anytime you download a new tool that you want to install, be sure to look for the developer's *hash* of their file. This hash provides a way of checking the integrity of the file you downloaded against what the developer says he or she created. For example, the owner or tool developer will use a tool like *md5sum* to generate an MD5 hash of their *tar.gz*, *.exe*, or *.zip* file. After you download a copy of that tool, run your own md5 hash of the program you downloaded. If the hash your tool generates matches the one the developer has published, then you know you have downloaded the same copy. Now, keep in mind that this does not mean that the program is free of malware; it just means that your copy matches whatever the developer created. You still have to rely on your common sense and remember to only download from reputable sites.

Here's an example of using md5sum to generate a hash for the Bilbo download file:

```
host1:/home/beckyp # md5sum bilbo-0.12.tar.gz
b12b3cd0ae2498c65837da00210c7999 bilbo-0.12.tar.gz
```

If we compare this hash to the information published on the Bilbo website http://doornenburg.homelinux.net/scripts/bilbo/#download, we can determine that the integrity of our download package matches what the developer created:

```
September 24, 2005: version 0.12
MD5 from this version: b12b3cd0ae2498c65837da00210c7999
```

Example Usage

Let's copy (`cp`) the file to a new file, `bilbo-infile`, add in our small subnet, create some simple Nmap-specific settings and clean it up. Now our infile looks like this:

```
# Add ip-addresses:
10.0.0.0/24
# Even change the behaviour of nmap on the flight:
<OPT> -sS
```

Running the Bilbo scan itself is nice and straightforward. If you type in ./Bilbo and hit enter, you can read the usage instructions:

```
Bilbo-server:/software/download # ./bilbo

Usage (as root): ./bilbo
        -i      <infile> File with hosts or networks to scan
        -r      <reportfile> Filename where the report will be
        -t      <tune> Limit the amount of simultanous scans (default: 5)
        -d      <debug> 0, 1 or 2 for more debug-info (default:0)
        -m      <Match-mode> 0, 1 or 2 for not, compare or compare-and-update
                the open-port-database (default: 2)
        -h      <help> This text
```

Let's try it and see what happens.

```
Bilbo-server:/software/download # ./bilbo -i bilbo-infile -r bilbo-test
New nmap_options: -sS --append_output -oG /tmp/bilbo-infile.tmp
```

It looks like our scan completed successfully; you can see how Bilbo kept track of the results by writing a temporary file in the /tmp directory. If you try to find that file once the scan completes, you will find that it has disappeared. The results get written to the report we named in the command line. We can view the results of our bilbo-test report file (edited for brevity):

```
Bilbo-server:/software/download # cat bilbo-test
Scanning host 10.0.0.0/24 for open ports.
Host: 10.0.0.1 () has open ports:
  Port: 23 - tcp - telnet
  Port: 80 - tcp - http
Host: 10.0.0.2 () has open ports:
  Port: 135 - tcp - msrpc
  Port: 139 - tcp - netbios-ssn
  Port: 1026 - tcp - LSA-or-nterm
Host 10.0.0.3 up, but doesn't show open ports.
Host 10.0.0.4 up, but doesn't show open ports.
Host: 10.0.0.5 () has open ports:
  Port: 22 - tcp - ssh
  Port: 111 - tcp - rpcbind
  Port: 631 - tcp - ipp
Host: 10.0.0.6 () has open ports:
  Port: 135 - tcp - msrpc
```

```
  Port: 139 - tcp - netbios-ssn
  Port: 445 - tcp - microsoft-ds
  Port: 1025 - tcp - NFS-or-IIS
```

According to the Bilbo usage instructions, the port database is set to update automatically if we scan these hosts again and any changes have occurred. The server listening at 10.0.0.3 was setup with a firewall, so we'll disable that first and see what Bilbo reports:

```
Bilbo-server:/software/download # cat bilbo-test
Scanning host 10.0.0.0/24 for open ports.
Host: 10.0.0.1 () has open ports:
  Port: 23 - tcp - telnet
  Port: 80 - tcp - http
Host: 10.0.0.2 () has open ports:
  Port: 135 - tcp - msrpc
  Port: 139 - tcp - netbios-ssn
  Port: 1026 - tcp - LSA-or-nterm
Host: 10.0.0.3 () has open ports:
  Port: 80 - tcp - http
  ** New host 10.0.0.3 found, no ports to compare.
  ** Host added.
  Port: 135 - tcp - msrpc
  ** New port found on host 10.0.0.3 : port 135
  ** Port added to database.
  Port: 443 - tcp - https
  ** New port found on host 10.0.0.3 : port 443
  ** Port added to database.
Host 10.0.0.4 up, but doesn't show open ports.
Host: 10.0.0.5 () has open ports:
  Port: 22 - tcp - ssh
  Port: 111 - tcp - rpcbind
  Port: 631 - tcp - ipp
Host: 10.0.0.6 () has open ports:
  Port: 135 - tcp - msrpc
  Port: 139 - tcp - netbios-ssn
  Port: 445 - tcp - microsoft-ds
  Port: 1025 - tcp - NFS-or-IIS
```

Bilbo successfully identified that new ports were added for the 10.0.0.3 host. Let's conduct one more test by using netcat to open a fake listening port on one of the systems and see if Bilbo catches it. On the 10.0.0.5 SUSE laptop, we'll set up a very easy listener like this:

```
netcat -l -p 53
```

Now let's kick off Bilbo with the same infile and see what results we get this time:

```
Bilbo-server:/software/download # cat bilbo-test
Scanning host 10.0.0.0/24 for open ports.
Host: 10.0.0.1 () has open ports:
  Port: 23 - tcp - telnet
  Port: 80 - tcp - http
Host: 10.0.0.2 () has open ports:
  Port: 135 - tcp - msrpc
  Port: 139 - tcp - netbios-ssn
  Port: 1026 - tcp - LSA-or-nterm
Host: 10.0.0.3 () has open ports:
  Port: 80 - tcp - http
  Port: 135 - tcp - msrpc
  Port: 443 - tcp - https
Host 10.0.0.4 up, but doesn't show open ports.
Host: 10.0.0.5 () has open ports:
  Port: 22 - tcp - ssh
  Port: 53 - tcp - domain
  ** New port found on host 10.0.0.5 : port 53
  ** Port added to database.
  Port: 111 - tcp - rpcbind
  Port: 631 - tcp - ipp
Host: 10.0.0.6 () has open ports:
  Port: 135 - tcp - msrpc
  Port: 139 - tcp - netbios-ssn
  Port: 445 - tcp - microsoft-ds
  Port: 1025 - tcp - NFS-or-IIS
```

Notice that the changes to 10.0.0.3 from our last scan are no longer highlighted, but we do see that Bilbo found a listening TCP port 53 on the 10.0.0.5 host. It appears that Bilbo's strength is in open port detection and high-level service identification. Incorporating –O into the Nmap options (to perform operating system identification) did not return any OS information in the subsequent report. However, it is a quick and efficient tool to use for comparing high level port scans.

Nmap-Parser

The Nmap-Parser has the ability to parse Nmap scan data using Perl, and based on user-crafted and supplied scripts, output specific scan data. Essentially the administrator can feed it Nmap output, parse it, and then interpret the parsed results.

Source and Install

The creator of *Nmap::Parser*, Anthony Persaud, has made the application available via *CPAN*.

> **Tools & Traps...**
>
> ### Using the Comprehensive Perl Archive Network
>
> CPAN stands for Comprehensive Perl Archive Network and is also a Perl module (CPAN.pm) that is used to download and install packages from CPAN. Like many online software repositories, CPAN depends on its end-users to keep it running like a well-oiled machine. Or in the words of the CPAN site itself:
>
> *How does the CPAN work?*
>
> *With dark magic, evil-looking sacrificial knives and scantily clad virgins under pale moonlight.*
>
> *It actually works with the generosity and cooperation of hundreds of developers, over 100 participating mirrors, funet.fi donating the network bandwidth, storage space and computing power, volunteers who help keep everything together and users whose interest in Perl keep the archive alive and growing.*

If you have a fairly recent Linux platform installed, odds are you already have Perl and can type in CPAN and hit enter to get to the CPAN prompt. From here, it really is as simple as typing `install Nmap::Parser` (edited for length of output):

```
cpan> install Nmap::Parser
CPAN: Storable loaded ok
LWP not available
CPAN: Net::FTP loaded ok
Fetching with Net::FTP:
  ftp://ftp.perl.org/pub/CPAN/authors/01mailrc.txt.gz
```

```
Couldn't fetch 01mailrc.txt.gz from ftp.perl.org
Trying with "/usr/bin/wget -O -" to get
  ftp://ftp.perl.org/pub/CPAN/authors/01mailrc.txt.gz
  -23:37:04- ftp://ftp.perl.org/pub/CPAN/authors/01mailrc.txt.gz
               => `-'
Resolving ftp.perl.org...64.27.65.115, 209.221.142.118
Connecting to ftp.perl.org|64.27.65.115|:21...connected.
Logging in as anonymous...Logged in!
==> SYST...done. ==> PWD...done.
==> TYPE I...done. ==> CWD /pub/CPAN/authors...done.
==> PASV...done. ==> RETR 01mailrc.txt.gz...done.
Length: 139,180 (136K) (unauthoritative)

100%[=====================================================================>] 139,180
365.97K/s

23:37:05 (364.99 KB/s) - `-' saved [139180]

Going to read /root/.cpan/sources/authors/01mailrc.txt.gz
<snip many, many pages of output>
  CPAN.pm: Going to build A/AP/APERSAUD/Nmap-Parser-1.12.tar.gz

cp Parser.pm blib/lib/Nmap/Parser.pm
Manifying blib/man3/Nmap::Parser.3pm
/usr/bin/make -- OK
Running make test
PERL_DL_NONLAZY=1 /usr/bin/perl "-MExtUtils::Command::MM" "-e"
"test_harness(0, 'blib/lib', 'blib/arch')" t/*.t
t/callback....ok
t/instance....ok
t/parser  ....ok
t/scanner.....ok
All tests successful.
Files=4, Tests=176, 3 wallclock secs ( 1.17 cusr + 0.66 csys = 1.83 CPU)
   /usr/bin/make test -- OK
Running make install
Installing /usr/lib/perl5/site_perl/5.8.7/Nmap/Parser.pm
Installing /usr/share/man/man3/Nmap::Parser.3pm
Writing /usr/lib/perl5/site_perl/5.8.7/i586-linux-thread-multi/auto/Nmap/Parser/.
packlist
Appending installation info to /usr/lib/perl5/5.8.7/i586-linux-thread-multi/
perllocal.pod
   /usr/bin/make install -- OK

cpan>
```

If you prefer to install on a Windows system, Anthony Persaud has made a *win32* package available as well.

NOTE

You will need to have a copy of *ActiveState Perl 5.8.x*, which can be found at www.activestate.com/Products/activeperl/. You can purchase the ActivePerl DVD for USD $39 + shipping and handling or download a copy for free. The Microsoft Installer (MSI) is only 15.8MB and a quick download on a DSL or cable modem line. After you get the MSI downloaded, it is a simple double-click to install *ActivePerl* to your workstation.

The README file contained in the UNIX package indicates that installation is as simple as:

```
ACTIVESTATE PERL (Perl Package Manager) - MSWin32
Run this in the command prompt:
   ppm install Nmap-Parser

This should contact the ActiveState repository, download the file and install it
automagically.
```

However, the ActiveState repository could not locate the file when attempting the installation in this manner. Fortunately, the latest Nmap-Parser version (1.12) was discovered on another repository found at trouchelle.com. Using this site, it is possible to use the *Perl Package Manager* (PPM) to quickly and easily install Nmap-Parser and XML-Twig, a required package for the parser. Here's an example of installing both:

```
C:\Perl\bin>ppm install http://trouchelle.com/ppm/Nmap-Parser.ppd
ppm install failed: Can't find any package that provide XML-Twig for Nmap-Parser

C:\Perl\bin>ppm install http://trouchelle.com/ppm/XML-Twig.ppd
Downloading XML-Twig-3.32...done
Unpacking XML-Twig-3.32...done
Generating HTML for XML-Twig-3.32...done
Updating files in site area...done
18 files installed

C:\Perl\bin>ppm install http://trouchelle.com/ppm/Nmap-Parser.ppd
Downloading Nmap-Parser-1.12...done
Unpacking Nmap-Parser-1.12...done
Generating HTML for Nmap-Parser-1.12...done
Updating files in site area...done
   2 files installed
```

At this point, we are set with Nmap-Parser on our SUSE server and also installed on an XP Pro laptop. Let's run some Zenmap scans from the XP Pro laptop and use our win32-installed Nmap-Parser to help interpret the results. We'll be using a sample script provided in the Nmap-Parser documentation found at http://search.cpan.org/~apersaud/Nmap-Parser/Parser.pm.

Example Usage

To showcase how much easier it is to use a tool like Nmap-Parser to pinpoint deltas in our Nmap scans; we must keep in mind that even our small scan of 6 hosts generates over 150 lines in the Nmap results XML file. Here is a sample of some of that output for only 1 host found in our report:


```
<?xml version="1.0" ?>
<?xml-stylesheet href="nmap.xsl" type="text/xsl"?>
<!- Nmap 4.53 scan initiated Wed Jan 16 00:30:47 2008 as: nmap -T
Aggressive -sV -n -O -oX nmap-results.xml -v 10.0.0.1-10 ->
<nmaprun scanner="nmap" args="nmap -T Aggressive -sV -n -O -oX nmap-results.xml -v
10.0.0.1-10" start="1200465047" startstr="Wed Jan 16 00:30:47 2008" version="4.53"
xmloutputversion="1.01">
<scaninfo type="syn" protocol="tcp" numservices="1714" services="1-1027,1029-
1033,1040,1043,1050,1058-1059,1067-1068,1076,1080,1083-1084,1103,1109-1110,1112,112
7,1139,1155,1158,1178,1212,1214,1220,1222,1234,1241,1248,1270,1337,1346-1381,1383-
1552,1600,1650-1652,1661-1672,1680,1720,1723,1755,1761-1764,1827,1900,1935,1984,198
6-2028,2030,2032-2035,2038,2040-2049,2053,2064-2065,2067-2068,2105-2106,2108,2111-
2112,2120-2121,2201,2232,2241,2301,2307,2401,2430-2433,2500-2501,2564,2600-
2605,2627-2628,2638,2766,2784,2809,2903,2998,3000-3001,3005-3006,3025,3045,3049,305
2,3064,3086,3128,3141,3264,3268-3269,3292,3299,3306,3333,3372,3389,3397-
3399,3421,3455-3457,3462,3531,3632,3689,3900,3984-3986,3999-4000,4002,4008,4045,412
5,4132-4133,4144,4199,4224,4321,4333,4343,4444,4480,4500,4557,4559,4660,4662,4672,4
899,4987,4998,5000-5003,5009-5011,5050,5060,5100-5102,5145,5190-
5193,5232,5236,5300-5305,5308,5400,5405,5432,5490,5500,5510,5520,5530,5540,5550,555
5,5560,5631-5632,5679-5680,5713-5717,5800-5803,5900-5903,5977-5979,5997-6009,6017,6
050,6101,6103,6105-6106,6110-6112,6141-6148,6222,6346-6347,6400-6401,6502,6543-
6544,6547-6548,6558,6588,6662,6665-6670,6699-6701,6881,6969,7000-
7010,7070,7100,7200-7201,7273,7326,7464,7597,7937-7938,8000,8007,8009,8021,8076,808
0-8082,8118,8123,8443,8770,8888,8892,9040,9050-9051,9090,9100-9107,9111,9152,9535,9
876,9991-9992,9999-10000,10005,10082-10083,11371,12000,12345-12346,13701-
13702,13705-13706,13708-13718,13720-13722,13782-13783,14141,15126,15151,16080,16444
,16959,17007,17300,18000,18181-18185,18187,19150,20005,22273,22289,22305,22321,2237
0,26208,27000-27010,27374,27665,31337,31416,32770-32780,32786-32787,38037,38292,431
88,44334,44442-44443,47557,49400,50000,50002,54320,61439-61441,65301" />
<verbose level="1" />
<debugging level="0" />
<taskbegin task="ARP Ping Scan" time="1200465047" />
<taskend task="ARP Ping Scan" time="1200465047" extrainfo="2 total hosts" />
```

```
<taskbegin task="SYN Stealth Scan" time="1200465047" />
<taskend task="SYN Stealth Scan" time="1200465056" extrainfo="3428 total ports" />
<taskbegin task="Service scan" time="1200465056" />
<taskend task="Service scan" time="1200465100" extrainfo="5 services on 2 hosts" />
<taskbegin task="SCRIPT ENGINE" time="1200465107" />
<taskend task="SCRIPT ENGINE" time="1200465107" />
<host><status state="up" reason="arp-response"/>
<address addr="10.0.0.1" addrtype="ipv4" />
<address addr="00:0F:B5:DF:AB:59" addrtype="mac" vendor="Netgear" />
<hostnames />
<ports><extraports state="filtered" count="1711">
<extrareasons reason="no-responses" count="1711"/>
</extraports>
<port protocol="tcp" portid="23"><state state="open" reason="syn-ack" reason_
ttl="64"/><service name="telnet" method="table" conf="3" /></port>
<port protocol="tcp" portid="80"><state state="open" reason="syn-ack" reason_
ttl="64"/><service name="tcpwrapped" method="probed" conf="8" /></port>
<port protocol="tcp" portid="1723"><state state="closed" reason="reset" reason_
ttl="64"/><service name="pptp" method="table" conf="3" /></port>
</ports>
<os><portused state="open" proto="tcp" portid="23" />
<portused state="closed" proto="tcp" portid="1723" />
<osclass type="WAP" vendor="Netgear" osfamily="embedded" accuracy="100" />
<osmatch name="Netgear WGR614v6 wireless broadband router" accuracy="100"
line="15462" />
<osmatch name="Netgear WGR614v7 wireless broadband router" accuracy="100"
line="15479" />
<osfingerprint fingerprint="
SCAN(V=4.53%D=1/16%OT=23%CT=1723%CU=%PV=Y%DS=1%G=N%M=000FB5%TM=478DA4D3%P=i686-pc-
windows-windows)
SEQ(SP=18%GCD=FA00%ISR=9D%TI=I%II=I%SS=S%TS=1)
OPS(O1=M5B4NW0NNT11%O2=M5B4NW0NNT11%O3=M5B4NW0NNT11%O4=M5B4NW0NNT11%O5=M5B4NW0NNT11
%O6=M5B4NNT11)
WIN(W1=2000%W2=2000%W3=2000%W4=2000%W5=2000%W6=2000)
ECN(R=Y%DF=N%TG=40%W=2000%O=M5B4NW0%CC=N%Q=)
T1(R=Y%DF=N%TG=40%S=O%A=S+%F=AS%RD=0%Q=)
T2(R=N)
T3(R=N)
T4(R=N)
T5(R=Y%DF=N%TG=40%W=0%S=Z%A=S+%F=AR%O=%RD=0%Q=)
T6(R=N)
```

```
T7(R=N)
U1(R=N)
IE(R=Y%DFI=S%TG=40%TOSI=S%CD=S%SI=S%DLI=S)
" />
</os>
<uptime seconds="713125" lastboot="(null)" />
<distance value="1" />
<tcpsequence index="24" class="unknown class" difficulty="Good luck!" values="FE65C
5BD,FE66BFBD,FE67B9BD,FE68B3BD,FE69ADBD,FE6C9BBD" />
<ipidsequence class="Incremental" values="3FE8,3FEA,3FEC,3FEE,3FF0,3FF2" />
<tcptssequence class="2HZ" values="15C33C,15C33C,15C33C,15C33C,15C33C,15C33D" />
<times srtt="0" rttvar="87" to="100000" />
</host>
```

The value of a tool like Nmap-Parser, with its ability to utilize scripts to parse and evaluate Nmap results, becomes readily apparent after attempting to manually review the previous Nmap XML output. With Nmap-Parser, we can run a quick script to compare our two results files and discover the following:

```
C:\perl\bin\perl NP_test3.pl
10.0.0.5 has these new ports open: 53 seems to be domain
```

The NP_test3.pl script incorporated one of the example scripts from Anthony Persaud's documentation and ultimately we simply compared one set of Nmap results to another. Review the bolded area of the script below:

```
use Nmap::Parser;
use vars qw($nmap_exe $nmap_args @ips);
my $base = new Nmap::Parser;
my $curr = new Nmap::Parser;

$base->parsefile('nmap-results.xml'); #load previous scan results
$curr->parsefile('nmap-results2.xml'); #load current scan results

for my $ip ($curr->get_ips )
{
        #assume that IPs in base == IPs in curr scan
        my $ip_base = $base->get_host($ip);
        my $ip_curr = $curr->get_host($ip);
        my %port = ();
        #find ports that are open that were not open before
        #by finding the difference in port lists
```

```
        my @diff = grep { $port{$_} < 2}
                    (map {$port{$_}++; $_}
                    ( $ip_curr->tcp_open_ports , $ip_base->tcp_open_ports ));
        print "$ip has these new ports open: ".join(',',@diff) if(scalar @diff);
        for (@diff){print "$_ seems to be ",$ip_curr->tcp_service($_)->name,"\n";}
}
```

The full power of Nmap-parser provides the administrator with the ability to craft new and enterprise-specific parsing, scanning, and interpretive scripts. The only negative with this approach to interpreting Nmap results is that if the administrator is not Perl-savvy, they will be getting a crash course in the language.

Summary

In this chapter, we discussed four different tools that were developed to assist with running, collecting, interpreting and comparing Nmap results. We discussed NDiff, which is great for taking output from one scan and very quickly comparing it to another scan of the same environment. It functions much like any other diff command. Next we covered a client/server tool called RNmap or Remote Nmap. RNmap helps by creating a centralized Nmap scanning server and provides the capability to authenticate remote users to the service. We discussed another open source help-application called Bilbo. It provides a flat-file database of scan results and a configuration file for controlling scan data. The database keeps track of results and from one scan to the next and can alert the administrator to changes in IP address, port, or service. Finally we reviewed a Perl module called Nmap-Parser which provides a way to create scripts and parse Nmap output in a multitude of ways. The administrator is limited only by their imagination and potentially their Perl expertise.

Discovering a user community that creates and supports good quality helper-apps like these is one of the great advantages to working with open source software. In the enterprise architecture, you may find that as your Nmap capabilities grow, your reliance on the information output also grows. You will have the potential to incorporate Nmap results into security reviews, system inventory lists, production change control tickets, malware analysis, and the list goes on. Knowing that add-on tools exist for Nmap and using the examples in this chapter as a guide, you will be able to design and implement your own enterprise solutions.

Solutions Fast Track

NDiff–Nmap Diff

- ☑ NDiff is useful for comparison assistance when working with large numbers of ongoing Nmap scans that have a high degree of output.
- ☑ Nmap machine parseable files have an extension of `.nm`. They are created with the `-m` switch.
- ☑ NDiff can be used to construct a desired baseline and then compare Nmap scans to it in order to determine your infrastructure compliance.

RNmap–Remote Nmap

- ☑ RNmap provides client/server architecture for centralizing the use of Nmap in your enterprise.
- ☑ Python is a requirement to successfully install and run RNmap.
- ☑ The RNmap administrator must set up each user and associated password in the users.list file.
- ☑ Passwords are stored as one-way hashes in the users.list file.

Bilbo

- ☑ Bilbo uses Perl to read in an input file that contains instructions for performing Nmap scans and creating output reports in a port database.
- ☑ The Bilbo port database is automatically updated with any changes that are discovered during subsequent scans.
- ☑ Bilbo operates best as a fast, high-level port scan comparison tool.

Nmap-Parser

- ☑ A savvy Perl administrator can use Nmap-Parser to read in Nmap results, parse them, and output any variety of desired data.
- ☑ Nmap-Parser comes with some simple examples that can help new users get a feel for the tool's capabilities.
- ☑ Nmap-Parser can be installed using the Perl Package Manager (PPM).

Frequently Asked Questions

Q: How do I know which one of these tools will work in my infrastructure?

A: NDiff is probably the easiest tool to get started with as it takes the least amount of configuration and advanced programming knowledge. The cool thing is that you can grow your NDiff solution as your infrastructure needs increase. As you gain more comfort both with Nmap and the results it produces in your environment, you will be able to test other Nmap add-on applications.

Q: I'm really interested in the Nmap-Parser tool and I would like to learn more about programming Perl scripts for it. Where do you recommend I learn more about Perl?

A: There is a great 6-part **Beginner's Introduction to Perl** series hosted on the Perl website at www.perl.com/pub/a/2000/10/begperl1.html. Good luck!

Q: Argh! I can't get this tool to work! Help!

A: First, look for any online forums that are specific to the tool you are having problems with. Next check out the Nmap forums–you might find that your question has already been posted there. Finally, you can always politely describe your issue in the Nmap forum and see if you can get some assistance from one of the more experienced folks on the forum.

Chapter 8

Nmap Scanning in the Real World

Solutions in this chapter:

- **Detecting Nmap on your Network**
- **Discovering Stealthy Scanning Techniques**
- **Discovering Unauthorized Applications and Services**
- **Testing Incident Response and Managed Services Alerting**

☑ **Summary**

☑ **Solutions Fast Track**

☑ **Frequently Asked Questions**

Introduction

Now that you have learned how Nmap works and how to use it, you are armed and ready to perform real world scans and analyze the results. In this chapter we discuss real-world network scanning scenarios that you could encounter on your systems or network. It is also possible that you may be called upon to perform some of the advanced and stealthier types of scans in your environment, whether to see how your security measures react or to test the attentiveness of outsourced monitoring. You will learn how to interpret the scan results, how to discover more information, and how to act on the results.

Detecting Nmap on your Network

There may be times when an attacker or malicious insider uses Nmap against you. This may be reconnaissance preceding an attack or other information gathering purposes. This section shows you how to detect Nmap scans on your network. Each of the scans are detected and analyzed using the Wireshark network protocol analyzer. You could also use tcpdump or another protocol analyzer of your choice.

TCP Connect Scan

The first scan that we will analyze is the Nmap TCP Connect (-sT) scan. This type of scanning is the most basic because it completes the TCP three-way handshake with open ports and immediately closes them. Nmap first sends a SYN packet to each target port. A response packet with the Reset (RST) and Acknowledgment (ACK) flags set indicates that the port is closed. If a SYN/ACK is received, it indicates that the port is open and listening. Nmap will then respond with an ACK to complete the connection followed by an RST/ACK to immediately close the connection. This aspect of the scan makes it easily detectable at the system level because the error messages made during attempts to connect to a port will be logged.

Figure 8.1 shows the Nmap scanner system, 192.168.100.2, sending SYN packets to the target, 192.168.100.5. Most ports respond with an RST/ACK packet; however, packet 2904 shows the SYN/ACK response from port 139.

TIP

When you start sniffing TCP/IP traffic and working with packet captures, it can be very useful to have a TCP/IP Pocket Reference Guide by your side. Luckily for us, the SANS Institute has just such an item! You can download your copy here: www.sans.org/resources/tcpip.pdf.

Figure 8.1 TCP Connect Scan

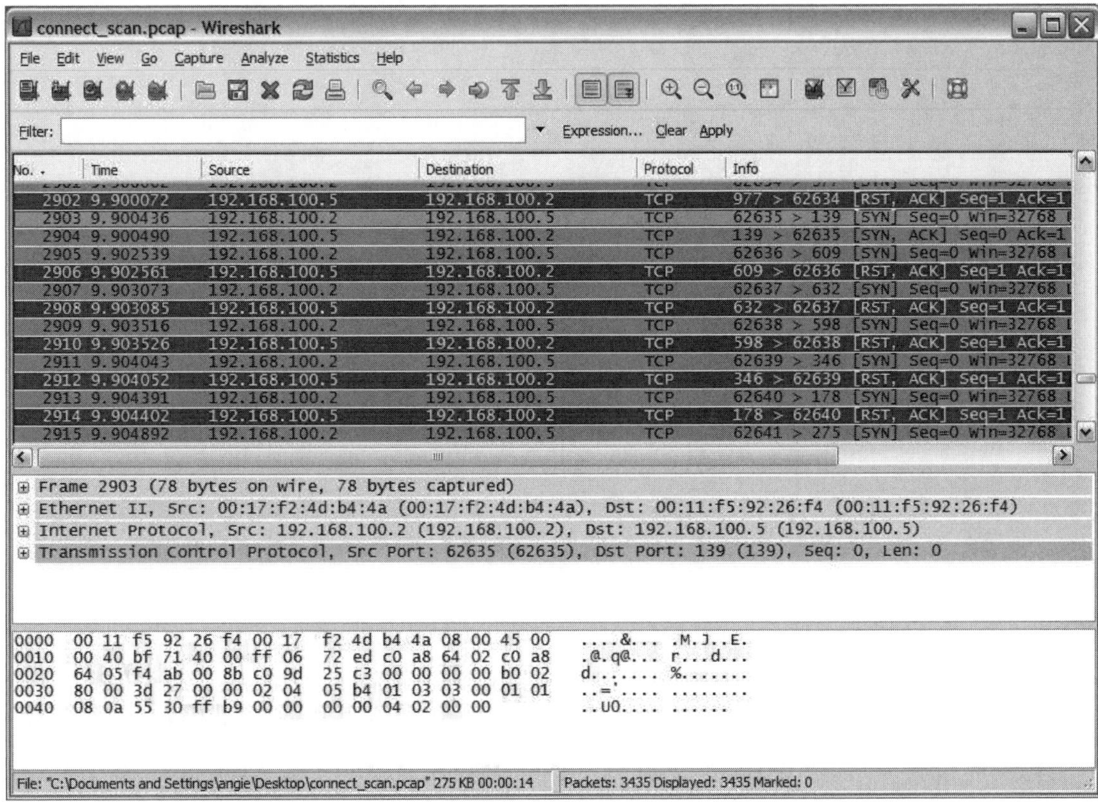

You can right click on the packet in the Wireshark output and choose Follow TCP Stream. This Wireshark feature shows only the packets affiliated with any particular connection. In our example, as shown in Figure 8.2, the extracted session shows the initial SYN packet, response SYN/ACK, and the subsequent ACK followed by the RST/ACK exchange on port 139.

Figure 8.2 Follow TCP Stream

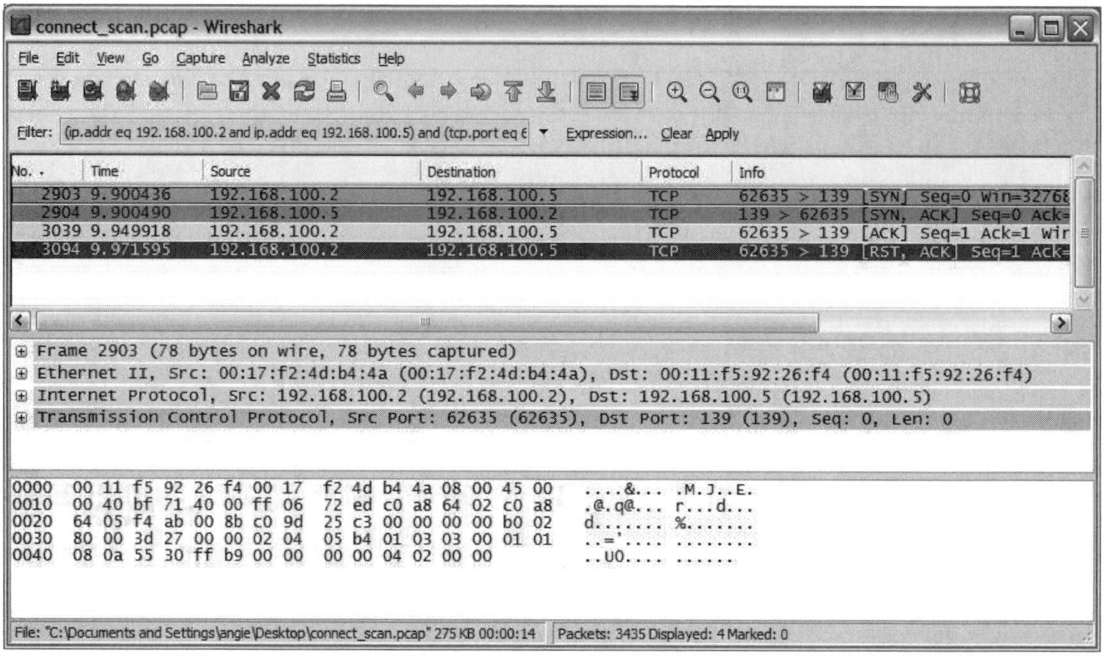

```
connect_scan.pcap - Wireshark
File  Edit  View  Go  Capture  Analyze  Statistics  Help
Filter: (ip.addr eq 192.168.100.2 and ip.addr eq 192.168.100.5) and (tcp.port eq 6   Expression...  Clear  Apply

No.  Time      Source         Destination    Protocol  Info
2903 9.900436  192.168.100.2  192.168.100.5  TCP       62635 > 139 [SYN] Seq=0 Win=32768
2904 9.900490  192.168.100.5  192.168.100.2  TCP       139 > 62635 [SYN, ACK] Seq=0 Ack=
3039 9.949918  192.168.100.2  192.168.100.5  TCP       62635 > 139 [ACK] Seq=1 Ack=1 Wir
3094 9.971595  192.168.100.2  192.168.100.5  TCP       62635 > 139 [RST, ACK] Seq=1 Ack=

⊞ Frame 2903 (78 bytes on wire, 78 bytes captured)
⊞ Ethernet II, Src: 00:17:f2:4d:b4:4a (00:17:f2:4d:b4:4a), Dst: 00:11:f5:92:26:f4 (00:11:f5:92:26:f4)
⊞ Internet Protocol, Src: 192.168.100.2 (192.168.100.2), Dst: 192.168.100.5 (192.168.100.5)
⊞ Transmission Control Protocol, Src Port: 62635 (62635), Dst Port: 139 (139), Seq: 0, Len: 0

0000  00 11 f5 92 26 f4 00 17  f2 4d b4 4a 08 00 45 00   ....&... .M.J..E.
0010  00 40 bf 71 40 00 ff 06  72 ed c0 a8 64 02 c0 a8   .@.q@... r...d...
0020  64 05 f4 ab 00 8b c0 9d  25 c3 00 00 00 00 b0 02   d....... %.......
0030  80 00 3d 27 00 00 02 04  05 b4 01 03 03 00 01 01   ..='.... ........
0040  08 0a 55 30 ff b9 00 00  00 00 04 02 00 00         ..U0.... ......

File: "C:\Documents and Settings\angie\Desktop\connect_scan.pcap" 275 KB 00:00:14   Packets: 3435 Displayed: 4 Marked: 0
```

Figure 8.3 shows the active ports on the target device. You can find these by using a filter such as `tcp.flags==18` to view packets with both the SYN and ACK flags set.

NOTE

TCP flags are located in the 13th byte of the TCP header (remember to begin counting into the header starting from 0). The flags are ECN ECN URG ACK | PSH RST SYN FIN. The ECN bits represent explicit congestion notification and are normally 0 unless implemented by the network infrastructure. The remaining flags stand for Urgent, Acknowledgement, Push, Reset, Synchronize and Finish and serve to describe the various parts of the TCP handshake and session process.

The filter `tcp.flags==18` will display packets with the SYN and ACK flags set because the binary value of the TCP flags field of a SYN/ACK packet is `0001 0010`, which equals `0x12` or `18` in decimal format.

Figure 8.3 SYN/ACK Responses

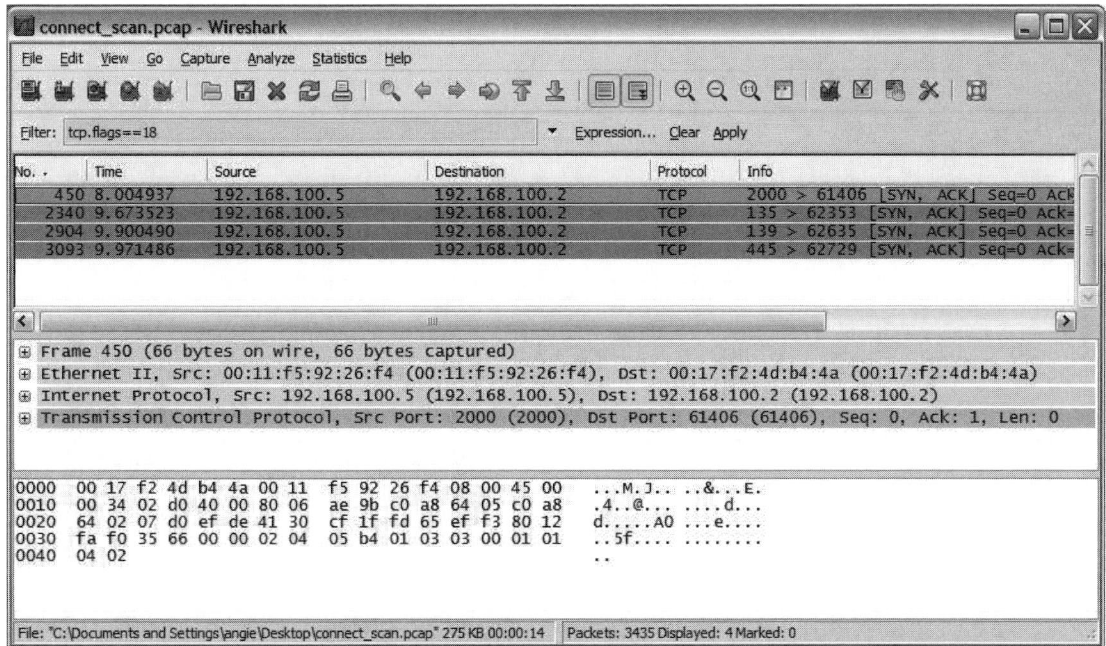

You are going to see a lot of TCP connect activity on your network as a result of normal network communications. However, the fact that the source IP address is connecting to so many ports and/or systems potentially indicates a scan. Also, unless stealth techniques are used, it is also another indicator of scanning activity to see a high number of connections within such a short time frame. IDS and IPS systems will oftentimes maintain a signature to detect scanning that looks for a certain number of sessions within a limited amount of time. If this limit is exceeded, the intrusion system will alert or respond accordingly. One example is to look for X number of SYN requests from a single host within a set number of seconds. This type of signature can generate false positives, but with customization to your specific infrastructure, it can also be a great alert for scanning activity.

The Snort sfPortscan preprocessor will detect Nmap TCP connect scanning activity. The previous scan generated the following entry in the Snort alert file:

```
[**] [122:1:0] (portscan) TCP Portscan [**]
01/13-20:30:31.107599 192.168.100.2 -> 192.168.100.5
PROTO255 TTL:0 TOS:0x0 ID:0 IpLen:20 DgmLen:161 DF
```

You may also use the Basic Analysis and Security Engine (BASE), which is a Web-based front-end for Snort. Figure 8.4 shows BASE with the portscan alerts generated from an Nmap TCP Connect scan.

Figure 8.4 BASE Alerts

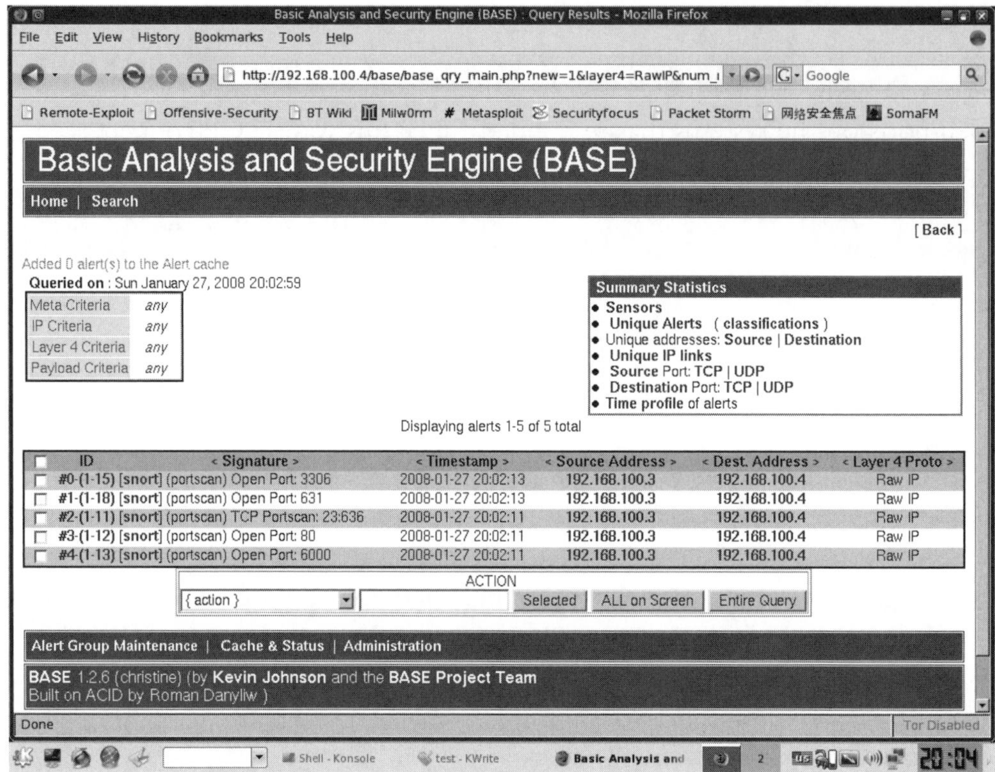

Tools & Traps…

Basic Analysis and Security Engine (BASE)

BASE is a highly-regarded Snort add-on tool that provides an easy way to review your Snort alerts. From the BASE about page:

"BASE is a web interface to perform analysis of intrusions that snort has detected on your network. It uses a user authentication and role-base system,

so that you as the security admin can decide what and how much information each user can see. It also has a simple to use, web-based setup program for people not comfortable with editing files directly."

You can download BASE from http://base.secureideas.net/.

Now you know the IP address of the system that was performing the scanning, and the open ports on the systems that responded. Since this was a TCP connect scan, the source IP address is not likely spoofed since it received and replied to packets. What else can we do with this information? If the scanner is an internal system, you should physically track it down to determine why it is sending this scan-like traffic. Notice we say "scan-like". The reason is that there could be a legitimate purpose for the traffic being generated by the internal system and it is wise to approach your search calmly, without starting a fire-drill. Many an administrator has been embarrassed by going off half-cocked in pursuit of an alleged attacker or hacked box, only to later find that the suspected malicious traffic was in fact, benign.

If this is a system external to your network, review your firewall policy to see how and why the scans are making it into the internal network in the first place. You should also look for other events and traffic targeting the host or indicating further reconnaissance. Depending on what you find, it might be a good idea to also evaluate the host for signs of compromise. If the system has been compromised, you should rebuild it. If this appears to be initial reconnaissance against the target, make sure that all patches are up to date on the system. If you are still seeing traffic from this source IP address, you may need to add a temporary rule to block packets from and to this source system. You should also investigate the open ports that responded to the scan. The attacker may have been looking for a particular open service (possibly because it has a new discovered vulnerability) or a Trojan port of some type.

SYN Scan

The next scan that we will analyze is a TCP SYN scan, also known as a *half-open scan* because a full TCP connection is never completed. Nmap first sends a SYN packet to each target port. If a RST/ACK is received, it indicates that the port is closed. If a SYN/ACK is received, it indicates that the port is open and listening. The part that makes this scan a half-open scan is that Nmap will then follow with an RST to close the connection (instead of the final ACK in the complete 3-way handshake). SYN scans were originally known as stealth scans because few systems would notice or log them because they never created a full connection. However, many current operating systems, firewalls and intrusion detection systems (IDSes) will notice and even log this type of activity.

In Figure 8.5, the attacker, 192.168.100.2, is sending SYN packets to the target, 192.168.100.5. Most ports respond with an RST/ACK packet; however, the highlighted packets 511 and 516 show the SYN/ACK response and the subsequent RST exchange on port 135.

Figure 8.5 SYN Scan

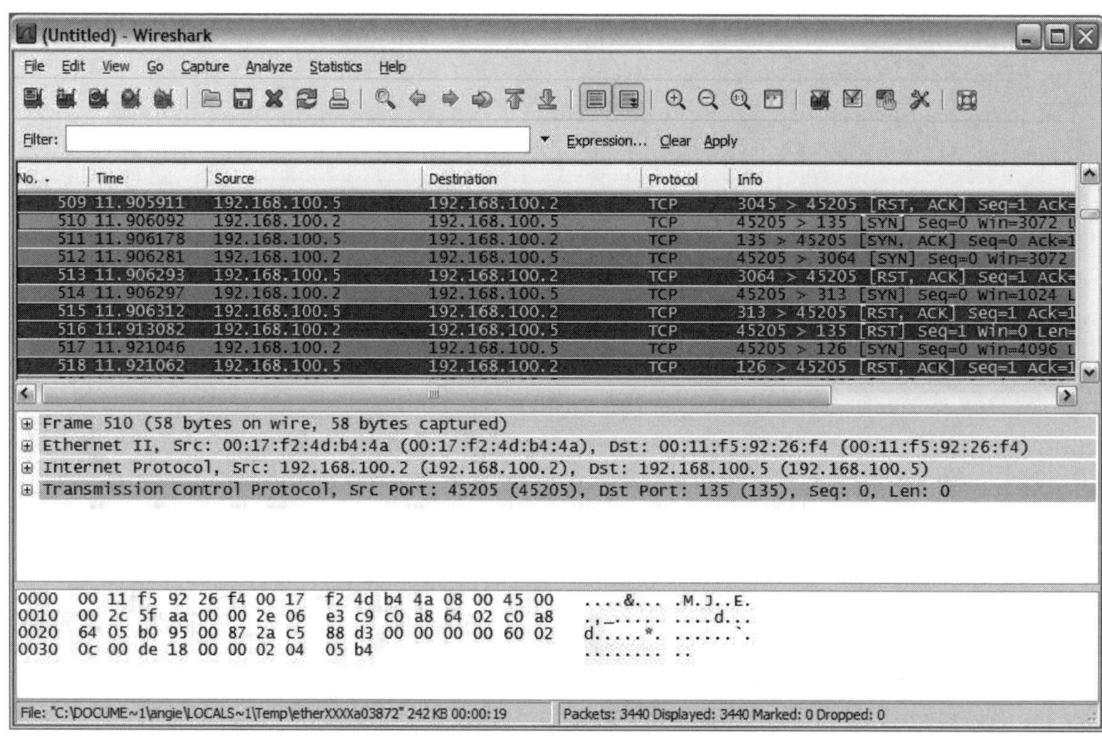

As with the TCP Connect scan, the Snort sfPortscan preprocessor will detect Nmap SYN scanning activity and generate an entry in the Snort alert file. You should follow the same response and mitigation recommendations as stated with the TCP Connect scan.

XMAS Scan

The XMAS scan determines which ports are open by sending packets with invalid flag settings to a target device. It is considered a stealth scan because it may be able to bypass some firewalls and IDSes more easily than the SYN scans. The Nmap XMAS scan sends packets with the Finish (FIN), Push (PSH), and Urgent (URG) flags set. Because this flag combination is invalid and should never occur in normal traffic, there is no established convention for dealing with these types of packets. Different TCP stacks will respond in different ways. Typically, closed ports will respond with a RST/ACK, and open ports will drop the packet and not respond. However, some TCP stacks will respond with RST packets from all ports, even open ports, and some systems will not respond to any packets. Personal firewalls and packet filters will also alter responses to this scan.

Notice that in Figure 8.6 the attacker, 192.168.100.5, is sending packets to the target, 192.168.2.1, with the FIN, PSH, and URG flags set. This scan is not receiving any responses to the XMAS packets.

Figure 8.6 XMAS Scan

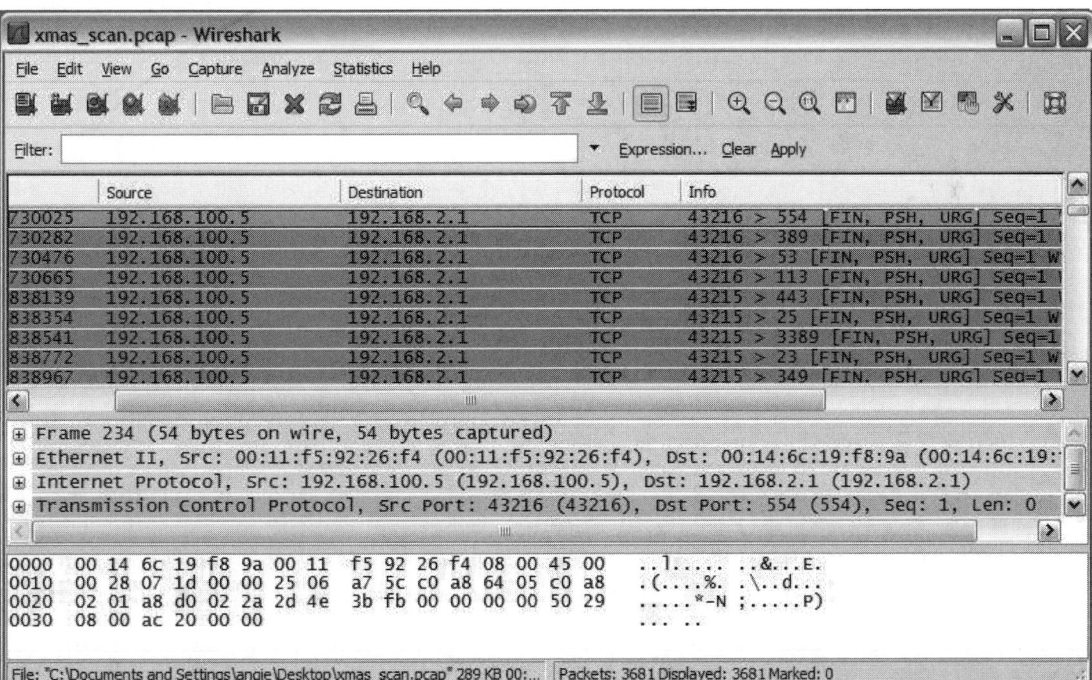

As previously mentioned, you should not see packets in normal traffic with the FIN, PSH, and URG flags set. The Snort SCAN nmap XMAS rule will detect Nmap XMAS scanning activity. The previous scan generated the following entry in the Snort alert file:

```
[**] [1:1228:7] SCAN nmap XMAS [**]
[Classification: Attempted Information Leak] [Priority: 2]
01/13-20:49:13.408003 0:11:F5:92:26:F4 -> 0:17:F2:4D:B4:4A type:0x800 len:0x36
192.168.100.5:55661 -> 192.168.100.2:23 TCP TTL:55 TOS:0x0 ID:12511 IpLen:20
DgmLen:40
**U*P**F Seq: 0x68134FB6 Ack: 0x0 Win: 0x1000 TcpLen: 20 UrgPtr: 0x0
[Xref => http://www.whitehats.com/info/IDS30]
```

You should follow the same response and mitigation recommendations as stated with the TCP Connect scan.

NOTE

In a well-documented, but little known fact, XMAS scans are so called because every flag is flipped on, like the lights on a Christmas tree. Notice however, that with the Nmap XMAS scan, only the FIN, PSH and URG flags are enabled.

Null Scan

The Null scan determines which ports are open by sending packets with invalid flag settings to a target device. Actually, the invalid flag settings are packets with all flags turned off (hence the name for the scan). Null scans were also originally considered very stealthy because of their ability to easily bypass operating system logging, firewalls and IDSes. However, much like the SYN scan, the prevalence of scan-specific signatures on network-based appliances and host intrusion prevention and detection applications have contributed to administrators' awareness with regards to this scan. Closed ports will respond with a RST/ACK, and open ports will drop the packet and not respond. However, some systems will respond with RST packets from all ports, even open ports, and some systems will not respond to any packets. Personal firewalls and filters will also alter responses to this scan.

In Figure 8.7, the attacker, 192.168.100.5, is sending packets to the target, 192.168.100.2, with all flags turned off, as indicated by the empty brackets [].This scan is not receiving any responses to the NULL packets. Notice that the intruder is using a static source port of 80. Specifying a popular source port that is often allowed through firewalls (such as Web port 80 or DNS port 53) is a common way for the Nmap scan to evade firewall restrictions.

Figure 8.7 Null Scan

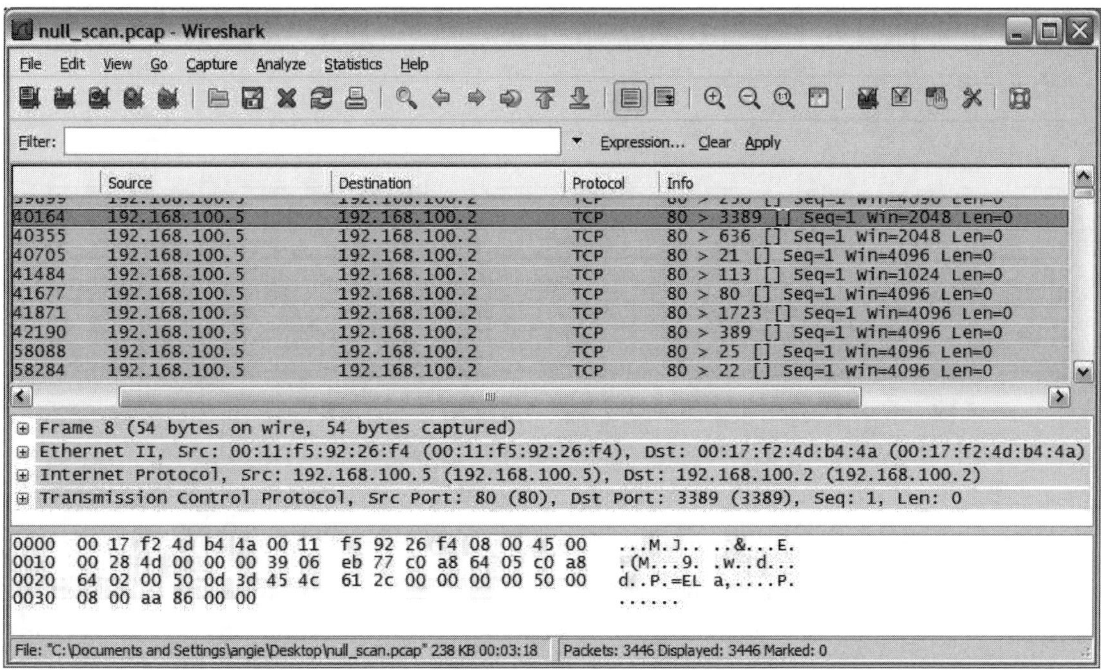

You should not see packets in normal traffic without any flags set.The good news is that Snort has a rule to detect null scans; be sure it is integrated into your rule set and test its responsiveness.You should follow the same response and mitigation recommendations as stated with the TCP Connect scan.

Discovering Stealthy Scanning Techniques

In this section, we'll cover some Nmap examples of packet fragmentation, decoy and evasion techniques to see what they look like from the sniffer perspective and to see if our IDS can detect them.

We discussed fragmentation and address spoofing in Chapter 4, but we'll readdress briefly here. Packet fragmentation is a common evasion technique that splits the packet header across many smaller packets. When used maliciously, this technique has the ability to break up distinguishing characteristics across packets and evade pattern matching detection techniques. Nmap can fragment packets by using the `-f` option. After the IP header, this option breaks data in the packets apart into 8 byte chunks. If you use this option twice, Nmap will break the packets into a maximum of 16 bytes after the IP header. The `--mtu` (Maximum Transmission Unit) option can also be utilized instead of the `-f` option to specify packet size for fragmentation in multiples of 8. For example, the following command line options perform the same fragmentation:

```
nmap -f -f 192.168.100.0/24
nmap --mtu 16 192.168.100.0/24
```

TIP

The MTU, or Maximum Transmission Unit, of a link determines whether or not a packet will have to be fragmented. Packets created on networks with larger MTUs will be fragmented by routers in front of networks with smaller MTUs. The MTU for Ethernet is 1500 bytes.

Packet fragmentation doesn't always evade security controls these days because controls have built in techniques to detect and handle fragmentation. However, because packet reassembly can be quite processor intensive, it is also common for administrators to disable or turn down the responsiveness of this functionality. You will have to determine a happy medium for your own infrastructure and processing capabilities.

As an additional reminder, spoofing is another evasion technique where you mask your IP address by pretending to be another system on the Internet or network. The Nmap decoy scan (`-D`) combines source address spoofing and multiple, fake host IP addresses (the decoys) in an attempt to evade true source detection. You can specify multiple decoys as a comma separated parameter. You can also specify your source IP address by using the word *ME* in the list to represent the position for your actual scanning system; otherwise Nmap positions your system randomly. The theory is that positioning your system further into the list increases the chances that you will not be detected because the victim will be too busy researching the first IP addresses that scan them.

Attackers often use real IP addresses of innocent, active hosts on the Internet, but for enterprise auditing this may not be necessary, and may even get you into trouble if the owners of the active systems take action. Remember, they will receive any traffic responses to their addresses that are generated by your scan. For security testing purposes you can specify other IP addresses in your network, maybe even ones set up in a development or lab environment for this purpose. If the scans in question are originating from the same subnet that the victim resides on, one simple way to determine whether or not the IP addresses are decoys is by looking closely at the layer 2 details of the packet capture. If it reveals the same Media Access Control (MAC) address for all IP addresses, you are dealing with spoofed IP addresses. Why would this answer not be applicable if the scan is originating from another subnet? Keep in mind that the upstream router's MAC address will appear as the source MAC in this case.

Nmap Fragment Scan

Let's test a personal firewall running on a fully-patched Windows 2000 Pro server that is sitting in our DMZ. This particular system should only have port 80 accessible as it is serving up a small, static Website. We'll try a fragmentation scan against the server and since we'll be testing from the same subnet, we'll also incorporate some decoy IP addresses and see what the MAC addresses look like in our Wireshark results.

The intended victim, our personal firewall-protected W2K server, has several typical Windows services listening. However, the firewall is configured to only allow DNS queries, ping traffic and inbound HTTP requests, as shown in Figure 8.8.

Figure 8.8 Personal Firewall Rules for W2K Test Server

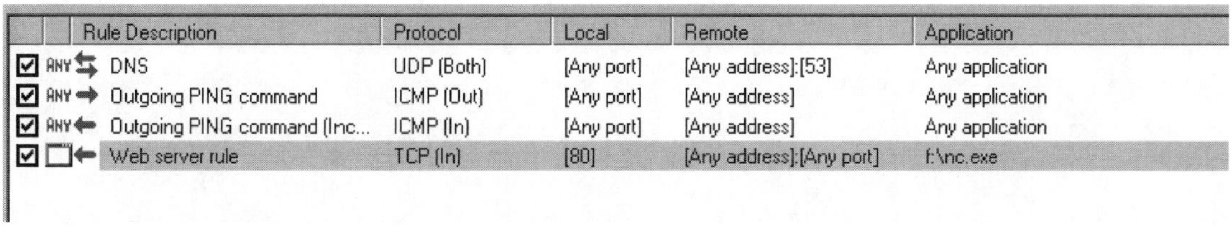

	Rule Description	Protocol	Local	Remote	Application
☑ ANY ⇆	DNS	UDP (Both)	[Any port]	[Any address]:[53]	Any application
☑ ANY →	Outgoing PING command	ICMP (Out)	[Any port]	[Any address]	Any application
☑ ANY ←	Outgoing PING command (Inc...	ICMP (In)	[Any port]	[Any address]	Any application
☑ ☐ ←	Web server rule	TCP (In)	[80]	[Any address]:[Any port]	f:\nc.exe

We want to see how this personal firewall handles an Nmap fragmentation scan. Here is the Nmap command for performing our test:

```
C:\downloads>nmap -f -D 10.0.0.10,10.0.0.15,10.0.0.33,ME,10.0.0.67,10.0.0.99 10.0.0.2
```

Notice in the Nmap command above, we used the word *ME* to place the scanning system after the decoy 10.0.0.33 in the list. We inserted several non-existent IP addresses into the decoy list. The IP address that we are scanning is the last item shown in the command, 10.0.0.2. The scan is being performed from a host with the IP address of 10.0.0.7. Wireshark was also set up to capture the details of this scan. Here are the results from Nmap:

```
Starting Nmap 4.53 (http://insecure.org) at 2008-02-01 16:39 Central Standard Time
All 1714 scanned ports on 10.0.0.2 are filtered
MAC Address: 00:02:E3:13:36:4B (Lite-on Communications)

Nmap done: 1 IP address (1 host up) scanned in 72.672 seconds
```

It looks like our personal firewall is doing a pretty good job against this type of scan! Nmap was able to determine that all of the ports scanned (we used Nmap's default port scanning list) are in the filtered state. If you recall from our previous chapters, this state implies the fact that Nmap can determine some type of filtering is occurring based on the results received from the scan. Now, let's check out our Wireshark output and see what those decoy IP addresses look like.

Nmap Decoys

In the first Wireshark screenshot, we can see the details from one of the decoy IP addresses. If you look at the packet details in the lower half of the screenshot, you can see the MAC address information captured by Wireshark, as shown in Figure 8.9.

Figure 8.9 Wireshark Output of Nmap Fragment Scan: Decoy Source

No.	Time	Source	Destination	Protocol	Info
19	0.317638	10.0.0.99	10.0.0.2	IP	Fragmented IP protocol (proto=TCP 0x06, off=8)
20	0.317895	10.0.0.99	10.0.0.2	IP	Fragmented IP protocol (proto=TCP 0x06, off=16)
21	0.318116	10.0.0.10	10.0.0.2	TCP	42699 > 80[Unreassembled Packet]
22	0.318348	10.0.0.10	10.0.0.2	IP	Fragmented IP protocol (proto=TCP 0x06, off=8)
23	0.318618	10.0.0.10	10.0.0.2	IP	Fragmented IP protocol (proto=TCP 0x06, off=16)
24	0.318809	10.0.0.15	10.0.0.2	TCP	42699 > 80[Unreassembled Packet]
25	0.319042	10.0.0.15	10.0.0.2	IP	Fragmented IP protocol (proto=TCP 0x06, off=8)
26	0.319261	10.0.0.15	10.0.0.2	IP	Fragmented IP protocol (proto=TCP 0x06, off=16)
27	0.319460	10.0.0.33	10.0.0.2	TCP	42699 > 80[Unreassembled Packet]
28	0.319654	10.0.0.33	10.0.0.2	IP	Fragmented IP protocol (proto=TCP 0x06, off=8)
29	0.319858	10.0.0.33	10.0.0.2	IP	Fragmented IP protocol (proto=TCP 0x06, off=16)
30	0.320137	10.0.0.7	10.0.0.2	TCP	42699 > 80[Unreassembled Packet]
31	0.320328	10.0.0.7	10.0.0.2	IP	Fragmented IP protocol (proto=TCP 0x06, off=8)
32	0.320520	10.0.0.7	10.0.0.2	IP	Fragmented IP protocol (proto=TCP 0x06, off=16)
33	0.320717	10.0.0.67	10.0.0.2	TCP	42699 > 80[Unreassembled Packet]
34	0.320974	10.0.0.67	10.0.0.2	IP	Fragmented IP protocol (proto=TCP 0x06, off=8)
35	0.321169	10.0.0.67	10.0.0.2	IP	Fragmented IP protocol (proto=TCP 0x06, off=16)
36	0.321409	10.0.0.99	10.0.0.2	TCP	42699 > 80[Unreassembled Packet]
37	0.321685	10.0.0.99	10.0.0.2	IP	Fragmented IP protocol (proto=TCP 0x06, off=8)
38	0.321933	10.0.0.99	10.0.0.2	IP	Fragmented IP protocol (proto=TCP 0x06, off=16)

```
⊞ Frame 24 (42 bytes on wire, 42 bytes captured)
⊞ Ethernet II, Src: 00:14:a5:13:17:75 (00:14:a5:13:17:75), Dst: 00:02:e3:13:36:4b (00:02:e3:13:36:4b)
⊞ Internet Protocol, Src: 10.0.0.15 (10.0.0.15), Dst: 10.0.0.2 (10.0.0.2)
⊞ Transmission Control Protocol, Src Port: 42699 (42699), Dst Port: 80 (80)
  [Unreassembled Packet: TCP]
```

Now we'll compare this MAC address information (00:14:a5:13:17:75) to the IP address that we know is the real source of the Nmap scan, as shown in Figure 8.10.

Figure 8.10 Wireshark Output of Nmap Fragment Scan: Real Source

No.	Time	Source	Destination	Protocol	Info
19	0.317638	10.0.0.99	10.0.0.2	IP	Fragmented IP protocol (proto=TCP 0x06, off=8)
20	0.317895	10.0.0.99	10.0.0.2	IP	Fragmented IP protocol (proto=TCP 0x06, off=16)
21	0.318116	10.0.0.10	10.0.0.2	TCP	42699 > 80[Unreassembled Packet]
22	0.318348	10.0.0.10	10.0.0.2	IP	Fragmented IP protocol (proto=TCP 0x06, off=8)
23	0.318618	10.0.0.10	10.0.0.2	IP	Fragmented IP protocol (proto=TCP 0x06, off=16)
24	0.318809	10.0.0.15	10.0.0.2	TCP	42699 > 80[Unreassembled Packet]
25	0.319042	10.0.0.15	10.0.0.2	IP	Fragmented IP protocol (proto=TCP 0x06, off=8)
26	0.319261	10.0.0.15	10.0.0.2	IP	Fragmented IP protocol (proto=TCP 0x06, off=16)
27	0.319460	10.0.0.33	10.0.0.2	TCP	42699 > 80[Unreassembled Packet]
28	0.319654	10.0.0.33	10.0.0.2	IP	Fragmented IP protocol (proto=TCP 0x06, off=8)
29	0.319858	10.0.0.33	10.0.0.2	IP	Fragmented IP protocol (proto=TCP 0x06, off=16)
30	0.320137	10.0.0.7	10.0.0.2	TCP	42699 > 80[Unreassembled Packet]
31	0.320328	10.0.0.7	10.0.0.2	IP	Fragmented IP protocol (proto=TCP 0x06, off=8)
32	0.320520	10.0.0.7	10.0.0.2	IP	Fragmented IP protocol (proto=TCP 0x06, off=16)
33	0.320717	10.0.0.67	10.0.0.2	TCP	42699 > 80[Unreassembled Packet]
34	0.320974	10.0.0.67	10.0.0.2	IP	Fragmented IP protocol (proto=TCP 0x06, off=8)
35	0.321169	10.0.0.67	10.0.0.2	IP	Fragmented IP protocol (proto=TCP 0x06, off=16)
36	0.321409	10.0.0.99	10.0.0.2	TCP	42699 > 80[Unreassembled Packet]
37	0.321685	10.0.0.99	10.0.0.2	IP	Fragmented IP protocol (proto=TCP 0x06, off=8)
38	0.321933	10.0.0.99	10.0.0.2	IP	Fragmented IP protocol (proto=TCP 0x06, off=16)

```
⊞ Frame 30 (42 bytes on wire, 42 bytes captured)
⊞ Ethernet II, Src: 00:14:a5:13:17:75 (00:14:a5:13:17:75), Dst: 00:02:e3:13:36:4b (00:02:e3:13:36:4b)
⊞ Internet Protocol, Src: 10.0.0.7 (10.0.0.7), Dst: 10.0.0.2 (10.0.0.2)
⊞ Transmission Control Protocol, Src Port: 42699 (42699), Dst Port: 80 (80)
  [Unreassembled Packet: TCP]
```

It's a match! Just remember that this test will only work for scans originating from the same subnet. Otherwise, you would find the MAC address of the upstream router for the source MAC. Now, hopefully you also noticed the fact that our packets were indeed fragmented. For example in packets number 31 and 32 you will notice the offset is equal to 8 and 16 respectively, indicating 8 byte increments. Wireshark shows that the `-f` Nmap option performed as expected and split our outbound packets into 8 byte fragments.

Detecting Nmap Fragment Scans

Since we are using Snort as our IDS of choice, we want to set it up to detect fragmented traffic. Out of the box, Snort does not have any rules that trigger solely on packet fragmentation, so we'll have to create one. Here it is:

```
alert ip $EXTERNAL_NET any -> $HOME_NET any (msg:"TRAFFIC-ALERT more
frag\ bits set"; fragbits:M; classtype:misc-activity; rev:1;)
```

This tells our Snort sensor to alert on any IP-based traffic (regardless of the layer 4 protocol), coming from any port on anything defined by our `$EXTERNAL_NET` variable and destined for any port on our `$HOME_NET` variable that has the *More Fragments* (`M`) flag set. We assigned a revision number of `1` to the signature since we just created it. Depending on your network infrastructure, you might find that a rule such as this will provide interesting insight into fragmentation you might have otherwise overlooked. For our purposes though, it is hopefully going to trigger on our Nmap `-f` scan.

After running another Nmap fragmentation scan, we can check our Snort alert file to see if the *more frag bits set* signature fired. Digging into the alert log file, we find:

```
[**] [1:5555:1] TRAFFIC-ALERT more frag bits set [**]
[Classification: Misc activity] [Priority: 3]
02/02-00:13:43.176044 10.0.0.99 -> 10.0.0.7
TCP TTL:58 TOS:0x0 ID:2130 IpLen:20 DgmLen:28 MF
Frag Offset: 0x0000     Frag Size: 0x0008

[**] [1:5555:1] TRAFFIC-ALERT more frag bits set [**]
[Classification: Misc activity] [Priority: 3]
02/02-00:13:43.176239 10.0.0.99 -> 10.0.0.7
TCP TTL:58 TOS:0x0 ID:2130 IpLen:20 DgmLen:28 MF
Frag Offset: 0x0001     Frag Size: 0x0008

[**] [1:5555:1] TRAFFIC-ALERT more frag bits set [**]
[Classification: Misc activity] [Priority: 3]
02/02-00:13:44.534995 10.0.0.10 -> 10.0.0.7
TCP TTL:52 TOS:0x0 ID:11159 IpLen:20 DgmLen:28 MF
Frag Offset: 0x0000     Frag Size: 0x0008

[**] [1:5555:1] TRAFFIC-ALERT more frag bits set [**]
[Classification: Misc activity] [Priority: 3]
02/02-00:13:44.535143 10.0.0.10 -> 10.0.0.7
TCP TTL:52 TOS:0x0 ID:11159 IpLen:20 DgmLen:28 MF
Frag Offset: 0x0001     Frag Size: 0x0008
```

Notice that our signature did indeed work. Snort created alerts about the packets that only had the *More Fragments* flag set. Notice the `Frag Offset` field in each packet and the `Frag Size` – these both give an indication of the placement and length of the fragment seen by Snort. The thing to keep in mind with this particular signature is that it will capture any fragmented traffic, regardless of whether it was generated by Nmap or not. If you want to try and create an Nmap-specific signature, you will have to run several fragment scans and look for consistencies in the way that your particular version of Nmap crafts the fragmented packets. These patterns could then used to create an Nmap version-specific signature for fragment scans. With older versions of Nmap, signatures could be created based on static IP ID numbers, predictable timing controls, ACK sequence numbering, etc. Fyodor and the Nmap team have worked diligently to avoid patterns that could assist with intrusion detection signatures however, so you have your work cut out for you!

TIP

If you are interested in learning more about working with Snort, check out the how-to for writing Snort rules. It can be found at www.snort.org/docs/writing_rules/chap2.html. This is an excellent write-up with lots of easy-to-follow examples for the Snort novice. As you work through the chapter, you will find yourself building more and more complex rules.

Discovering Unauthorized Applications and Services

We have previously discussed Nmap's capability for service and version detection against open ports. What really helps to put it into perspective is discussing real-life scenarios and that is what we'll do in this section. This feature of Nmap is commonly used to discover unauthorized or outdated applications and services. What happens when you are tasked with finding all the open file shares in the network? How about when the boss calls you and requests a count of how many FTP servers are running in your lab? What if one of your yearly goals is to make sure all SSH versions are up-to-spec? And finally, how about being tasked with tracking down users who are obscuring internal Web sites under atypical port numbers? Here's a list of some other items you might find yourself tracking down or keeping inventory of, depending on your organization's policy:

- P2P software
- Chat applications
- Samba servers
- Remote desktop services

- Unauthorized database services
- Open mail relays
- Unauthorized proxy servers
- Unmanaged printers
- Virtual operating systems, like VMware
- Unauthorized operating systems, like MAC OS X or Linux

The nice thing about using Nmap in this capacity is that the service and version detection capability is built right into the tool. Earlier in the book, we covered the `-sV` or version option, as well as the OS detection capability, called with the `-O` option. In more recent Nmap versions, you also have the luxury of running both simultaneously by utilize the `-A` option.

We'll run a sample scan and take advantage of the version detection capability. Looking back on our usage chapter, we can test out some of the following additional service and version detection options:

```
SERVICE/VERSION DETECTION:
  -sV: Probe open ports to determine service/version info
  --version-intensity <level>: Set from 0 (light) to 9 (try all probes)
  --version-light: Limit to most likely probes (intensity 2)
  --version-all: Try every single probe (intensity 9)
  --version-trace: Show detailed version scan activity (for debugging)
```

As a test, we'll run the version-intensity at 0 and then at 9 to compare the results. Let's test against our trusty SUSE system:

```
C:\downloads>nmap -sV --version-intensity 0 10.0.0.5

Starting Nmap 4.53 (http://insecure.org) at 2008-02-01 23:30 Central Standard Time
Interesting ports on 10.0.0.5:
Not shown: 1709 closed ports
PORT      STATE    SERVICE       VERSION
22/tcp    open     ssh           OpenSSH 4.1 (protocol 1.99)
111/tcp   open     rpcbind       2 (rpc #100000)
139/tcp   open     netbios-ssn   Samba smbd 3.X (workgroup: LAB)
445/tcp   open     netbios-ssn   Samba smbd 3.X (workgroup: LAB)
631/tcp   open     ipp           CUPS 1.1
MAC Address: 00:0C:29:E0:54:1B (VMware)
```

```
Host script results:
|_ Discover OS Version over NetBIOS and SMB: Unix
Service detection performed. Please report any incorrect results at http://insecure.
org/nmap/submit/.
Nmap done: 1 IP address (1 host up) scanned in 13.422 seconds
```

This looks great and exactly like the kind of information we would need to complete an inventory of TCP/IP services available on this system. We ran the command again using a version-intensity of 9 and received the same results. Let's see if we can trip up Nmap a little bit by starting up a netcat listener on TCP port 135 on the SUSE server. This port is normally associated with the Windows MS-RPC service. On the SUSE system, we'll run this command:

```
vmware1:/home # nc -l -p135
```

To verify that the port is now open, we can also run a quick *netstat* on the SUSE server:

```
vmware1:/home # netstat -na | grep ':135'
tcp     0     0.0.0.0:135     0.0.0.0:*     LISTEN
```

Looks great so far. Now we'll kick off the service and version detection scan with the most intense setting, a level 9, and specific to our port 135:

```
C:\WINDOWS\system32>nmap -sV --version-intensity 9 -p135 10.0.0.5
Starting Nmap 4.53 (http://insecure.org) at 2008-02-01 23:55 Central Standard Time
Interesting ports on 10.0.0.5:
PORT    STATE    SERVICE    VERSION
135/tcp open msrpc?
MAC Address: 00:0C:29:E9:43:0A (VMware)
Service detection performed. Please report any incorrect results at http://insecure.
org/nmap/submit/.
Nmap done: 1 IP address (1 host up) scanned in 13.000 seconds
```

Looks like the trick is somewhat successful. Nmap's best guess is that the port is indeed running the MS-RPC service. However, since Nmap is unable to provide any real version information, and we see the question mark in the results, we know that this service will require more intensive and possibly, hands-on, investigation. This really demonstrates the importance of remaining objective with regards to your Nmap results. Most likely, the majority of services in your infrastructure will be easily and properly identified by Nmap's service and version detection scan; however if an end-user really wants to cover up their tracks, you will have to be more vigilant in your own discovery efforts.

Tools & Traps...

Netcat

Netcat is a fantastic tool for reading and even writing data across TCP/IP connections. It has the capability to listen on any port and even to execute a command for that port. It has long been referred to as the TCP/IP Swiss Army Knife and is considered a must-have for the security analyst. As we saw in the example case in this chapter, it provides an extremely simple way of setting up a listener on any port to watch and collect traffic from any system that attempts to connect to that port. In this capacity, it provides a very simple, honeypot-like capability in that the service is obviously not really running, but from the attacker's viewpoint appears to be available. You can download the tool for UNIX systems from the original site here: http://netcat.sourceforge.net/. A windows port was also developed and is maintained here: www.vulnwatch.org/netcat/. There is a great readme.txt on the *vulnwatch* site that describes several different tips and tricks for working with the tool. You can check it out here: http://www.vulnwatch.org/netcat/readment.txt.

Testing Incident Response and Managed Services Alerting

Nmap can be very useful when you have been tasked with testing your enterprise incident response plan or team. Another example of using Nmap to test responsiveness is when you are working with a managed service provider, who is tasked with monitoring your organization's IDS or IPS environment. It can be very enlightening to discover whether or not your service level agreements are being adhered to in these types of arrangements. We'll discuss an example of using Nmap in such a way to trigger a known signature in your intrusion detection environment.

Scanning to Test Alert Procedures

It is critical to test your internal network alerting facilities and/or your outsourced managed services alerting. Both can be tricky to test. This is due in part to technical issues, but also from a political standpoint. You want to make sure you have your management's approval to conduct such a test in case the end result does not meet expectations or even worse, you cause a system crash or network instability. You must also conform to any existing contractual agreements with your managed service providers that specify the rules of engagement before you test their monitoring and alerting measures for your infrastructure.

Nmap has many types of scans and scan options that have been well-documented by IDS and IPS vendors over the years. Many signatures and heuristics have been devised to detect scanning and even to detect scanning from specific tools, like Nmap. As a result, there are most likely several ways to kick off an Nmap scan that will cause alerts to trigger on the monitoring stations of your managed service provider. The issue is finding a scan pattern that should attract enough attention because of its difference to the normal ebb and flow of traffic. Any intrusion analyst can testify that after a few million packets or so, you start to tune out common scans, service version queries and many other forms of general broad-range reconnaissance that happen on a daily basis and are commonly accepted as part of being "connected to the Web". Therefore, your job in performing this alert testing is to pinpoint an appropriate target in your network infrastructure in conjunction with the right attention-getting scan. When performed by a legitimate attacker, this process would be considered *targeted reconnaissance*. The attacker most likely has a preferred exploit in their arsenal or is looking for a certain type of target based on the latest vulnerability information. Your managed service provider should be tasked with staying on top of cutting edge vulnerability information and exploit signatures. You should also have in your contract some information about risk priorities specific to your protected oranization assets, in addition to guidelines for response timeliness. With our Nmap testing, we'll zero in on a specific target and utilize what should be some eye-catching scan techniques in order to test gaining the attention and response of our monitoring and managed services analysts. Keep in mind that we are talking about external-facing hosts. Unless otherwise instructed, your provider should immediately alert you to any internally-protected assets that come under Nmap scan-related fire.

Targeted Reconnaissance with Nmap

Targeted reconnaissance refers to the ever-tightening circle of information-gathering that occurs in the primary phase of an attack. To demonstrate how an attacker might perform this targeting using Nmap, we'll start off with a broad-based scan, looking for servers with Web ports. We're going after Web ports because that is one of the most published entry-points for the attacker into your infrastructure. Other external-facing servers of interest typically include DNS servers, mail servers, routers and unprotected desktops. With a Web server, if an attacker can exploit their way onto the system, odds are they will have access to further pathways into your infrastructure. This ties into the need for segregated server networks, server hardening, separation of duties, and the principle of least privilege – but that is a different book!

Working out of our demo lab, we'll only be scanning the 10.0.0.0/24 network, but in the real world an attacker would either be scanning multiple, miscellaneous subnets looking for certain ports or if they were targeting your organization specifically, then they might already have your subnet/s in their sites. As a reminder, here's what a basic Nmap port 80 scan would look like:

```
nmap -p80 10.0.0.0/24
```

There are certainly ways we could make this port 80 scan less obvious, the biggest one being the timing switch. Remember Nmap has the capability to slow down the speed with which it scans utilizing the `-t`, timing, option. Keep in mind though we are mimicking an attacker who is scanning from the Internet and servers that have an internet-exposed address receive numerous scans of this type on a daily, if not hourly, basis. At this stage in the reconnaissance game, these scans are typically ignored by managed services providers.

Why didn't the attacker incorporate the version detection option into this port 80 scan? The primary reason is for scan speed. They can come up with an extensive list of servers with an available HTTP port in a very short amount of time by using a pared down scan such as this one. If the attacker is already focused on a certain company or subnet, it is also likely that they want to minimize the number of probes being sent to the targets.

Now we have a listing of IP addresses that have an Internet-accessible port 80 listening. The attacker will feed this list of IP address back into a tool like Nmap and perform the next phase of targeted reconnaissance; determining what service versions are running on the open ports. The reason for this step is that most likely the attacker has exploit code ready to use against the matching, vulnerable service version. Hence the reason for staying on top of your patching and security hardening efforts.

Our scan discovered five active hosts, three of which have listening HTTP ports:

```
C:\Downloads>nmap -p80 10.0.0.0/24

Starting Nmap 4.53 (http://insecure.org) at 2008-02-03 16:01 Central Standard Time
Interesting ports on 10.0.0.1:
```

```
PORT    STATE    SERVICE
80/tcp open http
MAC Address: 00:0F:B5:6D:EF:F1 (Netgear)

Interesting ports on 10.0.0.2:
PORT    STATE    SERVICE
80/tcp open http
MAC Address: 00:02:E3:14:47:5C (Lite-on Communications)

Interesting ports on 10.0.0.3:
PORT    STATE    SERVICE
80/tcp closed http
MAC Address: 00:12:3F:FD:18:67 (Dell)

Interesting ports on 10.0.0.4:
PORT    STATE    SERVICE
80/tcp closed http
MAC Address: 00:0D:0B:BE:2C:67 (Buffalo)

Interesting ports on 10.0.0.5:
PORT    STATE    SERVICE
80/tcp open http
MAC Address: 00:0C:29:E0:54:1B (VMware)

Nmap done: 256 IP addresses (6 hosts up) scanned in 6.797 seconds
```

Now we'll run the -sV version scan against IP addresses 10.0.0.1, 10.0.0.2, and 10.0.0.5 to see what information Nmap can collect about the HTTP services found on the systems with the open HTTP ports:

```
C:\Downloads>nmap -sV -p80 10.0.0.1-2,5

Starting Nmap 4.53 (http://insecure.org) at 2008-02-03 16:10 Central Standard Time
Interesting ports on 10.0.0.1:
PORT    STATE    SERVICE    VERSION
80/tcp open tcpwrapped
MAC Address: 00:0F:B5:6D:EF:F1 (Netgear)

Interesting ports on 10.0.0.2:
PORT    STATE    SERVICE    VERSION
80/tcp open http?
MAC Address: 00:02:E3:14:47:5C (Lite-on Communications)

Interesting ports on 10.0.0.5:
PORT    STATE    SERVICE    VERSION
80/tcp open http Apache httpd 1.3.23 ((Unix))
MAC Address: 00:0C:29:E0:54:1B (VMware)
```

```
Service detection performed. Please report any incorrect results at
http://insecure.org/nmap/submit/.
Nmap done: 3 IP addresses (3 hosts up) scanned in 11.266 seconds
```

Now we're getting somewhere. From an attacker's perspective, we have one system, 10.0.0.1, that doesn't appear to be a viable target because the HTTP port is potentially protected. Our next option, 10.0.0.2, looks promising except for the fact that Nmap doesn't have any feedback on the HTTP version that is running. For the attacker, this could indicate a non-HTTP service masquerading on port 80. We actually ran a netcat listener on this system and collected the Nmap queries. The `-l` command tells netcat to listen on a port and we used the `-p` option to specify port 80. Here is a copy of the Nmap query data that was received on the console of the netcat listener:

```
F:\Netcat_for_Windows>nc -l -p80
GET /HTTP/1.0
OPTIONS /HTTP/1.0
OPTIONS /RTSP/1.0
l ? GET /nice%20ports%2C/Tri%6Eity.txt%2ebak HTTP/1.0
Ç (r¦??        ? ?åá ?ù|      ? ?? ? version?bind ? ? ? ? HELP
?? S? O? ?G+~¦,eO¦'~= ²é{¦+û+w¢µ-¦<=¦on?n (? ?
f ? ? e d c b a ' § ? ¶ ? ?? ñ SMBr ?@ @? ? ü ?PC NETWORK PROGRAM 1.0 ?MICROSOFT
NETWORKS 1.03 ?MICROSOFT NETWORKS 3.0 ?LANMAN1.0 ?LM1.2X002 ?Samba ?NT LANMAN 1.0
?NT LM 0.12 ?default
0????'???? Ç OPTIONS sip:nm SIP/2.0
Via: SIP/2.0/TCP nm;branch=foo
From: <sip:nm@nm>;tag=root
To: <sip:nm2@nm2>
Call-ID: 50000
CSeq: 42 OPTIONS
Max-Forwards: 70
Content-Length: 0
Contact: <sip:nm@nm>
Accept: application/sdp
TNMP? TNME ? ? ??a DmdT ? ? ?? ? ?: / ? @?¤ ? =? / @? <NTP/1.0>
? ²+.?¦á MMS¶ ? ? ? ====? ? ? ? N S P l a y e r / 9 . 0 . 0 . 2 9 8 0 ; {0 0 0
0 A A 0 0 - 0 A 0 0 - 0 0 a 0 - A A 0 A - 0 0 0 0 A 0 A A 0 A A 0} am-_ Z ?
?6?, ¦ ? : 4µ ? (CONNECT_DATA=(COMMAND=version))
```

As you can see, Nmap runs several different types of tests in its attempt to determine the service version of what it thinks should be a Web-enabled port. We can easily spot queries for headers, version.bind type, Server Message Block (SMB) and even Session Initiation Protocol (SIP) checks. Keep in mind that from the attacker's point of view, they would never see this output. It is included here only for the purpose of demonstrating Nmap's service version scan against this host.

The last host scanned, 10.0.0.5, is going to be the most interesting to the attacker at this point. Not only is it reporting a live host with an open port 80, but Nmap was also able to determine the version of Web server running on the port! In this case, it appears to be a rather outdated version of Apache, 1.3.23. If we do some basic searches online for vulnerability information pertaining to this version, we find that not only does it have vulnerability issues; one of those issues is incorporated into a Metasploit exploit, shown in Figure 8.11.

Figure 8.11 Metasploit Vulnerability Information

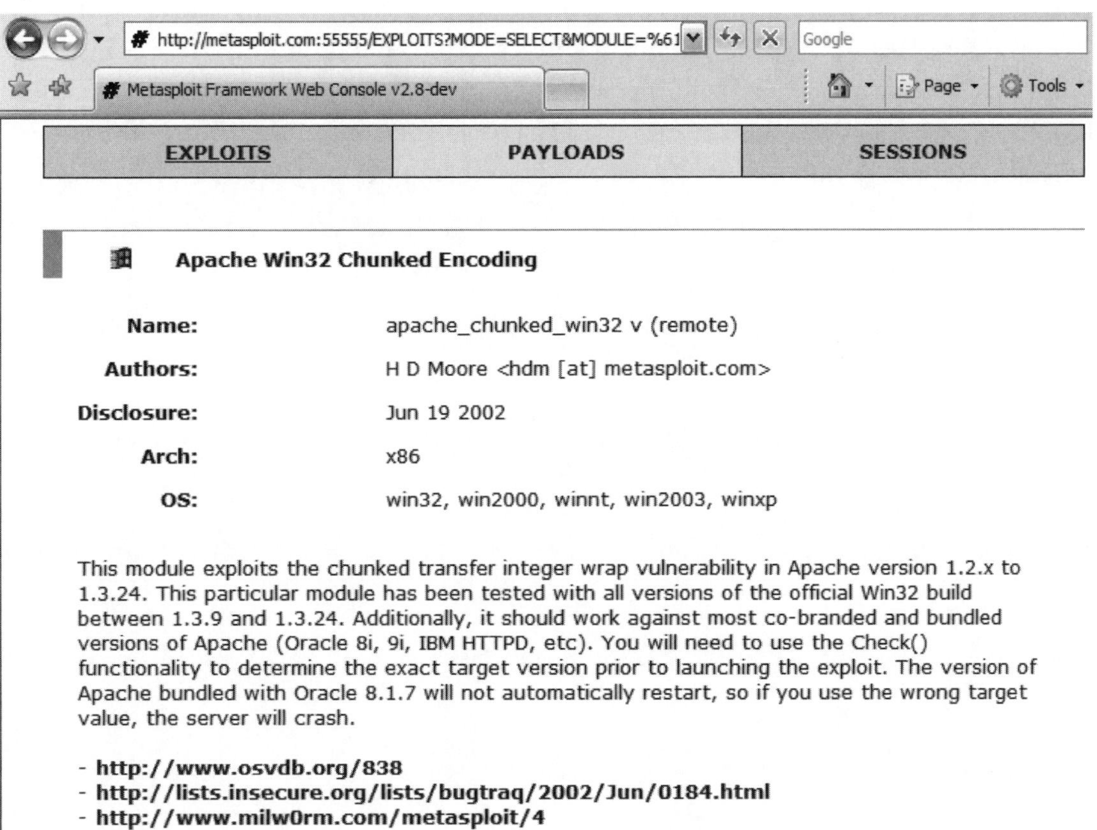

Luckily for us, this particular exploit appears to only work against vulnerable Apache versions installed on Windows machines. Nmap reported that this particular version is running on a UNIX-based platform:

```
Interesting ports on 10.0.0.5:
PORT STATE SERVICE VERSION
80/tcp open http Apache httpd 1.3.23 ((Unix))
MAC Address: 00:0C:29:E0:54:1B (VMware)
```

At this point, you might expect to see further Nmap queries from the attacker while they attempt to determine whether or not the operating system really is UNIX-based (although in the author's experience, they should save themselves the time and just trust Nmap's assessment). However, this doesn't necessarily mean that the attacker won't still attempt to run the exploit against your UNIX-based Apache server. Their mileage may even vary in terms of whether or not they cause any service disruption. Regardless, it is definitely time to update the Apache server. This also proves how easily an attacker could use Nmap to narrow down on a particular system. Back at your managed service provider, the analyst's alerting workstation should have generated several Events of Interest (EOI) pertaining to these scans. Hopefully you have received a notification by now of a potential intrusion attempt! If your targeted reconnaissance scanning efforts do not generate notifications of any type, it is definitely time to investigate the monitoring performance agreement with your vendor.

Summary

This chapter introduces some different problems you might run into while managing systems and networks in an enterprise networking environment. We discussed four common issues and provided insight into utilizing Nmap as a solution or part of the solution for each issue. As a reminder, here are some of the capabilities and possible uses we have discussed throughout this chapter and the this book, for using Nmap to meet the needs of your enterprise infrastructure:

Compliance:

- Testing for open ports on the interfaces of a firewall.
- Performing scans across workstation IP address ranges to determine if any unauthorized networking applications are installed.
- Determining if the correct version of Web service is installed in your DMZ.
- Locating systems with open file sharing ports.
- Locating unauthorized FTP servers, printers or operating systems.

Auditing:

- Auditing firewalls by verifying the firewall filters are operating properly.
- Searching for open ports on perimeter devices. Perimeter being anything from Internet-edge, to extranet or intranet boundary lines.
- Performing reconnaissance for certain versions of services.
- Performing vulnerability and patch management.
- Utilizing the OS detection feature to pin-point outdated or unauthorized systems on your networks.
- Identify an unknown, but "suspicious" system - whether thought to be infected or acting in a "strange" manner on the network.
- Identify a certain port across multiple subnets of IP addresses: For example, if a file sharing-based worm hits, performing Nmap scans looking for port 135.
- Utilizing an Nmap add-on tool like NDiff: when performing enterprise scanning to compare scan results. There are often times you want to run the same scan more than once and compare results. For example, you may be

interested in running Nmap before and after you install a patch or apply new software to a system, make a firewall or router access control list change, or making configuration changes.

- Identify all open ports and perform service and OS identification on Web servers that are going through the security review process before being allowed into production.
- Discovering unauthorized applications and services.

Advanced scanning:

- TCP scan flags customization.
- Packet fragmentation.
- IP and MAC address spoofing.
- Adding decoy scan source IP addresses.
- Source port specification.
- Ability to add random data to sent packets.
- Manipulatable time-to-live field.
- Ability to send packets with bogus TCP or UDP checksums.

Solutions Fast Track

Detecting Nmap on your Network

☑ A network protocol analyzer, such as Wireshark, is a good tool to use to monitor your network and detect network scanning.

☑ The Snort sfPortscan preprocessor will detect Nmap TCP connect and SYN scanning activity.

☑ If you detect scanning activity on a specific host, you should investigate other events and traffic targeting the host and evaluate the host for signs of compromise.

☑ Some attackers will use a popular source port that is often allowed through firewalls (such as Web port 80 or DNS port 53) to evade firewalls.

Discovering Stealthy Scanning Techniques

- ☑ Packet fragmentation is oftentimes used as a method for evading intrusion detection systems.
- ☑ Nmap can insert decoy IP addresses into the scan with the `-D` option.
- ☑ Snort can detect fragmented Nmap scans if you include a signature with the `M`, or *More fragments*, flag enabled.

Discovering Unauthorized Applications and Services

- ☑ Nmap's service and version detection scan is called by the `-sV` option.
- ☑ The intensity of the service/version detection scan can be controlled by applying the `--version-intensity` option.
- ☑ If Nmap is uncertain of its results regarding a service or version, it will include a question mark (`?`) next to the output.

Testing Incident Response and Managed Services Alerting

- ☑ You must ensure that appropriate agreements are in place with your managed services vendor before attempting to test their monitoring and alerting capabilities of your infrastructure.
- ☑ Targeted reconnaissance is the primary phase of a directed attack. The attacker will first locate a broad range of targets and then, utilizing a scanner like Nmap, begin to narrow down their attack scope to the most vulnerable systems.
- ☑ Many IDS and IPS signatures have been created for Nmap scans. Check with your managed services provider to determine which ones they include and monitor for.

Frequently Asked Questions

Q: If I am seeing scanning activity on my network how can I tell if it is Nmap?

A: Snort has some rules to detect Nmap scans, but it is very difficult to tell by passively monitoring network traffic what tool is being used. You can sometimes detect Nmap because some scan types send a TCP ACK packet to port 80 by default.

Q: I have never seen any fragmented packets on my network. Should I worry about looking for them?

A: In modern networks, fragmented packets can indeed be uncommon to find. However, that actually provides more reason to watch for them. If you ever actually find fragmented traffic, this could indicate some serious networking problems or as we saw in our examples, IDS or IPS evasion attempts. This certainly isn't to say that every fragmented packet is indicative of a malicious event, but rather that it should be investigated and understood in your infrastructure.

Q: It sounds like I need to be a TCP/IP guru in order to fully understand Nmap?

A: You can reap a multitude of benefits from Nmap without becoming a TCP/IP top gun. However, learning more about the intricacies of TCP/IP will also help you become a better security analyst and all-around network troubleshooting genius. The authors always like to recommend TCP/IP Illustrated, Volume 1: The Protocols by W. Richard Stevens. Even though the book was published in 1994, it is still one of the best references you will find.

Q: I'm tired of only being able to run Nmap scans and tests in my lab or home network. Do you think I'll get caught if I start scanning valid IP address space?

A: As common sense-sounding as the answer should be for most, the authors have actually been asked this question on numerous occasions. Will you get caught? No one knows for sure. Could you get caught? You bet. And if you do, there could be any number of consequences depending on whether or not your scanning caused any downtime or damage. Simply put, don't chance it. They don't get a lab at all in jail.

Index

Linux User account commands:

pwck - checks & warns if account has no pw.

passwd -l or -u - locks or unlocks an account
-n - sets # of minimum days between pw changes.
-w - Sets # of days warning of pw expire
-i - Sets # of days After pw expires before account is locked
-c - Allow viewing of account info. in clear text.